The Eagle

ALASDAIR FOTHERINGHAM is a freelance journalist based in Spain. He has covered twenty two Tours de France and twenty Tours of Spain, as well as numerous other major races. He first interviewed Federico Bahamontes in 1993. The *Independent* and the *Independent on Sunday's* correspondent on Spain and cycling, he is also a contributor to *ProCycling* magazine and the website www.cyclingnews.com.

of Toledo

The Eagle of Toledo

The Life and Times of Federico Bahamontes

Alasdair Fotheringham

Aurum
Press

First published in Great Britain
2012 by Aurum Press Ltd
74–77 White Lion Street
London N1 9PF
www.aurumpress.co.uk

This paperback edition first published in 2014 by Aurum Press Ltd

Copyright © Alasdair Fotheringham 2012

Alasdair Fotheringham has asserted his moral right to be identified as
the Author of this Work in accordance with the Copyright Designs
and Patents Act 1988.

All rights reserved. No part of this book may be reproduced or utilised in
any form or by any means, electronic or mechanical, including photocopying,
recording or by any information storage and retrieval system,
without permission in writing from Aurum Press Ltd.

Every effort has been made to trace the copyright holders of material quoted in
this book. If application is made in writing to the publisher, any omissions
will be included in future editions.

A catalogue record for this book is available from the British Library.

ISBN 978 1 78131 049 6

1 3 5 7 9 10 8 6 4 2
2014 2016 2018 2017 2015

Typeset in Dante MT Std by SX Composing DTP, Rayleigh, Essex

Printed and bound by CPI Group (UK) Ltd, Croydon, CR0 4YY

This book is dedicated to the memory of María José Antón Jornet, and to Mar.

Contents

Author's Note

For the sake of clarity for non-cycling fans and also because that is what the people of Catalonia call it, I have used *Volta a Catalunya* or *Volta* to describe the region's premier stage race (also known, outside Spain, as the Tour of Catalunya or Tour of Catalonia). For similar reasons I have used *Vuelta al País Vasco* rather than the Tour of the Basque Country, *Giro d'Italia* or *Giro* rather than the Tour of Italy, and the *Vuelta* or the *Vuelta a España* for the Tour of Spain. Given its overriding importance, the Tour de France is sometimes referred to simply as the Tour. (As Bahamontes likes to say: *'Le Tour is le Tour.'*)

On a completely different note, this biography contains extracts from a number of interviews with Federico Martín Bahamontes but it is not an authorised version of his life. As Bahamontes put it: 'You can do it, provided you leave me in peace.' And, by and large, I did.

Alasdair Fotheringham
March 2012

Acknowledgements

First and foremost, my greatest thanks goes to Naomi, for making this book both possible and worth doing.

Steve Farrand has been a rock of support throughout, and Jacinto Vidarte has provided everything from photographs of Bahamontes to a much-appreciated dry sense of humour about the whole project. To these two in particular, thanks.

I am also very grateful to my mother, Alison Harding, for her support, knowledge and advice on reading and writing books, thinking about books and getting them published; to my brother William, for sound advice about the same, useful phone numbers, specific comments and general encouragement (not to mention getting me interested in cycling in the first place); to my late father, Alex, for his interest and comments, as well as sharing the odd invaluable memory about 1950s and 1960s cycling; and to all three of them for helping to keep me motivated. Thank you.

Thanks also to Spanish cycling historian Javier Bodegas, for his support, comments, information and interest; to Philippe Bouvet of *L'Equipe* for phone numbers, advice, and infectious enthusiasm; to Josu Garai for allowing me to take over *MARCA's* photocopy machine for several hours; to Alex Hoskins, for being the ideal co-pilot around a large part of Spain and France in search of elderly former bike riders and the right kind of Patxaran; to Richard Moore for much-needed encouragement when the book was beginning to take shape; and at the other end of affairs, to Sam Harrison of

Aurum and Martin Smith for their hard work and skilful editing when the book was being hammered into its final form. Also to (in alphabetical order) Geoff Brown, Alberto Contador, Pedro Delgado, Raul Esgueva, Hugh Gladstone, Rupert Guinness, John Herety, Miguel Indurain, Graham Jones, Alain Laiseka, Unai Larrea, Margarita Lobo, Edward Pickering, Dave Prichard, David Randall, Jorge Quintana, Phil Sheehan, Francois Thomazeau, Benito Urraburu, Antonio Valdivia Molina and Graham Watson. Finally to my agent, Mark Stanton of Jenny Brown Associates, both for his astute handling of all the boring bits of getting a book published as well as keeping the nerves of a first-time author from becoming overly jangled.

Prologue
The Reference Point

Before Alberto Contador made his mark on stage racing in the late 2000s, his hometown of Pinto, outside Madrid, was best known for being the geographical centre of Spain. Following his rise to fame, every time that Contador stood on the town hall balcony, waving at the cheering crowds after taking his latest Grand Tour, the people of the humdrum dormitory town must have felt they were at the centre of the sporting world, too.

During one of these celebrations, someone tried to gatecrash the party. As Contador left the balcony and walked down the stairs to a reception, the bell at the main doors locked to keep out intruders, began to ring furiously. At the same time a voice could be heard shouting: 'Let me in! Let me in! It's Bahamontes!' Sure enough, it was. Smartly dressed in his usual dark suit and tie, his shock of wavy, unruly hair as neatly combed as it could be, Federico Martín Bahamontes was outside bestowing embraces on friends and fans alike, signing autographs and grinning from ear to ear. After Bahamontes was admitted, Contador duly obliged by having his photograph taken for the press alongside the man known as the Eagle of Toledo. It was a symbolic moment: Spain's first winner of the Tour de France, and arguably the greatest climber the sport has known, and his latest heir (albeit a somewhat controversial one given Contador's positive test for the banned performance-enhancing drug clenbuterol).

In his home country, Bahamontes is considered to be the man

who paved the way for future generations of Spanish cyclists who dreamed of taking the sport's most prestigious trophy. Unlike similarly iconic figures in other countries, and double Tour winner Fausto Coppi in Italy and Britain's 1965 World Champion Tom Simpson spring to mind, Bahamontes is anything but historically remote. Time and again he pops up, giving away prizes at race finishes, making statements to the press, and in the case of top riders like Contador or 2008 Tour de France winner Carlos Sastre, giving them reams of sound, often longwinded, advice from the other end of a mobile telephone. Even though that advice may be unsolicited, Bahamontes seems boundlessly confident that as the most important original source of inspiration for Spanish professional cycling, his presence and comments will always be appreciated. And is that so surprising given that his Tour de France win had such an enormous impact in post-Civil War Spain that it extended far beyond sport?

Bahamontes' Tour win in 1959 was the biggest international sporting breakthrough for Spain in a year when the country was, at long last, making advances socially and economically as well. The most important of these was undoubtedly the definitive end of the international isolation which had followed the victory of General Franco's forces over a democratically elected Republican govern-ment in the 1936–39 Civil War, and his regime's support in the first part of World War Two for Nazi Germany and Fascist Italy while technically neutral. Both Hitler and Mussolini had backed the General's coup and it was nearly two decades before the United States and the other Allies were fully willing to welcome Spain back into their midst.

On a sporting level, as arguably the country's biggest individual success at any point since Franco took power, Bahamontes' victory in the Tour 'proved' to the man on the street that Spain was returning to full membership of the international community, and marked an important watershed. Bahamontes' success coincided with the end of two devastating decades of economic recession, so bad they are still referred to as 'the years of hunger'. On 21 July, 1959, with Bahamontes' Tour glory less than a week old, the

Government introduced their 'Stabilisation Plan', a series of radical reforms that heralded the modernisation of the Spanish economy.

Bahamontes, then, was not just opening a new chapter in Spanish sport, he was a surefire sign that the country's worst years were over, and that at home and abroad times were changing for the better. It was therefore small wonder that Franco's regime provided no less than fourteen military bands for the victory celebrations in Toledo. That Bahamontes' triumph in Paris came on 18 July, the anniversary of the start of Franco's uprising against the Republic, was an even happier coincidence for the country's rulers, not least because it reinforced that hallowed date in the Spanish calendar.

Even better, winning the Tour was viewed as beating the despised French at their own game. France was resented by Franco for being the sporadic political ally of the defeated Republic and the closest example of democratic prosperity, as well as the alleged source of the liberal, subversive and modernist values that had corrupted his idealised view of traditional, authoritarian Roman Catholic Spain. Such a strong political interpretation of sporting achievement may strike twenty-first century readers as odd; however it continued to infect Spanish cycling right up until the 1990s when Miguel Indurain's string of victories in the Tour was seen as proof positive that Spain had finally made it into mainstream Europe. Indurain's runaway victory in the 1992 Tour, which visited all the European Union member states who had signed that year's Maastricht Treaty – including Spain – was the icing on the cake.

Back in 1959, Bahamontes' Tour win represented a massive breakthrough. And like any breakthrough it would also shape the future. Victory in the greatest multi-day race of all left Spain's cyclists obsessed with stage racing. Even today, one-day Classics and track racing, two other major facets of the sport, barely receive the media attention or sponsorship they deserve. 'The mountains [are] the basic truth of cycling for Spaniards,' wrote Carlos Arribas, longstanding sports correspondent for *El País*, as recently as January power, they said, that he once attacked in the Alps then stopped at the top of a col to eat an ice-cream while waiting for the pack. Or, so it was rumoured, he would tell his team-mates they could all abandon and head for the team hotel at the foot of the last climb because he could handle the ride to the summit finish alone. His sense of honour could be so touchy that, allegedly, he once got off his bike during a race and attacked a spectator with a bike-pump for insulting him. His temper was so fierce, they said, that he abandoned a Vuelta a España after officials refused to re-admit a disqualified team-mate. He rode so deliberately slowly that day that he was booed and whistled along the route, and he finished more than an hour behind the rest of the field.

However, for all he might be surrounded by stories and anecdotes, Bahamontes was also a solitary figure, and remains so. Once asked if he had ridden for a team who supported him, Bahamontes snapped back: 'Never. I was always alone.' Through- out his career he never had a full-time manager, no personal mechanic, no long-standing faithful *soigneur*: none of the typical trappings top professional cyclists build up over the years. Given to fits of child-like petulance, Bahamontes often accused fellow riders and race directors of betraying his trust and abandoning him to his fate. Even the Spanish state, he claims, was prepared to sacrifice his chances of victory in the Vuelta a España for the sake of its political interests. Barring a handful of allies, such as team worker Julio San Emeterio, Bahamontes was widely regarded as self-centred and self- isolating, convinced of his own sporting genius but rarely capable of appreciating efforts made to help him.

'Federico?' former team-mate, and Tour of Spain winner, Bernardo Ruiz once said to me. 'He was never grateful to anybody for anything.' The Tour's quasi-official newspaper *L'Equipe* called him: 'A sombre, melancholy figure like the El Greco figures from his native region of Castille,' adding bitingly: 'Bahamontes was too whimsical, too Bohemian, too capricious to win the Tour more than once.' Others are less polite. '[As a racer] he was what we could call "madness personified,"' says Josu Loroño, a former cycling journalist and son of Bahamontes' deadliest rival, Jesús Loroño. Josu elsewhere claims: 'It's always been about "me, me, me" . . . Yes, he [Bahamontes] was great, but he never appreciated what others could do.'

However, this image of Bahamontes the eccentric individualist was far from being completely unintentional: while convinced that the world, by and large, was out to get him, this self-imposed isolation also contained ingredients of a craftily designed publicity stunt that allowed him to pursue his real objectives under a smokescreen. As Bahamontes never tires of pointing out, his 1959 Tour win came about partly because the other favourites, notably the French, thought his only interest was in the King of the Mountains jersey. By the time they realised their mistake, the Eagle of Toledo had flown.

Bahamontes still cannot resist the opportunity to add to the myth. During interviews, he will bring down from the shelves a copy of the book he had specially produced for the half-century celebrations of that success. Though a kind enough gesture, you cannot help noticing there are two or three dozen identical volumes still sitting on the bookshelf awaiting future admirers. In an adjacent room, the dust-enshrouded personality cult continues with another vast photograph of Bahamontes. This time, close to the end of his career, he is in full flight on a mountain climb: typically, his head and body jut forward, arms locked in an 'L' position, fingers splayed wide over the handlebars and legs beating out a relentless rhythm as he seeks one last win.

Even after retiring following his last Tour in 1965, which he abandoned little more than a week in because his team allegedly refused to pay him, the almost manic energy that had driven him throughout his career remained intact. For years he ran amateur and professional teams. In the off-season, Julio Jiménez, who won the King of the Mountains title three times in the 1960s, would join him in cruising around Spain in Bahamontes' gleaming Mercedes, milking a series of invitations as guests of honour at criteriums, winter club meets and inaugurations. Indeed, Bahamontes' restless energy seems to increase rather than diminish. When I met him early one morning in the spring of 1993, he walked so fast through the streets of Toledo, shouting at anybody who looked remotely sleepy that they should 'wake up, it's day-time', it was almost impossible to keep up.

Visiting him never fails to produce dramatic moments. I once spent half an hour waiting in his Mercedes as he went into the local police station to nag them to fix a drain cover that was sticking up in the road. He was so keen to get into the building he forgot to put the handbrake on and the car, parked on a roundabout with me in it, rolled ten yards downhill and collided with a traffic bollard. He got back in and drove away as if nothing had happened.

Yet behind this nervous bundle of energy, the regrets and barely concealed bitterness remain. Bahamontes firmly believes he was the best climber cycling has seen; all that prevented him from winning more Tours was the lack of a decent team, a surfeit of loyal team-mates and the absence of summit finishes, which was fatal for a poor descender like him. However, the truth is far more complex. Bahamontes' Tour victory in 1959 was at least partly assisted by an internecine power struggle between France's top riders, who secretly preferred a Spaniard to win rather than one of their home rivals. And too often his impulsive nature, his sometimes excessive ambition and his bizarre abandons, left him overly isolated, even in the context of the cut-throat world of 1950s cycling.

'If Bahamontes had been different, he'd have won a whole lot more,' reasons Jiménez. The problem as Jiménez saw it?: 'He [Bahamontes] wanted everything.' However, Bahamontes' single-mindedness should not detract from his successes, nor what he represents. It is fair to say that he is both one of the last great surviving figures from an era Spain wishes to forget, and one of the few living legends from a time for which cycling fans remain relentlessly nostalgic.

In Spain, quite apart from the political exploitation of his victories, Bahamontes' achievements became part of popular culture across the generations. 'He was a god in a country that, after the Civil War, was desperate for myths,' said Angel Arroyo, second in the 1983 Tour, in an interview. Older Spaniards remember clustering around the radio in the village bar to listen to his exploits in the 1959 Tour, the first live broadcast of a sporting event in Spain. Decades later, the Eagle of Toledo would still form part of children's street games. 'We'd cut out pictures of cyclists from magazines and put them inside the caps of Coca-Cola bottles with a piece of glass on top to keep them stuck in there,' recalls 1988 Tour de France winner Pedro Delgado. 'If you were lucky, you'd get Bahamontes. Then in your street – which usually wasn't paved – you'd make a circuit out of the sand with curves and hills and you'd flick the cap around it with your finger. The first one across the line won. Sometimes you'd secretly file down the edges to make the lid go faster. I suppose you'd call that our equivalent of doping!'

Curiously enough, this game of *chapas* is first mentioned in connection with Bahamontes in the sports daily *MARCA* on 19 July, 1959, the day after he won the Tour. It claimed that children across Spain have 'changed from playing at footballers to playing with lids of pop bottles with their favourites glued to them . . . the lucky ones get Bahamontes, of course'. More than a decade later, as Delgado points out, Spanish children were still doing it.

'That game was how I first heard of Bahamontes. In the 1970s there weren't many televisions in Spain, it was just what your parents had told you about him when the Tour came round. When Luis Ocaña won the Tour in 1973, everybody in the neighbourhood would pile down to watch the TV in the local bar and say, "It's like Bahamontes all over again". It made you think, "Well, if Ocaña was like this, then what must Bahamontes have done?"'

As tarmac and television spread across Spain, games like *chapas* have long since disappeared from the lives of Spanish children, but Bahamontes remains the key reference point for his country's cycling. Others would follow, but none has had the dramatic potency of the lone climber, soaring high in the mountains, oblivious to the rest of the field and at the centre of his own universe.

'I talk a lot to him, or rather he talks a lot to me, but I've always liked to listen to him,' says Carlos Sastre, who grew up in Ávila, close to Toledo. 'When I was a junior, I was on the point of signing for his team, and he would go on to me about what I should and shouldn't do, saying I should sign with him because I'd be treated as if I was going to race for Real Madrid. I didn't sign, I wanted to race in the same team as José María Jiménez [Sastre's now late brother-in-law, another top climber] but I can remember him buzzing around in the races he'd organised, pointing out which riders were good. He's very direct, he calls a spade a spade and if he thinks you're a bastard, he'll tell you. He's given me loads of advice. He'd ring me up in a Vuelta and tell me, "Don't trust him, he's a bastard", or "do that". And I'd say to myself, "If Fede's said that, it has to be for a good reason".'

'He is synonymous with cycling at its highest level,' says Contador. 'Bahamontes' personality is unique, not just because he opened up Spanish cycling to the world but because he has an innovative, inexhaustible way of seeing life in general.'

Delgado believes: 'Bahamontes was the father of the sport and above all you'd think, my goodness, if there was such a big difference even in my time between what we had in Spain and abroad in terms of material and training techniques, how much bigger must the difference have been back then? It was cycling at its most epic, its most legendary. Another world.'

As with any legend, though, contradictions abound. Yet perhaps this is not so surprising. Getting accurate reports of what has happened in a bike race can be complicated, even now. There may be up to two hundred starters and television tends to focus on the leading few. This fact is something all riders, not just Bahamontes, cheerfully exploit to ensure they come out looking the best. As one top Spanish cycling journalist put it to me: 'It used to be impossible to be sure of what really happened before the live TV coverage came on, which was only when there were a couple of hours left to race. If the newspaper's sports desk asked you for an on-the-spot mid-stage report of what was going on, you'd just dive into the nearest public phonebox and make it up.'

More than half a century ago, that potential for being 'economical with the truth' was far greater. Before cycling was televised, and with fifty years separating the riders from the races, their versions of events tend to be even more disparate. At the same time, the clouds in the memories of men almost all in their ninth decade grow steadily thicker. As for Bahamontes, he has only had one full-scale biography published about him. That was back in 1969 and it has long been out of print. All the more reason, then, to dust down tales of those exploits, and to do so now before the hammering on the town hall doors falls silent for good.

Chapter One
'Nunca Ha Sido Niño'
('He Never Was A Child')

On the outside wall of the church of Val de Santo Domingo, the village in the province of Toledo where Federico Bahamontes was born on 9 July, 1928, is a half-metre high plaque that reads 'Fallen for God and Spain'. It is embossed with Spanish Fascist Party symbols and the name 'José Antonio Primo de Rivera', the party's leader until he was executed in the first months of the Civil War. Beneath are listed the fourteen men from the village who died for General Franco's Nationalist Spain during the bitter three-year conflict. For the Republicans of Val de Santo Domingo, there is still no similar memorial. As was the case until Franco's death in 1975, even now, more than three decades later, the opponents to his rule have no tangible commemoration here.

If the divisions that split Spain for forty years remain unchanged on Val de Santo Domingo's church wall, time has stood still in other ways in Bahamontes' home village: the plaque on the central square, too, has not changed its name from Plaza del Generalísimo. However, this is not as uncommon as it seems. In many of the pueblos of deepest Spain, not just Val de Santo Domingo, remnants of Franco's Spain linger on in street names, plaques on church walls. A few even have his honorific 'El Caudillo' [The Leader] added to the village name itself. And hidden from sight there are far grimmer reminders: the bodies of one hundred and forty thousand Republicans murdered in mass executions are still buried in unmarked graves along roads and in ravines across the country.

The names and memorial still on display in Val de Santo Domingo are also apt reminders that without Franco and the Civil War, the Eagle of Toledo might never have achieved his status as one of Spanish cycling's greatest legends. Curiously, though, public recognition of Bahamontes' links with the village are almost non-existent. There is one street named after him, but nothing on the signs at the village entrances to indicate that this is his birthplace. Certainly there is nothing as sophisticated as a museum, as there are in many famous bike riders' home towns. Moreover, the house where Bahamontes was born, situated on a slight rise just outside the town and opposite a huge restaurant built principally to feed workers from a nearby iron foundry, was knocked down a few years ago. Demolishing what might have become a site of pilgrimage for cycling fans was hardly a profitable move. The humble house made way instead for an unintended monument to the country's new economic malaise: one of Spain's myriad phantom industrial estates, where the tarmac, street lights and traffic signals are all in place, but the recession took hold before any factories were actually built.

In fact, Val de Santo Domingo is like hundreds of anonymous agricultural villages in the remoter regions of Spain. Its centre is a huddle of single-storey, century-old, terraced houses on poorly maintained roads around the main square and church. Farther out there are more recently-built, garish, double-storey residences, each with its own concreted garden space, tiny swimming pool and garage. Beyond that are a clutch of factories, none of which look particularly active, and in the background, the vast, windswept, uncultivated, unfenced and unchanging fields of central Castille.

Val de Santo Domingo's deserted streets, even at 11 o'clock on a weekday summer's morning, give the place a decidedly spooky feel. But near a hermitage church overlooking the village at least one inhabitant is visible: an old man, Pablo Rodríguez, is walking his dog. Rodríguez vividly recalls Bahamontes coming back from the 1959 Tour and visiting Val de Santo Domingo for a celebration dinner at his school. He still has the photograph taken of all the schoolchildren, himself included, then aged eight, with Bahamontes in the middle. 'He used to come here a lot after he retired,' Rodríguez recalls, 'to visit a friend of his, Marcelino, who ran the bar on the corner next to the main road. But when Marcelino died, that was it. I've barely seen him since, except on the telly.'

Indeed, just the day before, Bahamontes had popped up on the nation's screens when he appeared on the podium of the 2011 *Vuelta a España* in nearby Talavera, helping France's Sylvain Chavanel don his red jersey as race leader. But in Val de Santo Domingo nowadays Bahamontes is barely a memory. His family left for Toledo when he was eight, and Rodríguez claims there are hardly any of Bahamontes' relatives left in the village: 'Just a cousin or two' . That is only true in the living sense: the graves in the local churchyard are jammed together, just a few centimetres apart, and perhaps one in every four of those buried there has Martín, the surname of Bahamontes' father, either for their first or second name.

Rodríguez followed Bahamontes' career closely, and like so many of his fans he feels that despite winning so much Bahamontes' achievements are a fraction of what they could have been. 'It was Coppi who really guided him,' Rodríguez says in a convinced tone of voice, referring to the all-too-brief period when Bahamontes rode for the Italian champion's team. 'Without him, he wouldn't have won that Tour in 1959. Bahamontes should have won more though. But with the sort of head he has, could you really have expected it?'

Too far from Toledo to become one of the typical Spanish dormitory towns with their avenues of high-rise housing, the church tower is still the highest landmark in Val de Santo Domingo, just as it was in 1928. Behind the locked church doors the font where Bahamontes was baptised remains in place, and so too does the parish register of births, baptisms, marriages and deaths. Perhaps appropriately for a rider whose career was often shrouded in conflicting accounts, myths and half-truths, there is even some uncertainty about Bahamontes' name: in the register of baptisms he is called Alejandro. Equally strangely, though his two surnames are Martín Bahamontes, he is not known by his first, as is customary in Spain, but by his second. 'My uncle Federico was younger than my father, Julián, but Federico was the head of the family,' Bahamontes explains. 'And after the baptism he said, "This one's going to be called after me". So I was. As for Bahamontes, I used my mother's name because there were lots of Martíns out there.'

After Federico was born, his parents had three more children, all girls, each born a year apart from 1929 to 1931. It was not a large family for the time, but thankfully in those days a road-mender's job came with a rent-free house next to the section of highway for which he was responsible. In early 1936 a position came up for a foreman on a large estate just outside Toledo owned by a local aristocrat, the Duke of Montoya. Julián's parents had run a farm in his youth and his agricultural knowledge was enough to land him the more profitable job.

Initially the move was a real step up for Bahamontes' family, even if his father still earned only 3.5 pesetas a month (around 48 euros today). The family's income was supplemented by eggs, milk, meat and vegetables from the farm, and rabbits would appear on the kitchen table some mornings thanks to Julián's poaching. As for Federico, he was able to attend a charity school in Toledo run by nuns. Not surprisingly for someone as restless as Bahamontes, formal education was not something he remembers fondly. 'We spent hours sitting at desks trying to join up fancy-looking letters in blue-lined exercise books, and that was pretty much it,' Bahamontes recalls. 'It was boring as hell.'

Tedious as learning copperplate handwriting might have been, life on the Montoya estate was good for Bahamontes and his family. They had food on their plates, a roof over their heads and his father's job looked secure. However, in the space of one summer morning, a few months after they had arrived, this new-found stability was to shatter permanently.

*

At 7 a.m. on 21 July, 1936, an infantry captain named Vela-Hidalgo stood in the vast Alcázar fortress in Toledo, reading out an official declaration of war. If that was not startling enough, this declaration was especially momentous because it was being made against the Spanish Republic, an institution the Army was sworn to protect. Doubtless, Vela-Hidalgo drew on the same justifications for this armed rebellion as one of its main ringleaders, General Franco, had used shortly after the uprising started four days earlier. Franco claimed that Spain was in mortal danger because 'revolutionary hordes, backed by foreigners, were destroying our monuments and paralysing the nation with their strikes'. To make matters worse, Franco argued, the Constitution had all but disintegrated and anarchists were stalking the country. If the rebel general was to be believed, Spain was hell-bent on self-destruction and in such dramatic circumstances it was up to the Armed Forces, as the country's moral guardians, to restore order. Seizing power in the process was merely a necessary evil – or a cynical and brutal abuse of military force, depending on how you looked at it.

Military rebellions were far from uncommon in Spain, with thirty-seven attempted uprisings between 1814 and 1874 alone, twelve of them successful. Spain's only previous Republic, in the 1870s, had been brought down by the Army's intervention, and the still fledgling Second Republic (1931–39) had succeeded the military dictatorship (1923–30) of Primo de Rivera. As recently as 1931, there had been another attempt by the Army to overthrow the Republic, led by Franco's colleague General Sanjurjo.

At the time Spain was one of the poorest and least industrialised countries in Western Europe. Her established political classes were largely more interested in maintaining their own status than in improving the lot of the country's underprivileged workers. During the first five years of the Republic – Spain's first full-scale democracy – there had been some limited improvements for the working class, particularly in the education and status of women. But the country had also suffered a steady increase in political murders and general strikes as well as several attempts at all-out revolution, the most significant erupting in Asturias in October 1934.

Meanwhile, the bulk of the Spanish Army's vast surplus of officers – at the start of the century there was one general for every hundred rank-and-file soldiers – did little but conspire for the restoration of traditional, authoritarian government. The working class, for its part, was increasingly frustrated by the Republic's failure to implement the urgently-needed land, education and legal reforms that would iron out some of the tremendous social inequalities in the country, and help reduce levels of unemployment running at almost twenty per cent.

Adding to this simmering political tension were the Nationalistic movements in Spain's peripheral regions: Galicia, the Basque Country and Catalonia. Culturally very different to the rest of the peninsula, these areas were strongly separatist and large parts of their populations dreamed of splitting away from what they viewed as a corrupt and inept central government. In the wealthy Basque Country and Catalonia, the separatists also possessed the financial clout to make their case.

The social and political turmoil came to a head when a loose alliance of left-leaning political parties, the Popular Front, ousted the right-wing Government in the February 1936 general election. For the right, losing power democratically was like an open invitation to begin their latest military-led plot to return to government by force. As early as February, Franco even tried to convince the caretaker Prime Minister, Manuel Portela Valladares, not to allow the Popular Front to take power. At the opposite end of the political spectrum, hundreds of left-wing prisoners were freed even before a general amnesty was decreed. The incoming Popular Front, meanwhile, was disappointed to find that Spain's economic problems were even worse than in 1931. Sabotage of the peseta's value by right-wing industrialists had produced a radical drop in foreign investment, and the right-wing press churned out reports claiming the country was completely ungovernable, often fabricating political crimes as a means to justify the imminent uprising. Indeed, street violence, even if much of it was deliberately provoked by the Fascist-inspired Falange, was steadily growing. By 1936, even Spanish parliamentary deputies started attending debates armed; in April, a bomb was thrown, allegedly by a member of Spain's militarised Civil Guard police force, at President Manuel Azaña during the Republic's anniversary celebrations. More shooting broke out at the civil guard's funeral.

On the streets strikers and demonstrators were regularly attacked by right-wing gunmen in hit-and-run raids. In Madrid in June, for example, the Falange machine-gunned pickets during a seventy thousand-strong building strike. Others would regularly drive through working-class districts, shooting indiscriminately. At the same time, land raids on the giant *latifundia* estates in the south by local socialists and anarchists intent on farming them as cooperative communes free from money, religion and marriage, were becoming more commonplace.

The right-wing coalition opposed to the Republic (the Fascists, to their enemies) included the Monarchists, and the majority of right-wing parties including Spain's Falange. Later this alliance would became known, albeit in an amalgamated form, as *El Movimiento Nacional*, or *FET de la JONS*, the only political organisation permitted under Franco's dictatorship. The driving forces, as usual, were the upper echelons of the Armed Forces, with the support of the majority within the Spanish Catholic Church.

The final straw for the Right – even though the uprising was already well planned by this stage – was the retaliatory murder of a leading right-wing politician, Calvo Sotelo, on 13 July, 1936. Four days later, the *coup d'etat* began; first among the garrisons in Spanish Morocco, where the Republic was weakest, and then, on 18 July, by the Army in mainland Spain.

Broadly speaking, the Nationalists' common goals were an authoritarian state, the defence of the interest of the industrialists and landowners, the continuing domination of Spain by the Catholic Church and strongly centralised government. The Republicans, however, fought for a wide-ranging and diametrically opposed set of goals, from anarchist or socialist revolution through to independence for the Basque Country and Catalonia, to a simple desire to resist the continuing rise of the extreme Right across Western Europe.

Alongside the anti-interventionist stance of the democratic governments of Britain, France and the United States, and the support for the Nationalists provided by Hitler and Mussolini, the diversity of political aims among the Republicans was one of the main causes of their eventual defeat. In July 1936, in cities like Seville and Oviedo where the authorities refused to arm the workers quickly enough, the military rebellion triumphed. However, in others, like Madrid and Barcelona, Army barracks were quickly surrounded and the uprising crushed within a few days. Indeed, the coup met with far more resistance than Franco and his co-conspirators had anticipated. A mixture of trade union militiamen, a handful of regular army units, Basque and Catalan separatists, and foreign volunteers known as the International Brigades, rose to the defence of the troubled Republic. The result was the three-year Civil War that devastated Spain.

The Toledo that the Bahamontes family moved to in early 1936 was little more than a large town of around thirty thousand inhabitants. However, both militarily and historically it was far more significant. Singled out by the Roman historian Livy as being a well-fortified town as early as 192 BC, it was later the Visigoths' capital of central Spain. Following the Moorish conquest of most of Spain in the eighth century it was viewed as one of Europe's most culturally advanced and ethnically tolerant cities. Through much of the Middle Ages, Arab, Jewish and native Spanish communities lived side by side, and its market places, craftsmen and university thrived on what was an unusual example of successful integration. Today the architecture in the older parts of Toledo, particularly its labyrinthine Jewish quarter, is a vivid reminder of its bedrock of different cultures. However, the city's tolerant ethos came to an abrupt end in 1480 when, during their process of uniting Spain for the first time, the 'Catholic Kings' Fernando II of Aragón and Isabella I of Castille announced that the Jewish residents of Toledo were forbidden to live in Christian areas. Far worse was to come in 1492. While across Spain the Arabs were forced to convert to Christianity, the Jews were expelled en masse.

Sixteenth-century Castille was Spain's industrial and commercial powerhouse, and while Toledo was only the country's capital for a brief period, it was the spiritual centre of Spain's Roman Catholicism for much longer. It had always been famous for its high quality metalwork, and as Spain's foreign policies grew increasingly belligerent following the country's unification in 1492, so too did the demands for the weaponry made in Toledo. 'Toledo blades' became world famous, and a symbol of the city: even today, winners of bike race stages that finish in Toledo will often receive a large commemorative sword.

Even though Toledo lost its political stature in 1561 when Felipe II adopted Madrid as his capital, the town remained of key military importance. At the time of the Civil War, the Alcázar fortress housed Spain's main military academy and Toledo's proximity to Madrid made it an ideal forward position for an assault on the Republican capital. Furthermore, as one of the largest military buildings in Spain, dominating the skyline of old Toledo, the Alcázar attained huge symbolic value. Perhaps unsurprisingly, then, as soon as the Civil War started, Toledo took a real hammering. Though by no means a major battle, the attempt by the Republicans to gain control of the Alcázar was bitterly fought, and its successful defence by Franco's supporters was raised to near-mystical levels on the Nationalist side.

The alleged execution of the 16-year-old son of the Alcázar commander after he refused to surrender (other reports say the boy was killed in reprisal for an air-raid) was seized on with zeal by Nationalist propagandists. Moreover, Franco's decision to divert his march on Madrid towards Toledo to ensure the Alcázar did not fall into Republican hands is widely believed to have provided the definitive consolidation of his hold on the Nationalist leadership.

All this came at a high price to the city, though. By the time Franco visited the Alcázar on 29 September after his supporters had held out for two months huge sections of Toledo held by the Republicans had been destroyed, both by artillery fire and inaccurate air-raids. Photographs from the siege's aftermath show the fortress looking like a sandcastle swept over by a succession of high tides. Towers lean at crazy angles, walls have caved in and foundations laid bare by vast craters. Little more than a quarter of the building above ground remained standing. Outside in the city itself, contemporary photographs show little more than a mass of tangled house beams, piles of bricks and gutted buildings. Destruction of this magnitude was far from uncommon in the Spanish Civil War, and the numbers of refugees ran into the millions. Among them were Bahamontes and his family.

A veteran combatant of the Spanish war in Cuba in the 1890s, Bahamontes' father was too old to be recruited by either side. However, he still came within a whisker of becoming one of the Civil War's earliest victims. As news broke that a Republican column of troops and militia was on its way, Franco's forces retreated to the Alcázar in Toledo and many civilians were enlisted to accompany the General's men to act as reinforcements, or more accurately cannon fodder. Julián was one of them. Realising his chances of survival were low – as it turned out, only half of the Alcázar's one thousand defenders made it through the siege uninjured – he managed to escape undetected. That was far from being the end of his troubles, though. The Duke of Montoya's estate was the ideal location for the Republic's artillery in their siege of the Alcázar. When Julián returned home, it was to find the whole area had been taken over by militiamen who, Bahamontes says scornfully, 'had come down from Madrid by taxi. And they called themselves Communists!'

Communists or not, Julián was ordered to open up the estate's storehouses so they could steal cooking oil. When he refused, they threatened to shoot him. Julián took to his heels for a second time that day and managed to shake off the ensuing manhunt by hiding in a doorway. By the time he reached the family house later that night, spent shell cases lay scattered across the surrounding farmland and the Republic's battalion of 102-millimetre guns was stationed in the middle of it, blazing away at the fortress. In a matter of hours, Toledo had gone up in flames and the whole area had become a war zone. Under the circumstances, Julián, his wife

Victoria and their family had only one option: to join the long line of refugees making their way towards Madrid and relative safety.

The family reached the Spanish capital in the back of a cart in late July 1936. Once there they settled in a vast refugee camp set up in the grounds of Madrid University. 'We were living like gypsies, under canvas,' Bahamontes recalls. 'There were people there in their thousands.'

For the first few months of the war, after the Army's attempt to take the city had failed, Madrid remained the seat of the Republican Government. By late September the city was under siege from Franco's best forces at which point the Republican Government decamped to Valencia. But the combination of armed workers' militias, a few regular army units and later the International Brigades, saved the city for the Republic. As the initial turmoil subsided, and despite air-raids and trenches across many of the main streets, Madrid regained something akin to pre-war normality. In the centre, restaurants and expensive shops reopened, even though the front-line was only a few kilometres away. Indeed, Gran Via, one of the city's main thoroughfares, was known as 'Howitzer Alley' because of the number of shells that fell there. While refugees in cities like Barcelona were often installed in the homes of middle-class families who had fled, in Madrid they were largely left to fend for themselves. The Bahamontes family was no exception.

As soon as possible Julián moved his family again, away from the refugee camp, to stay with his sister in a flat in a cul-de-sac near El Retiro Park in central Madrid. Julián went to register their new address – 'he had no choice if he wanted a ration card for the family,' as Bahamontes recalls – and this time he was promptly roped into the Republican Army. Julián's age meant he could only form part of the reserve and he was detailed to work in supplies. His experience with animals led to him being put in charge of a mule team hauling provisions from a vast depot at Atocha railway station on Madrid's south side up to the front at Brunete, a few kilometres outside the city. It was dangerous work, but it had some advantages. As Bahamontes points out, Julián could steal some of the Army's provisions.

Federico, meanwhile, was also busy contributing to his family's upkeep by pilfering firewood from trees cut down in El Retiro Park. As the park had been closed, Bahamontes remembers that the only way to get the wood out was to perch between the iron spikes of the railings. It was a tight squeeze for an eight-year-old, but just about manageable. 'Once I'd got there, I'd throw a rope with a hook on it into the park and drag the fallen branches towards me,' Bahamontes says. 'Then we'd heave the branches over the railings, drag them home, and use the rope again to haul them up to my aunt's flat for fuel for cooking.'

As the air raids increased, Federico, his mother and sisters were sent to stay with relatives in the village of Villarubia de Santiago, to the south of Madrid. 'We had an aunt with an olive tree plantation, that was enough of a reason to go,' Bahamontes explains. With an increasing lack of food in Madrid, the capital certainly held little attraction. Toledo, now in Franco's hands, was unreachable, so the Bahamontes family spent the rest of the conflict in a village in one of the last Republican zones to surrender.

When the war ended with Franco's victory on 1 April, 1939, the family were joined by Julián and remained in Villarubia de Santiago for another two years. There was nowhere else for them to go: the Duke of Montoya's estate had been swept away by the Civil War, and as a soldier on the losing side Julián was not entitled to any kind of pension. The only job he could find was breaking rocks as a road-mender's mate. Federico, now aged eleven, was expected to help him. 'His job was to split them up with a pick, and then I would break them up into smaller pieces,' Bahamontes recalls. 'That was it.'

For two years, Bahamontes' childhood consisted of little more than moving from one section of road to another and breaking stones. The monotony of the work can only be imagined. But as Bahamontes puts it, there was no other option. That said, since professional cyclists were dubbed 'the convicts of the road' by the media at the time, there is a slightly ironic edge to how he spent his early youth.

In early 1941 the Bahamontes family decided to return to Toledo. They could hardly have chosen a worse time.

When Bahamontes started winning top international cycle races he quickly became a sporting hero for Franco's regime. It is ironic, then, that Bahamontes' youth was so distorted by the consequences of the war that placed Franco in power: mass poverty, an economy in ruins, famine, widespread ill-health and disease.

Nor did things improve quickly for the Spanish after the Civil War. There are a number of reasons for this: poor economic management by Franco's government; the seemingly endemic corruption in the one-party, military dictatorship he created; and, finally, the conflict in the rest of Europe and the Allies' partial blockade of the country. Even the end of World War Two had little positive effect on Spain's economy. A report by *The Daily Telegraph*'s Spanish correspondent in the summer of 1946 from the city of Cordoba in the southern region of Andalusia leaves no doubt about the levels of poverty. 'All the usual revolting signs of famine are there: children with hideously swollen stomachs, fragile limbs and wizened, emaciated faces, women like human scarecrows with enormous eyes who are unable to move as their joints are swollen,' he wrote.

Hispanist Gerald Brenan, who travelled through the country in 1949, was equally graphic. 'The widespread corruption causes shame and dismay,' Brenan wrote in his account of his travels, *The Face of Spain*. 'The system of government controls is the despair of businessmen, whilst the severe inflation has reduced the middle and lower classes to great straits and the agricultural labourers to starvation. The feeling given out by Spain today is that of a country whose road to – I do not say prosperity – but simply any humanly tolerable condition is blocked.'

As for Toledo itself in the 1940s, Brenan describes it as 'a strange, dark, almost ominous city . . . built on a bare rocky hill in a loop of the Tagus – a fortress if there ever was one – it has, through the greater part of its history, been [a] citadel. What a rabbit warren its streets and houses and churches make! Like Fez it reeks of the

Middle Ages: like Lhasa, of monks. Yet the thing that most impressed me on this occasion was the proximity of the bare, rocky hills beyond the river gorge, walking in narrow, crooked lanes . . . that harsh, waterless sierra, with its iron-coloured boulders looks as if it rose from the end of the street. Toledo, one says to oneself – though it is not quite true – is a fortress built in a desert.'

But like the rest of Spain, Toledo had almost nothing left to defend. If many Spanish middle-class families, according to Brenan, could only afford one full meal a day if they wanted to buy decent clothes, for ordinary working-classes families like Bahamontes', life became a desperate hand-to-mouth struggle against starvation. While the cost of living was five times higher in the 1950s than it had been before the war, it was only in 1954 that average incomes in Spain returned to pre-Civil War levels.

'Federico never was a child,' his mother said on the eve of his greatest victory, the 1959 Tour de France. 'It just wasn't possible.' Like so many Spaniards under Franco, Bahamontes had to grow up far too fast for any notion of childhood.

The Bridge of Saint Martin, or *Puente de San Martín* to give it its name in Spanish, has always been one of Toledo's most popular attractions for travellers. That is partly because you cannot miss it. Built in the fourteenth century across the River Tagus to supplement the older, narrower *Puente de Alcántara*, *San Martín* boasts five giant arches, the largest with a massive forty-metre span. At each end of the bridge there are two more gigantic archways set into towers; each tower is heavily fortified and bristles with cannon. It is the first man-made landmark anyone sees when they approach the city's outskirts, and it would have been as unforgettable and unmistakable a sight for visitors in the Middle Ages as San Francisco's Golden Gate is for globetrotters today.

Six centuries later, as a child growing up in Toledo in the 1940s, Federico Martín Bahamontes looked on the *Puente de San Martín* rather more irreverently. True to his reputation for keeping an eye on the main chance, and particularly in pursuit of food in those days, the bridge was an ideal location for the odd spot of robbery.

'We'd climb up one of the towers just before a vegetable lorry went underneath,' Bahamontes recalls with an impish grin. 'When the lorry got there, it would have to slow because the archway's so narrow. And then we'd drop on top of the load and fill up a bag with beetroot. Or we'd slit open a sack with sugar or beets in it, fill up a bag, and steal those instead.' This kind of derring-do may sound like the stuff of Errol Flynn movies, but for Bahamontes and his teenage accomplices, stealing vegetables was no pastime: it was part of the daily fight to stave off hunger. 'Orange peel, stale bread, vine shoots, rotten fruit and cats – I ate them all in my childhood,' Bahamontes recalls. 'If I caught a cat, I'd cut off its paws and head, and skin it. Then my mother would gut it, fill up the cavities with salt, pepper and vegetables, and pop it in the oven. They tasted delicious. We called them "baby goats".'

While the family could afford few scruples about where they got their food from, they were equally practical about what they wore. 'My mother would make us clothes out of hand-me-downs, given to her by people who took pity on us. She'd get old shoes, and remake them with canvas undersoles so we had something to wear on our feet. It didn't get so bad we had to beg, but we were always in debt. Even if we managed to pay our bills, we were never out of the woods. Always *atascados* [bogged down].'

Bahamontes had one very dangerous way of making money: selling live ammunition dug out of old Civil War trenches around Toledo for scrap. 'It could have blown our heads off, but you don't think about that when you're starving.'

Though Bahamontes says he never saw anybody die of hunger in or after the war, it was not uncommon. A report from the American embassy in Madrid estimated that infant mortality rates in Spain's poorest areas in the early 1940s ran at fifty per cent or worse. Living so close to the edge for so long, and working from such a young age – 'I started at eleven and never stopped' – have clearly left their mark. Five decades on he can still recall exactly how much he was paid for one of his earliest jobs as a market worker.

Throughout his life Bahamontes has shown what some regard as an obsession with money and financial security. His longstanding 1960s rival and friend Raymond Poulidor recalls:. 'He came up to me in a criterium and said, "You remember that place where such and such happened" – he was capable of protesting about something that had happened two years before, too – "I bought you a stamp that day. You owe me for a stamp". He had it all written down in a little book. To be honest, it made me laugh.' Back in the 1940s, though, the struggle for even a stamp's worth of money was a far more serious matter. As Bahamontes says, 'When you talk about times like that, it sounds like a kid's battle. But you wait until it happens to you.'

Apart from road-mending and robbing lorries, Bahamontes was regularly taken out into the fields by his father to help cut wheat or hay. When the harvest was over, however, father and son had to look for whatever work they could find for the winter. 'We came back in 1941 and in Toledo it was the most desperate year of a desperate era,' Bahamontes recalls. There was barely enough food to be had for anybody. My mother would get a lump of bread and some garlic, boil it up in some water, and we'd have that for supper. You know those [tv survival] programmes where they eat cockroaches on desert islands? That was nothing compared to '40 and '41'

The family of six lived in a three-roomed flat, with no electricity, no heating and no running water. Fuel was rarely available; in any case, as 'the coal carts had to come all the way from Madrid and the roads were so bad they would only get through once every three or four days'. Gainful employment was difficult to find, and Bahamontes is convinced his father's personality often worked against him. As Bahamontes puts it: 'He was shy, too shy, a nothing, a zero. If it hadn't been for my mother, we'd have all died in a ditch.'

To describe a parent like this, particularly when Bahamontes says he got on well with his father, sounds unbelievably harsh. But in his defence, the family bordered on the brink of starvation for most of his childhood and the majority of his waking hours were spent in search of food. Under the circumstances, shyness simply meant you stayed hungry longer. Fortunately Bahamontes had a similar temperament to his mother, and he was tenacious and versatile with it. By hanging around Toledo market long enough, he was finally hired to unload a cart, receiving fifteen centimos per one hundred and fifty kilo load. This was a ridiculously low sum, around twenty-five pence in modern currency, but it was money nonetheless.

Slowly but surely Bahamontes became a regular hired hand at the market. 'You'd meet one person, make friends with them, and then you'd get to know another,' is how he explains it. 'It was all about contacts. And not wanting to be hungry.' Starting at six in the morning, he would begin his day by unloading lorries, then move on to picking out spoiled fruit and vegetables from the loads. He even had a nickname: *El Lechuga* – the Lettuce-boy. This second job in the market was much more to his liking, because he quickly opened up a sideline with private auctions of any fruit rejected as unsellable. 'I'd gather it all up and sell it out the front. It wasn't too hard; people were desperate,' he recalled. 'One peseta fifty centimos [£2 today], the box. Then after a while, I got enough together to buy a cart and I'd go around five different fruit shops selling produce to them direct.'

Bahamontes' business instincts were getting sharper and sharper, something that would prove invaluable later in his life. But with work in the market over by 10 a.m., by mid-morning he would find himself at a loose end again. So in 1946, when he was just eighteen, he decided to move into other, more illicit, business. To do that, though, he needed a more sophisticated mode of transport.

Bahamontes' first bike cost him one hundred and fifty pesetas (£250 in modern money). For an occasional market labourer, it was a small fortune. 'It was second-hand, too, and had no brakes or tyres either, which was a real worry because if you wanted to buy new ones you had to return the previous set,' Bahamontes recalls. However, he was convinced it was worth the investment. His plan was to ride from village to village, picking up illegal loads of bread, beans and flour, and selling them on in Toledo. Throughout Spain, villages had got off far more lightly in the Civil War, hiding stores of food from the authorities. With rationing still in force until the

1950s, the black market flourished. Typically, Bahamontes has no problem recalling how much money he made. 'The villagers would make a profit of at least two pesetas [£3] a bike load. If they'd sold it wholesale, they'd have made far less. Also, I could sell it cheaper than the official rate. So we were all on to a good thing.'

Bahamontes was not the only Spanish cycling star who started riding a bike for illegal profit. Carmelo Morales, a top Spanish rider of the 1950s, started riding a bike aged eleven to deliver fish his family had 'forgotten' to pay the municipal tax on. He earned his nickname of *El Jabalí* after he dodged the Civil Guard by diving into the bushes and wriggling away through the undergrowth so fast they told villagers that Morales was just as difficult to catch as a wild boar.

Bernardo Ruiz, the winner of the Vuelta a España in 1948, also admitted that he 'only began riding a bike to shift goods around'. When asked what kind of things he would transport, he gave an embarrassed smile, and said: 'Well, black market goods.' Bahamontes, on the other hand, positively delights in revealing his 'criminal' past. As he puts it: 'It's all part of the legend.'

Bahamontes' parents were initially opposed to him buying the bike. But when they realised it had been purchased with the sole aim of making money on the sly, they gave their approval. Of course, black marketeering had its risks. The Civil Guard, the semi-militarised police force who handled all rural crime, watched the roads and anyone caught in possession of illegal goods faced a prison sentence. Bahamontes, though, had bought a racing bike, complete with drop handlebars, with good reason: to ensure he could make a fast getaway. Like his fellow conspirators from Toledo, he had other tactics, too. 'We deliberately timed it so we'd go to the villages when it was hottest. That way we'd be on the roads when the police were asleep under a tree. And we'd warn each other if our paths crossed – you know, just like cars flash their headlights nowadays when there's a speed trap coming – so you'd know if you had to change roads. We knew all the shortcuts and we knew their schedules. It worked.'

Bahamontes had a few close shaves, but riding the back lanes on his bike gave him a considerable advantage over the Civil Guard, who were either on foot or horseback. 'And I reckoned,' Bahamontes says with slightly disturbing nonchalance, 'that they would never shoot at a black marketeer.' Fortunately, he never had to find out. He managed to steer clear of the Civil Guard for nearly two years, though he paid a high price for his nearest miss. 'One of my friends gave me a tip-off they [the Civil Guard] were coming up the road I wanted to use and I had to hide under a bridge. I managed to get there just in time, but I was standing in stagnant water for so long I got bitten by a mosquito and ended up with typhoid.' Typhoid is not actually transmitted by mosquitoes, but whatever led to Bahamontes' illness, and whatever the illness was, the effects were highly unpleasant. 'I ended up so ill I couldn't leave the house for two months. I had bouts of high fever that were so severe they thought I might die. When the fever came down I was so hungry I would break open the padlock my mother had put on the larder door to steal whatever I could get. I was as thin as an anorexic. I must have weighed about forty-five kilos [a little over seven stones] at the worst point. I was so weak I couldn't walk. Two of my sisters would carry me between them around the town so I could get some fresh air. All my hair fell out, too. Before it had been straight, and when it grew again after I was cured it came out much curlier.' He was given a doctor's certificate, which stated that he had chronic chest problems and recommended he avoid all types of physically demanding sports. As Bahamontes would delight in telling journalists in the years to come, that obviously included cycling. But, of course, he continued riding. After all, blind obedience to authority has never been in his nature.

So what led Bahamontes to move from black marketeer to bike rider? The simple answer is money, and the talent to make it.

But if the driving force was economic, it was pure chance that first pushed Bahamontes to enter a race. On Wednesday, 18 July, 1947, as they would do every year on the anniversary of the start of the Civil War until his death nearly three decades later, General Franco's supporters celebrated his victory and rise to power. The country would grind to a halt. But not everybody spent the so-called *Fiesta Nacional* in a public show of loyalty to the ruling regime. After his 1959 Tour win, the still severely censored Spanish media would claim that Bahamontes had made enough money from his market work to buy the bike on which he rode his first race a dozen years before. But, in fact, Bahamontes had spent that morning riding the thirty-one kilometres from Toledo to the town of Torres to pick up an illegal shipment of bread, flour and beans and bring it back in bags slung over his handlebars. For the black marketeers, 18 July was business as usual. The only difference for Bahamontes was that because the street market where he had his legal job was closed for the celebrations, he could make an earlier start.

By midday he was back in Toledo, his illicit consignment disposed of, and his bike pointing homewards. But a chance meeting with two other teenage black marketeers took Bahamontes' life in a different direction altogether. His partners-in-crime were competing in a bike race, organised as part of the *Fiesta Nacional* in the nearby village of Minasalbas. When they invited Bahamontes to join them, he jumped at the chance.

At this point it is worth recalling that Bahamontes had never taken part in a competition of any kind before. His one attempt to play a sport, in his case soccer, had ended when his father crept into his room in the middle of the night and cut his football to ribbons. He wanted to be sure his son had no distractions from work. However, when Bahamontes reached the start of his first race, he came up against an even bigger obstacle than his father: Spanish bureaucracy. It transpired he needed a licence to take part. Luck remained on his side. After a quick word with a government official, the required document was obtained and filled in. Even today in Spain, this kind of simple bureaucratic process can take weeks. That day, for Bahamontes at least, it took no time at all; perhaps because the race was sponsored by the Ministry of Education itself and was part of the official celebrations of Franco's victory, they felt the more riders they got to the start-line the better.

Now Bahamontes was the owner of his first race licence and had become a *bone fide* amateur bike rider. Unfortunately he had come completely unprepared. His work bike was a racer, true enough, but he had no sports clothes. Instead, as he was to recall thousands of times, he rode his first race in his usual trousers and a borrowed baseball shirt with reinforced shoulder pads. As for food, a lemon and a banana were his only sustenance; by the end of the event, he was so hungry he wolfed down the lot, banana skin and lemon peel included.

The race, around forty-five kilometres long, started well enough. As soon as the flag dropped, not knowing the textbook tactic was to conserve strength until the end, he made a move that was to become 'vintage Bahamontes'. As a handwritten note says on the first page in his privately published account of the 1959 Tour de France, 'my tactic from the beginning was attack, attack and attack again'. It would have caught the rest by surprise. Unfortunately there was a mechanical problem: Bahamontes' bike chain kept coming off. And not for the last time he was caught on a descent. Not all was lost, though. After sitting in the bunch for the rest of the race, Bahamontes amazingly finished second. Encouraged by this, he decided to come back the following week for more.

Bahamontes' next race was sixty kilometres long, and he still wore the same basketball shirt and trousers. At least he had sorted out the problem with his chain. On the downside, the opposition was far stronger. Of the twenty-five riders taking part, the youngest was Bahamontes' age, the oldest twenty-two or twenty-three. Fortunately Bahamontes had a secret weapon: 'Team Fede', a lorry-load of supporters. With his three younger sisters on board, as well as their respective boyfriends, the lorry drove along behind the race. Bahamontes could not see them, but knowing they were there was a major boost to his morale. The flag dropped. Almost immediately, he put his head down, stomped on the pedals and opened a gap. It was only his second race, but he already had a trademark move. By the halfway point, Bahamontes was still out in front, alone and pedalling his way slowly but steadily across the arid semi-desert which surrounds Toledo. His only company in the miles of featureless flatlands was a one-man police motorbike escort. A long way behind, a low dust cloud indicated the main pack of chasers. It had become a one-bike race. At one point, the outrider dropped back level with Bahamontes and looked across at him. 'Hey,' he shouted, 'aren't you bored out here by yourself?' Bahamontes looked back. 'Don't worry,' he replied, 'I'm doing just fine.'

Chapter Two
The Melon Thief

After victory in only his second race, Bahamontes endured another summer of backbreaking, poorly paid agricultural work with his father before deciding to start racing as a full-time amateur. The logic of the choice was almost purely financial. 'I could make more money out of winning one race than my father would make out of working in an entire harvest,' Bahamontes recalls.

However, piecing together his progress in the early years of his career is anything but simple. The economic dificulties that faced races he took part in as an amateur are largely responsible: frequently events already curtailed for three years by the Civil War in the 1930s would appear and disappear again. This endemic problem would even affect the country's flagship professional event, the Vuelta a España. Moreover, the erratic newspaper reporting in a country governed by a military dictatorship, and in the throes of its worst economic depression in a century, also contributed. 'The Spanish press makes a curious study,' writer Gerald Brenan observed in 1949. 'The first thing one notices is there is scarcely any news given in the Madrid papers about Spain. One is not told, for example, that the factories in Barcelona are only working two days a week. The foreigner casting his eye over the press might well suppose that nothing happens in the Peninsula except football matches, religious ceremonies and bullfights.' The arbitrary nature of the reporting meant that the Volta a Catalunya stage race, for example, was enormously popular in its own region and received

huge amounts of column inches in the local newspapers. Beyond
the Catalan frontiers, however, despite being Spain's biggest race
between 1951 and 1954, it barely made an impact. In 1953 *ABC*, the
leading Madrid-based newspaper of the time, published exactly
four paragraphs, all results, on the race's final stage.

The racing conditions themselves reflected Spain's extreme
poverty and almost non-existent infrastructure. An early
Government-funded documentary of the 1946 Vuelta a España,
designed to promote Spain in the best possible light and shown in
Spanish cinemas, cannot avoid revealing much of the country's true
condition. For nearly a month, and on a course lasting three
thousand eight hundred kilometres, the forty-six-strong peloton
raced the length and breadth of Spain: from Madrid, south through
Extremadura to Seville, then north and east to San Sebastian, via
Barcelona, and finally back, through Santander and Valladolid, to
Madrid again. Because it covered so much terrain, the
documentary is probably one of the most complete visual
'snapshots' of Spain since the Civil War ended seven years before.
The scars of the conflict are still clearly visible. Not just in the black-
clad widows, many of them young women, who form dark knots
in the crowds lining the route. The country itself is barely back on
its feet: none of the roads outside the cities are tarmacked; the
surfaces often just a tangle of ruts and badly spaced cobblestones.
The consequences of that disrepair are also evident: every two
minutes or so an injured rider is shown slumped on the side of the
road as orderlies bandage him up.

And not even a propaganda film can hide the occasional glimpse
of bombed-out buildings in the background as the riders pedal by.
The lack of infrastructure extends to the race itself where the black,
high-sided support cars look pre-War in appearance – pre-World
War One, that is. Handkerchiefs are used as flags, there are no
banners except at the finish line, no barriers or advertising on or
off the riders' dark clothing. The heavy-looking racing bikes have
no numbers; instead they are pinned to the riders' backs. Certainly
there is nothing like a winner's podium, no cups or bouquets, at
least until the twenty-nine riders who complete the Vuelta reach

the final stage finish at an athletics stadium in Madrid.

The poverty is unmissable, too. The wiriness of the spectators in the large crowds is visible even at a distance. In many cases their threadbare Sunday-best clothes hang off them, and a fair proportion of the women and children are barefoot, particularly outside the cities. One tall male spectator is wrapped in nothing but a blanket. Most telling of all is the difference in physical condition of the public and the cyclists: even after three weeks' hard racing the riders, traditionally scrawny alongside 'normal' people, look comparatively healthy and well-fed.

Cars, too, are a rarity. In one shot the few vehicles visible are outnumbered by horses and carts. Bikes, though, abound; many have been converted for carrying heavy loads. At one point three lads, very probably black marketeers to judge by the large, unmarked boxes and bags behind their saddles, look worriedly at the camera for a second before haring off at top speed. However, the biggest difference between these images of Spain and contemporary footage of, say, Great Britain, is the almost total absence of features you would take for granted in a twentieth-century European landscape: telegraph poles and wires, pavements, streetlights, parked cars, tarmac. There are barely any shops, few blocks of flats, no billboards, no parks. Remove the travelling circus of the Vuelta and you could be in the Spain of the 1840s: the sense of grinding economic misery is palpable.

In an interview in 1962, Spain's most successful racer of the 1940s, Julián Berrendero, recalled: 'We raced as if we had been abandoned by everybody. We had no help. We had bikes with just three gears rather than the ten you normally have now.' Asked how tough it was to race, he answered: 'If I suffered half now of what I had to put up with in my best years, I would be a millionaire. I put up with everything. In the 1937 Tour I fell and they gave me six stitches in my knee. The wound burst open, but I kept racing. They stitched me up, I went to bed, started again, it burst open again, and so on and so on until I completed the race. These days nobody could stand that sort of torture – nobody.'

Born in the village of San Agustín de Guadalix near Madrid,

Berrendero was toughened by his harsh youth which included working long hours at a clay pigeon shoot for two pesetas (six euros) a day. But Berrendero's recollection of his racing days show that life in the peloton made significant demands for very little reward. The races, he confirms, were run with minimal infrastructure, but the riders got on with it. 'We were much more resistant to everything – cold, heat, rain. I don't know if it was because we were so desperate for the money, but there were no wages, no start money, and if you abandoned you had to make your own way home. When we raced the Vuelta a España there were only half-a-dozen support cars and two or three journalists to keep the whole country informed. Now there are dozens of them.' Berrendero, amazingly, seemed to have a certain nostalgia for the savage racing conditions of two decades earlier. 'These days the trade teams have hugely improved things financially for the riders. Cycling has lost nothing as a spectacle, but it's lost the grandeur of those superhuman efforts. There are far more people involved, but their love of cycling has diminished.'

If the Vuelta a España was the country's premier bike race, what must the provincial races of Bahamontes' early years have been like? With the country's transport and communication infrastructure so poor, and such long distances between the major cities, the bike racing 'scene' in the late 1940s and early 1950s was a series of chronically disconnected hubs of activity. Some, like Catalonia, were very dynamic; others, such as Andalusia, only sporadically so. What they all had in common was scant knowledge about what was going on elsewhere in the cycling world. It was something Bahamontes exploited to the full, whether consciously or not.

Racing across the country, Bahamontes pops up under different names: first as Martín, secondly Martín Bahamontes, and thirdly, and most frequently, 'Bahamonde'. 'Bahamontes' only starts to appear in the newspapers with any degree of consistency in late 1953. Ask him these days about the name-changing and Bahamontes just grins. But he had reason to be happy with all of them. He should have used Martín, his father's surname, but preferred his mother's. General Franco's second surname was Bahamonde, and for an ambitious young man like Bahamontes, letting the public think he shared a family name with the *Generalísimo* was presumably appealing, if only because it caught the attention of the press. Most importantly, though, this ambiguity kept rivals in the dark about whether he was competing in a race until he appeared at the starting line. By then, of course, it was too late. Their concern was understandable since Bahamontes had discovered a formula that guaranteed him success: forming a combine with another rider, also from Toledo.

'His name was Ladislau Soria and we were both strong riders. He didn't climb well but was good on the flat, and with me it was the other way round,' Bahamontes recalls. 'His brother, who was a telegraph operator at [nearby] Aranjuez railway station, organised our trips. He was our manager, but he didn't charge us any money. He'd ring up the villages and towns where he knew the annual *fiesta* was coming up and he'd ask, "Are you going to put on a bike race as part of the celebrations?" If the answer was yes, then off we'd head. Nine times out of ten, we'd win.'

With cars scarce and the roads in terrible condition, there was only one way Bahamontes and Soria could travel between races: as hobos on the railways. 'We'd go in the guards van of goods trains so we wouldn't have to pay. [Soria's] mother would cook us up some breaded pork chops and omelettes, and we'd put them in a wicker basket for later.' With his transport, racing programme and sustenance all laid on by his colleague, Bahamontes was on to a winner. He did make a contribution, though, albeit a minor one: 'When I chipped in with a bit of bread that was us sorted for food.'

Sleepless nights and spectacularly long bike rides, often in the dark, were part and parcel of the dynamic duo's campaigns. 'There was the time we went from Toledo to Motilla del Palancar [three hundred kilometres] in one night. We travelled from Toledo to Aranjuez [60 kilometres] by bike, Aranjuez to Cinco Casas by train, then rode from Cinco Casas to Tomelloso [twenty kilometres] in the middle of the night in the pitch dark. Then it was back on the train again and we got to Motilla at seven in the morning. We ate a couple of bananas, drank a litre of milk, slept on four chairs pulled together for an hour, then went out to race.'

This 'hobo' image is not as surprising as it sounds. In many ways the Spanish cyclists of the late 1940s and early 1950s had more in common with other 'rootless' lifestyles of the time – like tinkers, itinerant musicians and theatre companies – than they did with professional sportsmen. The first time Jesús Loroño, one of Bahamontes' main rivals, ran into the Eagle of Toledo was in 1953 when they were both en route to a bike race. 'He was lying under a tree, sucking on a lump of fat, and looking like a tramp in scruffy workaday clothes.' Loroño's description was confirmed by another leading rider, Miguel Poblet. 'I first came across Bahamontes when I did my military service, and I competed in the military national championships in Toledo, riding for Catalonia. Suddenly riding along behind me I noticed this really scrawny kid wearing rag-tag clothes. He overtook us even though he had nothing to do with the race! Admittedly we had our rifles and bandoliers, but he still overtook us. And when I next saw Bahamontes, in a Volta a Catalunya, he told me it had been him.'

Hitching rides on goods trains meant there was little certainty about when the pair would get back to Toledo, or whether their supplies would last them. If money was tight the only solution was to steal fruit and vegetable crops from fields. Bahamontes recalls one nightmare ride from a race in Burgos to Toledo [400 kilometres] in which he and Soria ate nothing but purloined, half-ripe, watermelons. Bahamontes' partnership with Soria was a makeshift system but it was highly effective. 'We stitched them up time and again. I won one amateur Tour of Andalusia by over an hour, as well as four stages and a hill-climb to Sierra Nevada, then did the same all over again in the Tour of Cadiz. And I always finished alone. It got to the point that riders wouldn't want to start if they knew we were racing.'

This lucrative collaboration was interrupted in July 1949 when Bahamontes was summoned for National Service. Billeted at Canillejas, close to Madrid, the sudden loss of the freedom to travel more or less where he wanted, coupled with life in an army barracks after two years of making money hand over fist, came as a shock to Bahamontes. 'For eighteen months my life consisted of trying to eat as many black beans and lentils as I could,' he recalls. 'That's what I wanted to eat, anyway. But for some reason the saucepans in the barracks never seemed to hold anything bar water. We were always hungry. I'd ride over to Toledo to see my girlfriend [Fermina, who Bahamontes had met in the local market where she worked] and she gave me parcels of sausages and chocolate.'

In fact, financially, his life was picking up. He and his family had built their own house, principally out of rubble from bombed-out Civil War buildings. By 1950, aged just twenty-two, Bahamontes had opened a shop in Toledo, a one-roomed 'hole in the wall' where he rented out bikes. As he was doing his military service at the time, a former amateur rider who would become a life-long business associate, Faustino Suárez, took over as manager. Fermina manned the cash register, as she would do in a series of bike shops Bahamontes was to own in Toledo. 'She was there on the front-line for her whole life,' Bahamontes says. 'Wherever there's money, the women are always there. They're the ones who look after it the best.'

Bahamontes was breaking through in other areas as well, taking the King of the Mountains title in the amateur Tour of Ávila in 1948. The earliest reference to him in a national daily newspaper, albeit under one of his aliases, came in *ABC*'s sporadic coverage of the same race on 26 May, 1949. After three stages, the first two having gone unreported, one 'Bahamonde de Toledo' was lying fifth, a minute and a half down. The final stage, on 27 May, was won by Bahamontes, though most *ABC* readers may not have noticed: the story was tucked away in the bottom right-hand corner of page seventeen. Nonetheless, Bahamontes' win was there. A bold eight-line series of results records that at the end of a stage one hundred and nine kilometres long, which ran from Arevalo to Ávila, 'Bahamonde' outstripped the pack in his last chance for victory. Soria, his combine companion, was fifth.

Even if the media coverage was patchy, the prize money offered was still irresistible for even the least talented rider, and Bahamontes was far from that. Bernardo Ruiz recounts that when he first travelled to the Volta a Catalunya race in 1945, aged twenty-one, he had three hundred and fifty pesetas [£240 in modern money] in his back pocket and had never been outside the region of Valencia in his life. After winning the Volta a Catalunya, he came back home with several times that amount. Compared with Bahamontes' two peseta mark-up on each bike load from his black market trade in Toledo, there is no question which was the more profitable profession; it also explains why Bahamontes stuck at cycling so determinedly.

From the earliest days his preference for a spectacular racing style over an effective one shone through. 'He always had to win alone,' recalled Luis López Nicolas, an amateur rider at the time and later a journalist with *El Alcázar* newspaper. 'Sitting in and waiting for a sprint was too comfortable an option for him. He was a nervous rider who launched attack after attack, most of them inconsequential.' Bahamontes bought a lighter bike with his winnings: it weighed just twelve kilos rather than twenty, which increased his chances of victory. But he had a propensity to be involved in crashes, even if they were not all of his own making. According to *El Alcázar* one of the most spectacular was in the 1948 amateur national championships when a spectator crossing the road brought down the peloton. Bahamontes was in the thick of the ensuing pile-up, but still ran fifth. An animal was responsible for Bahamontes' next big crash, which took place when he was leading the 1948 Tour of Ávila: during a descent a pig ran into the road and right into the pack. 'As the crash happened just after a corner, more and more riders blasted round the bend at 60 k.p.h. and slammed into the mass of bodies,' *El Alcázar* reported. 'One, Isidro López de Salamanca, had his head split open like a watermelon and had to be taken to hospital. Fortunately he survived. The skin was ripped off the whole of Bahamontes left side – arm, leg, thigh and face – but fortunately he was all right apart from that.' Bahamontes made a supreme effort to try to catch an Asturian rider named Suárez, who was lying second overall and who had dodged the crash. In an eighty-kilometre pursuit, Bahamontes managed to overtake several other riders, but lack of food, coupled with exhaustion and the after-effects of the crash forced him to abandon. Nevertheless it was an indication of the innate tenacity which would pay him dividends in the future.

Bahamontes' narrowest escape in his amateur years, though, did not happen while he was racing, but when he was taking one of his late-night rides between events with Soria. After finishing first and third in a race near Toledo, the two had to make it to Cuenca, two hundred kilometres further east, for another event the following day. But there were no train connections. Having ridden more than one hundred and fifty kilometres in pitch darkness, Bahamontes hit a stone in the road and went over his handlebars. Bleeding heavily from two major wounds, one in the arm, the other in his shoulder, he was unconscious for half an hour. 'Soria was really nervous, he thought I'd killed myself,' Bahamontes told *El Alcázar*. The two arrived in Cuenca at 5 a.m., woke up four hours later and once again finished first and third, even though Bahamontes could only grip his handlebars with one hand. Sometimes Bahamontes' mishaps were caused deliberately by his rivals. At one race in Toledo, there were so many tin-tacks on the road he punctured eight times. But having sent his father home to get all the spare tyres he could find, Bahamontes still finished.

'In 1948 he raced in San Sebastián for the first time, at the Ministry of Education's national champomships, and that was when he first saw the sea,' López Nicolas recalls. 'Third overall, and second in the King of the Mountains competition, that was also where he told me he first felt really confident about his chances on the climbs.'

Sporadically, but steadily, more results for Bahamontes and his various aliases began to appear in the press: second in the opening stage of the Tour of Ávila 1950; second in a hilly stage of the Tour of Madrid in 1951. He also took two overall victories in a stage race: at the Tour of Ávila in 1951 and at the Tour of Cadiz the same year, rounding off his success in Cadiz with another stage win on the final day. Bahamontes also claims he won the Spanish Amateur

National Championships in 1949. However, according to Spanish Federation records, what would have marked a breakthrough victory never actually happened: instead the title went to Eduardo Gadea.

But winning races was not the only source of income to be found in cycling: Bahamontes recalls he threw the following year's Amateur National Championships to 'Luciano Montero, while [Juan] Campillo came third. I did it because I needed the money'. If Bahamontes had reached a position where he was selling a race as important as the Spanish Nationals, this was ample proof that he had mastered the game and was ready to compete at a higher level.

His first opportunity to take on the professionals came in the week-long Tour of Asturias in 1953. It was one of the toughest professional races on the Spanish calendar and was frequently decided in the daunting Picos de Europa mountain range. The initial challenge for Bahamontes, though, was actually getting to the start. 'It was a five hundred-kilometre journey from Toledo and I did it all by bike,' he remembers. 'That sounds bad, but the long trip north had given me a great opportunity to hone my form and find a good race rhythm. So when I got to Asturias I was more than ready to go.' Nonetheless, he faced strong opposition. Barring those participating in the Giro d'Italia, which ran concurrently, all Spain's top professionals were present, plus some powerful national teams from Italy and Belgium. None of this deterred Bahamontes. Riding as an *independiente*, or semi-professional, unsponsored, unaffiliated rider, he won the opening stage and the first professional King of the Mountains jersey of his career. He finished a more than respectable twenty-first overall out of the sixty-nine starters.

The stage win was no fluke, either. In a 120-kilometre run from Mieres to Luarca, incorporating three classified climbs, the 24-year-old took off halfway through. Sixty kilometres and two cols later, he was still alone at the head of the field. Just as in his amateur days, Bahamontes was determined to win in his trademark solo style. Also typical was his plummet in the overall classification on the next stage, held on the afternoon of the same day.

Following his triumph in Asturias, Bahamontes competed in more races in Madrid. In one of them, the one-day Vuelta a los Puertos, the first signs emerged of his decade-long conflict with Jesús Loroño, Spain's other top contemporary rider. Bahamontes and Loroño broke away on the Navacerrada pass outside Madrid, on the steeper side known as 'The Seven Hairpins'. However, after arguing about who was going to set the pace on the front, the duo were reeled in. It was a minor incident, but it set the tone for a rivalry that was to divide Spanish cycling fans into *Bahamontistas* and *Loroñistas*.

Now all this success meant it was time for Bahamontes to make the move to the richest area of Spain and the only region where bike racing was truly flourishing: Catalonia. For any self-respecting professional in Spain in the 1950s, a spell in Barcelona was inevitable. As the area least affected by the economic depression, Catalonia was 'where it was all happening', as Bahamontes put it. He explained: 'Catalonia had more money than the rest of Spain combined and it was much more advanced in all sorts of ways. Just take sport: in Madrid there was only one football stadium and one bullring, while Barcelona didn't only have that, it even had its own velodrome. [The singer-actresses] Lola Flores, Carmen Sevilla and [the boxer] Fred Galiana . . . all us big stars went there, artists and athletes alike. You could say my sporting roots are in Barcelona, and it was where I finally retired, too, with my last race [in 1965] in the Montjuic park.'

Barcelona was also where Bahamontes found the first of the two key backers of his career: Santiago Mostajo, a businessman and former rider who twice won the Spanish national championships. Mostajo was a hugely influential figure in Barcelona's cycling scene at the time, and not just as a race organiser and team director. He was also one of those shadowy figures so often found behind the scenes in cycling and without whom the sport would grind to a halt: an affluent fan who was happy to take a few riders under his wing, help finance their racing and provide everything from transport to moral support, all in exchange for a little reflected glory. Mostajo's set-up involved four or five riders who were, as

Bahamontes puts it, paid 'under the counter'. Indeed, Bahamontes suspected Mostajo was paying them using money that officials from Barcelona's town hall had given him to build a second velodrome. 'The velodrome was going to be an open-air one, but it never happened,' says Bahamontes. 'Basically he had us for nothing.'

Others, who are more generous to Mostajo, point out that the businessman put up riders in his own house, rent-free, with meals and laundry thrown in. And the second velodrome *was* built – it just took a very long time (until 1961) to happen. 'Mostajo just wanted to be part of the scene,' comments 1955 Tour of Spain runner-up Antonio Jiménez Quiles, who stayed in Mostajo's house as an amateur rider a few years after Bahamontes. 'He was a former rider himself and his son, also called Santiago, was a racer, but he wasn't very good. OK, he had a pretty dodgy used-tyre business and there was that stuff with the velodrome, but he never kept the prize money. Nobody else was doing what he did for cyclists in Barcelona. He just loved the sport.'

Mostajo directed Bahamontes' first professional squad, a small, eight-man team sponsored by Balanzas Berkel, a company who manufactured scales and weighing machines. Whatever the source, by the standards of his fellow Spaniards Bahamontes was now earning a reasonable wage of around five hundred pesetas a month. But the situation was not to his liking and his association with Mostajo did not last long. However, before the two parted company, the older man gave Bahamontes' career a significant boost. Despite his protégé's professional status, Mostajo helped Bahamontes into Europe's most prestigious training camp for amateurs, the *Campo Simplex*. The money may not have been good, but as Jiménez Quiles points out, the logistical and psychological support Mostajo provided for Bahamontes was crucial. And the closeness between them comes across clearly in one of the few photographs to survive from Bahamontes' early career. Taken after his biggest victory of 1953, the King of the Mountains jersey in the Volta a Catalunya, it shows the finish line of the race and there, waiting to fling his arms around the young rider, is Mostajo. Both men, the trainer and his star pupil, display huge grins.

It was symptomatic of the economic gulf that separated Catalonia from the rest of Spain that the Volta a Catalunya, the region's top stage race, was for a while Spain's biggest cycling event. Nine days' long, as top Catalan sports newspaper *El Mundo Deportivo* put it in its 1953 preview of the race, 'the Volta a Catalunya is our own little Tour de France'. Without the competition of the Vuelta a España, which did not run between 1950 and 1955 due to financial problems, the Volta enjoyed massive media coverage in Catalonia. At the time, *El Mundo Deportivo* published six or eight pages each day, and three or four of those would be dedicated exclusively to the Volta. And all written, its journalists were keen to point out, on typewriters provided free by Olivetti.

Even today, one of road-racing's greatest attractions is that it is free to watch, and in the grip of an economic recession the Catalan public turned out for the two-wheeled entertainment in their thousands. That was not all. Villages would sponsor prizes, known as *primes*, for the first rider through the main square; climbs would be jammed with spectators; and during the race newspapers would be plastered with advertisements for cycling-related products. At the end of the Volta a Catalunya, fourteen different sponsors were listed in the newspaper's reports as backing various prizes, from Cinzano for the King of the Mountains to Olivetti for the sprint competitions (as well as the journalists' typewriters).

If Asturias had seen Bahamontes fighting against a depleted field, that was not the case in the Volta a Catalunya of 1953, where nine four-man Spanish regional squads took part, as well as teams from Belgium, Germany and Holland. Only the French were absent after three of their single five man-squad failed to turn up. In controversial circumstances, the victor of the opening stage in Montjuic park was all-rounder Miguel Poblet, the previous year's winner and, in 1956, Spain's first leader of the Tour de France. Another rider, Miguel Bover, was actually first across the line, but he was penalised for accepting a wheel from a spectator. The rules were unclear at the time, stating that a rider could not receive 'a bike' from a spectator, and Bover's team claimed that a wheel was 'not a whole bike, but a part of one'. Unsurprisingly, the race officials disagreed, and Bover was demoted.

Though sprinting was never his strong point, Bahamontes had been active in a break and that afternoon, in the stage's second section to Gerona, he showed again he was undaunted by the calibre of the opposition. Midway through the stage, after an earlier break of eight had disintegrated when a massive rut in the road wrecked several of their bikes, the Italians Giancarlo Grosso and Donato Zampini broke away. The bulk of the chasing pack eased back and let the pair go, but Bahamontes and the young Belgian rider Marcel Janssens managed to bridge the gap. As the riders reached Gerona, the quartet were a mere twenty seconds ahead, and the peloton appeared confident they could pull them back on the four laps of the city centre that followed. However, to their surprise, it emerged that times for the overall classification were taken at the start of the first lap, not at the finish line, meaning Grosso could claim the lead and Bahamontes a prestigious result as first Spaniard. To make matters even more confusing, the four lapped the pack and sprinted for the stage victory in the middle of the main field. Afterwards the top Spaniards were furious, but as the lead home rider in his biggest race to date, Bahamontes was ecstatic. 'Bahamonde [sic] is the big news of the race,' commented *El Mundo Deportivo*, who brushed aside the protests about the rules with the testy comment 'although it would have been better if things had been explained to the pack before the race reached Gerona'.

Things reverted to normal the following day on stage three to Granollers when Francisco Alomar, of Spain, took over as leader. Grosso had unfortunately drunk some water from a public fountain and suffered a severely upset stomach, losing nearly forty minutes. Bahamontes, meanwhile, remained third overall and fourth in the King of the Mountains competition. However, the next day, stage four, he made his first appearance on the front page of a Spanish newspaper. The photograph shows him in a plain jersey, with inner tubes strapped across his back, and staring piercingly at the camera. He was fêted because he had performed above expectations on an exceptionally mountainous stage which followed the main road from Barcelona to Puigcerda and the French border before darting westwards to Andorra. Bahamontes did more than pull through, crossing the massive Collada de Tosas pass in the Pyrenean foothills in sixth place. He was then ninth into Andorra after a 200-kilometre trek through some of the wildest uplands of Catalunya.

Victory went to Salvador Botella, another Mostajo protégé. Botella had made a lone attack that enabled him to gain a four-minute forty-second lead on Alomar. But it was the performance of the little-known Bahamontes that everybody was talking about. He was 'one of the Spanish revelations of the race', claimed *El Mundo Deportivo*'s headline. His slide from third to seventh mattered little, the report insisting that by riding so well as a rookie professional 'even such defeats carry the whiff of victory'.

The next two stages developed into a phony war. Despite his racing against the clock being theoretically weak, Bahamontes lost just one place overall, dropping to eighth, in the fifty-four-kilometre midday individual time-trial that, incredibly by modern standards, was jammed between a forty-three-kilometre mass-start stage from Andorra in the morning, and a sixty-kilometre stage down to Lerida in the afternoon. Bahamontes continued to move up the mountains classification after he broke away briefly on stage seven to lead across the Collado de Lilla climb. However, it was on stage eight the next day that he really shone.

Bahamontes' achievements on the 251-kilometre ride from Tarragona on the coast to the Pyrenean town of Berga all but confirmed in a single day that he was capable of becoming Spain's greatest stage racer. There were some spectacular twists and turns in the overall battle. Against all expectations, Botella cracked completely, leaving the way open for Zampini to gain a seven-minute advantage and the lead. Once again, though, Bahamontes stole the show, with a 146-kilometre solo breakaway through the streets of Barcelona, culminating in a lone ascent of the capital's best-known climb, the Tibidalbo. What Mostajo must have thought when his protégé, sporting the bright pink jersey of the King of the Mountains leader, arrived in Barcelona a full five minutes ahead of the pack can only be imagined. The media were certainly impressed. 'We need a few riders like Bahamontes,' *El Mundo Deportivo*'s cycling correspondent wrote, 'who climb well, perform brilliantly on the flat and whose courage distinguishes them above all others. We need this type of rider, the kind who know how to fling themselves into the battle, with the sole intention of provoking a war. All the other teams' well-studied strategies went up in smoke thanks to one lone man's courage.' It was a story that would repeat itself time and time again.

After a break of nearly an hour for lunch – a tradition that would soon die out – the riders set off from the summit of the Tibidalbo, separated by time gaps based on when they had reached the top of the climb. Bahamontes knew he had to make the most of his four-minute advantage, and after scooping up prime after prime, it was only at the foot of La Trona, the third and final climb of the day, that he was finally reeled in. Exhausted by such a long early break, he trailed across the line twenty-fifth, fourteen minutes down on Zampini, the new leader. In a lesson perhaps too well learnt by Bahamontes, the impact of such an impressive breakaway far outlasted the moment he was caught by the pack. As *El Mundo Deportivo* pointed out: 'The crowds had heard about what he had achieved in the morning and applauded him even though he was dropped.'

Not for the last time, Bahamontes' sanity was called into question. The newspaper described his breakaway as 'the adventure of a madman', concluding: 'It would be no bad thing if cycling were full of madmen like him.' Nor was such 'lunacy' unprofitable: Bahamontes earned thousands of pesetas from his breakaway. In the town of Manresa alone, the fans offered their own 'prime' of five hundred pesetas (£600 in modern money) for the first rider to pass through the centre; that was as much as he earned from Mostajo in a month. Moreover, Bahamontes' maverick style was praised in the press as 'harking back to the golden age of our sport' when legend had it that impetuous lone attacks, rather than cold-blooded conservatism, were the order of the day.

Bahamontes had shown he could compete with the established riders of the time. Former national champion Francisco Masip, José Serra, who finished third in the 1950 Tour of Spain, and Antonio Gelabert, the 1950 Volta winner, were all in the race. However, they all preferred to play a waiting game than risk burning themselves out in breakaways. The younger generation, like Bahamontes and Botella, exploited their caution to the full. Botella finally regained the overall lead for good after Zampini cracked on the final day, conveniently, the skeptical might say, in the middle of nowhere.

If eclipsing the big names was a major coup for Bahamontes, so too was the way his triumph was presented to the public by the press as a throwback to a long-lost era. *El Mundo Deportivo* even went so far as to compare Bahamontes to Vicente Trueba – the 'Flea of Torrelavega' who won the Tour de France's first King of the Mountains jersey in 1933 – as well as other intrepid climbers from Spanish cycling history, like Federico Ezquerra and Julian Berrendero. Ezquerra, who was born in 1909, was the second Spaniard to win a Tour de France stage but is more widely remembered for his spectacular solo assault on the infamous Galibier climb in 1934. Berrendero, born three years later, won the Vuelta a España and the Volta a Catalunya twice, as well as the King of the Mountains jersey in the Tour and Vuelta a España. For Bahamontes to be compared with those two was high praise indeed, and suggested a country eager to recapture past glories. 'Bahamontes proves our heritage of climbers has not disappeared,' the paper said.

Just as today's cycling fans regard the 1950s and 1960s as a golden age of dashing heroics, so sixty years ago there was a sense that the sport had become excessively calculating. Bahamontes, therefore, was seen as a new hero who would break the mould, gain iconic status and increase newspaper sales in the process. Everybody, in short, was a winner.

Chapter Three
Cycling's Most Famous Ice Cream

Long before the days of budget flights, Spain had already become an important training destination for Britain's amateur cyclists. However, back in the early 1950s, while very few, if any, riders from the United Kingdom could say they had ridden alongside Federico Martín Bahamontes, one, at least, could claim to have shared jugs of red wine with the future Tour winner across a dinner table in Cannes. That rider was Morecambe-born Ian Brown. He was selected in 1954 to take part in the Simplex training camp, sponsored by a components company for top amateurs from around Europe, which was where he met Bahamontes.

In charge of the camp was the former French cycling great Charles Pelissier, who had won eight stages in a single Tour, in 1930, a record equalled only by two other riders. He had also been joint leader of the race in 1931, the year Brown was born. 'Pelissier had us ride alternate days hard and easier,' Brown recalls. 'The more straightforward ones were approximately 100-kilometre rides along the coast and the *corniches* in a big loop. The harder day was around one hundred and sixty kilometres, riding up through the Alps, then at a reasonably hard pace down to Cannes for lunch. The ride back from Cannes was supposedly an easy semi-individual ride along the coast road to the camp headquarters at Monte Carlo. Somehow Bahamontes and I always ended up at the same table for lunch in this really nice restaurant in Cannes. He didn't speak English, and I didn't speak Spanish and his French was even worse than my schoolboy French. Despite this we always ended up together, purposely the last two riders out of the restaurant. There'd always be this *pichet* of wine on the table so we'd down that.

'But it wasn't the wine. Really we'd stayed there so we'd be the last out and back on our bikes, which we were as soon as the last of the other guys had gone. The aim was to catch and pass all the others on the way back to Monte Carlo. We were jumping on to the back of trucks, scooters, motorbikes and any other vehicles we could tuck in behind, doing 'bit and bit' [taking turns to lead]. It was real fun, way better than riding on the wet slushy roads in England. I must admit the red wine we were allowed to have with lunch helped make it more fun, too. And we'd always catch everyone before we'd get to Monte Carlos. It was hilarious.'

It is somehow sobering to think of Bahamontes and his British friend, unable to communicate, but forming a loose, slightly inebriated alliance to score a few harmless points off the other amateurs. Up to that point, Brown and Bahamontes' careers had been curiously similar: neither had travelled abroad before, and both were still finding their feet outside their own country. British and Spanish cycling had been isolated from the rest of continental Europe, though for radically different reasons. For much of the 1940s athletes from Franco's Spain had been subjected to an extensive international boycott; Britain's sporting isolation was more cultural: before the pioneering Brian Robinson, in the 1950s, amateurs rarely ventured across the English Channel. 'Federico was always very open, very polite, a fun rider,' Brown says. 'But I also got the impression he was very glad to be out of Spain, what with Franco and the political repression.'

Brown, one of the five-man 'Northern' team in the 1953 Tour of Britain, was the top rider in his category in the race for several days 'until I went on a breakaway', he remembers wryly, 'and blew to bits'. Nonetheless, his high-profile ride secured Brown his invite to the month-long camp in Monte Carlo. 'A train ticket turned up in the post in late January 1954, and away I went,' he says. 'It was wonderful to get down south and see yellow mimosa and orange

blossom for the first time in my life. Then in Monte Carlo there
was the palace across the bay from our hotel. We weren't allowed
to dry our kit on the balcony, though – the royals might have seen
it.' The Spaniard with whom Brown would make friends, meanwhile, was also thanking his lucky stars he was there: technically an
independiente, or freelance professional cyclist, Mostajo had wangled
Bahamontes into the amateurs' camp thanks to his contacts within
the parent company. For both, Simplex represented a hugely
important rung on the ladder towards a full professional career.
Agents and teams from across Europe would be keeping an eye on
them and snap up those judged to be the most promising and
talented.

Brown recalls: 'During the last few days all the riders, including
me and Fede, were taken to a clinic and given medical tests to see
if we really had it in us physically. I had no idea what the tests were
for. Being an out-of-the-way northerner, I did not even know there
were such things as sports doctors. The next day we were all
individually interviewed by Pelissier, who told us who among us
were going to be super champions. Unfortunately I was not one of
them, but [in Pelissier's words] "that Spanish rider who you drink
a lot of wine with at lunch in Cannes, and race back to Monte Carlo
with, he is".'

Not only was Pelissier right about Bahamontes, but Brown says
he was spot on about other riders, too. '[He said that] the Italian
[Guido Messina] who was the oldest rider there, an ex-soccer player,
he was going to be a super champion, too – and he was world
pursuit champion that year. The Belgian rider [Jef] Planckaert, he
was going to be a super champion, and in fact he made second in
the Tour de France [1962]. And there was a Swiss rider, too, but
unfortunately he was killed in a race going through an unlit tunnel.'
Last but not least, Brown recalls Pelissier told him: 'The
Luxembourg rider you ride with, he will be a super champion, too.'
That was Charly Gaul, winner of the Tour de France in 1958 and
known as 'the Angel of the Mountains'. Unlike Gaul, though, who
became one of Bahamontes' most formidable rivals, Brown's path
only crossed once more with the Eagle of Toledo following their

slightly tanked-up training rides along the Cote D'Azur: in the 1955 Vuelta a España.

As the first Spaniard to attend a *Campo Simplex*, as Bahamontes called it, his presence represented a breakthrough for his country's cycling at international level. Even though his federation rather shortsightedly threatened to revoke Bahamontes' professional racing licence for attending a camp meant for amateurs, the fact that a former rider as prestigious as Pelissier had selected Bahamontes was a major step forward. So, too, was Bahamontes' first international victory. It came just before the camp finished when his Balanzas-Berkel squad took part in the early-season Mont Agel hill-climb on the France-Monaco border. Held on the last day of February, it had the standard format for these events of a short, flattish opening segment whose sole purpose was to warm up the riders' legs, followed by the main challenge: a lengthy grind up to a mountain-top summit, in the case of Mont Agel, 3,700 feet above sea level. In other words, it was a race designed for thoroughbred climbers like Bahamontes, who would win seventeen of this type in his career. For his first, after pulling out of the pack three kilometres from the top, Bahamontes overtook French favourite Peruggi less than one hundred metres from the finish.

The victory did not escape the notice of Franco's regime; Bahamontes' team made sure of that. When *El Mundo Deportivo* attempted to contact the team's director, Santiago Mostajo, by telephone at his Barcelona home to discuss the win, his daughter told them her father was already out at the Post Office sending a telegram about the success to General Moscardó, the Nationalist hero of the Alcázar siege, and by 1954 president of the Spanish Olympic Committee and the Government's sports minister. Equally remarkable was *El Mundo Deportivo*'s exploitation of the win to symbolise the renewal of Spain's moral and spiritual welfare. That a newspaper should try to forge such a far-fetched link between the two concepts is hard to conceive – until it is remembered that at the time the Spanish media was used by Franco's regime as a vehicle for its propaganda.

El Mundo Deportivo's front-page report of Bahamontes' Mont Agel victory in its edition of 1 March, 1954, proved to be a precursor to the same kind of elegiac, nationalistic theories of innate Spanish sporting and human talent that were rife in 1959 after his Tour de France win. The article starts off with a fairly predictable description of Bahamontes as a 'Quijote of Toledo', a comparison to one of the most traditional Spanish literary ideals of the warrior-knight from Castille. But then citing the theories of Adolf Hitler, of all people, on the relationship between humanity and history, followed by a paean to the natural greatness and civilising influence of the Iberian macho, was an indication of how Nazi ideology was still politically acceptable in 1950s Spain. Piling on this pseudo-grandiose significance on one small victory in France illustrates how desperate the Spanish authorities were to exploit any kind of international success by a local athlete. Headlined 'Bahamontes wins the European criterium of cycling', the report then claimed that: 'History repeats itself, the [new] generations are created with the good that they inherited. When this sacred truth disappears, society will be chaos and primitive brutality will return. As Hitler wrote in his memoirs, "He who is indifferent to history is a man with no ears, no face, of course that man can live, but what does his life have?"' After comparing Bahamontes again to Quijote, and 'giving a warm welcome to this young man from Toledo', the writer then claims that 'while many novels and films drag us towards the conventional and morbid, it's encouraging to find that sport has sparked the re-forging of an ancient lineage. What is good and uplifting for national pride reaches deeper places . . . and Bahamontes, a Spaniard, has spoken in one of the Alps' highest summits, giving a new example that the Hispanic race has not extinguished and that its desire to exist and triumph is reborn with new motivation, just as one day it was a civilising light in two worlds . . .'

Though the article can best be described as tepid Fascist propaganda wrapped up in a sports report, it demonstrated that right from the start Bahamontes' career was being exploited for political reasons. The role of sport, in any case, had become clear just a few years after the Civil War ended. By 1945 the running of sport in Spain was put into the hands of a specifically created delegation of the *Movimiento Nacional*, the only political party permitted by Franco's regime, containing both Fascists and Monarchists. A law introduced in 1945 had specified the sports delegation was to be 'a service provided by *El Movimiento*, and it is responsible for the direction and promotion of sport in all its aspects and modalities . . . it is the supreme authority'. The head of sport, or 'chief sports delegate', would also be named by Franco himself. The sports delegation's statutes rammed home the message about its importance with article 42 announcing that 'all the members of National [sports] Federations and the heads of clubs or sporting societies must have proven adhesion to the *Movimiento*'. In other words, on paper at least, only the party faithful would be allowed to have an officially approved career in Spanish sport. And there could be no doubt, either, as to who would take the credit for their success.

If nothing else, Bahamontes' victory showed that post-Civil War Spain was beginning to have an impact abroad in professional cycling. It had taken its time. The Spanish national team's first post-war participation in the Tour de France of 1949 ended with all six riders abandoning in less than a week. The riders were poorly equipped and given no expenses, though the Spanish Federation had promised seventy-five kilos of sugar in lieu of cash payment for their participation. But as Lucy Fallon and Adrian Bell point out in their book on the Vuelta a España, *Viva la Vuelta!,* the sugar disappeared into the black market before the riders saw it. That the sports director provided by the Federation was completely deaf was hardly a morale boost. Though the riders were criticised for lacking moral fibre when they pulled out – they were labelled 'dwarves of the road' by the Spanish press – their exits were not down to poor physical condition. Rather, they lacked decent logistical support, which in turn was due to a dearth in funding. When one Spanish rider, Dalmacio Langarica (Bahamontes' future team director), had a mechanical problem on stage five, the team car was in such poor condition it took nearly forty minutes to reach him. With the whole team instructed to wait for their leader, they failed to finish inside the time limit.

After turning down Tour director Jacques Goddet's invitation to return in 1950 to avoid repeating the embarrassment, the Spaniards were back in 1951 and did far better than expected. Bernardo Ruiz took two mountain stages, one in the Massif Central after a day-long breakaway, the second in the Alps, and finished ninth overall. If that was not impressive enough, in 1952 Ruiz became the first Spanish rider to make it into the top three of the Tour de France. However, he was never in a position to beat the winner, Fausto Coppi. The following year, the Basque climber Jesús Loroño clinched the King of the Mountains title by taking off alone on the Aubisque pass in the Pyrenees and winning at Cauterets, six minutes ahead of his closest pursuer, on the way to finishing fifth overall.

If the Spanish were beginning to make their mark in the Tour for the first time in twenty years, the country itself was slowly beginning to emerge from the economic consequences of the Civil War. By 1953 the Franco regime was starting to receive the huge loans it desperately needed after allowing the United States to build military bases there as part of their Cold War strategy against the Soviet Union. Another five years of recession followed, but at least by 1954 average Spanish incomes had finally regained pre-Civil War levels. Franco, though, showed no signs of ceding power, and constantly played up the alleged Communist threat to Spain, both for the benefit of the United States and internal rivals. 'Every newspaper gives the impression that war is imminent and that the whole of Europe down to the Pyrenees will be overrun by Russian armies,' Gerald Brenan commented. 'This anti-Red ballyhoo helps keep together the two parties on which the regime depends, the Monarchists and Falangists. But for the widespread fear of Communism . . . Franco would have left long ago.' Even if the country's economic position was no longer critical, the dictatorship was there to stay.

Though the 13.4-kilometre pass of the Col de la Romeyere is far from being the hardest Alpine climb the crowd gathered on Monday, 26 July, 1954, for the seventeenth stage of the Tour de

France, feeling a sense of mounting expectation. On this very hot day, the question foremost in their minds is, naturally, who will be first across the top? However, if any of them are expecting it to be Frenchman Louison Bobet, the 1953 Tour winner, who is lying second in the King of the Mountains competition, they are in for a big disappointment. Instead, the first rider across the summit, leading a break of four, is Spanish. And given that Federico Bahamontes has already made his mark in the Pyrenees, and has been on the attack in every mountain stage so far, there is no mistaking him, either. His shorts are rolled up high, and his head is raised and staring fixedly into the middle distance. Bahamontes is already well-known as the young leader of the King of the Mountains competition, even though there is not yet a distinctive jersey for the category. However, there is confusion in the crowd when Bahamontes crosses the summit first, claims the points and then immediately rides his bike off the road towards a metal cart selling ice cream. He gets off and without even so much as offering to pay, grabs a cornet. Bahamontes is mobbed by the crowd as he consumes his 'bonus prize', some trying to rip off his race number, and even his clothes, if the victim is to be believed. However, the story of Bahamontes licking away at an ice cream at the top of the Romeyere is guaranteed a permanent niche in the history of cycling.

Bike riders stopping for a snack in the middle of a race is not as uncommon an occurrence as might be thought. In one Vuelta a España in the early 2000s, the entire peloton apparently pulled over at a road-side hot-dog stall for a bite to eat. Yet there are key differences: the Vuelta a España's 'hot-dog moment' was early on an endlessly flat, tedious stage somewhere in the bleak, empty moorlands of northern Spain; it was not at the top of the first Alpine climb in the Tour de France of 1954. To stop for an ice cream while at the head of the biggest bike race in the world seems bizarre and utterly subversive; it is as if the rider is almost wilfully disconnecting himself from his sport. Small wonder that if there is one story that cycling fans know about Bahamontes, it is that he was 'the Spanish climber who ate that ice cream on top of a mountain during the Tour'. Or as Bahamontes put it to me two decades ago in an interview for the magazine *Cycle Sport*: 'I'm never going to hear the last of that ruddy ice cream.'

His explanation for what happened is very straightforward: 'I only stopped because two of my spokes were broken and I had to wait for assistance. I had got away with three guys, one of them a Belgian. The Belgian's team-car came up to him to tell him not to collaborate because that was only going to favour me. When his car came past me, it struck a stone, which bounced up and broke my spokes. The Romeyere was a shortish climb but very tough, with some very steep sections. When I got to the top, with my spokes broken, I was nervous and really angry. There was no sign of [Spanish team director Julián] Berrendero. So I stopped. The summit was packed, just like every summit of the Tour. But there were two ice cream carts. I picked up a cone from one of them and put in a scoop of vanilla ice cream. At the time, I was more angry with Berrendero than anything else.'

The impromptu ice cream stop was not the only unusual incident on top of the Romeyere, as Bahamontes reveals. 'As it was a good breakaway we had fourteen minutes' advantage – not like they call breaks these days, a proper one – but I didn't know that. I had to wait so long – the bunch had split apart and my director was stuck in race "traffic" – I actually got bored after eating the ice cream and went down to a stream a little way away. I got some water into a *bidon* and when the bunch came past me I threw the water all over them.' Dousing the peloton in water earned Bahamontes a fine. However, it was the ice cream incident that made it into sporting history.

Bahamontes knew he would be riding in his first Tour as early as the summer of 1953, almost a year before. 'Even then, [team director] Julián Berrendero told me to get ready for the Tour, and when I asked him what my objective would be when the time came to take part, he told me, "To try and win it",' Bahamontes recalls. Today, making overall victory a target for a rookie Tour de France rider a year in advance would be ridiculous. However, it is an indication of how fast Bahamontes was progressing. After his King of the Mountains jersey in the Volta a Catalunya in 1953, big results began to pour in. In mid-October Bahamontes won an astonishing five stages in the Tour of Malaga, and by the spring and summer of 1954 he had grown so successful he sold another victory, in exchange for a contract for the following season. Bahamontes claims that in the one-day Classic, the Vuelta a los Puertos, he let a rival from the La Solera team win. 'I had been first over two of the climbs that day, los Leones and another one, but I was interested in going to Barcelona because that was where the money was. The man in charge of La Solera said to me during the race, "If you let him [Bahamontes' rival] win, you've got a contract in Catalonia for next year", and I said, "That's a deal".' The deal-maker kept his word: after racing in 1954 for three Barcelona-based teams – Circulo Barcelonista-Yaste, Balanzas-Berkel and Splendid – in 1955 Bahamontes had a La Solera jersey on his back.

After his years as a black marketeer, swift negotiating came naturally to Bahamontes. As Mostajo's influence faded in late 1954, Bahamontes insists he became much more of a one-man show, just like his early days. 'It's true I received advice from another Catalan businessman, Evaristo Murtra – and I called him *"padrino* [godfather]". He sponsored me sometimes, like when I had my bike shop in Toledo. But basically I fought every battle by myself. I did the deals by myself, and if I won it was all by myself as well. Always. I work alone better than anybody else can.' The Spanish expression he uses is *me muevo solo,* or 'I move alone', which implies the physical sense of riding without back-up. It is a phrase that neatly sums up his career and even his life. And in the mountains of France, and for the first time on a worldwide stage, Bahamontes was going to prove that he could 'move alone' better than any other bike rider.

Predictably, even though he had been told he would be racing in the 1954 Tour so early, Bahamontes' final selection was not without a minor drama. After winning the King of the Mountains in the Tour of Asturias for a second year, as well as in the Bicicleta Eibarresa in the Basque Country, Bahamontes claims that

Berrendero came up to him and without further ado confirmed his promise with the words: 'You, you're going to the Tour de France.' Somewhat implausibly, Bahamontes recollects his initial reaction was to refuse to go because he had no suitcase and did not speak French. However, after demanding to be allowed to telephone his parents to discuss his dilemma, Bahamontes quickly changed his mind, raising suspicions that his initial refusal was merely attention-seeking. Given this definitive invitation to ride had only come in the third week of June, and the Tour started on 8 July, Bahamontes did little specific training for the race. In any case, his role was what the Spanish call 'a free electron', meaning he had no responsibility to his team leaders, and had complete freedom to concentrate on his own speciality, the mountains. So with eleven other Spanish riders, one of them a reserve, he flew from Barcelona to Amsterdam for the start of the Tour: Bahamontes' twelve-year relationship with the race that defined his career was about to begin.

The French sports daily, *L'Equipe*, rated the Spanish line-up in 1954 as one of the strongest because it combined relative youth with experience. It says a great deal about the speed with which Bahamontes was progressing that despite being the youngest team member at nearly twenty-six, his presence was taken for granted by the Spanish media. 'Of the ten riders, there are no possible doubts about four of them: [1948 Vuelta winner] Ruiz, [former national champion Francisco] Masip, [1953 Volta a Catalunya winner Salvador] Botella and Bahamontes,' argued El Mundo Deportivo before criticising the inclusion of others who had not performed well enough to merit selection. 'I don't think we can win,' Berrendero said, 'but we'll do our best to get as high up the overall classification and I have high hopes for the mountain stages.' Berrendero even attempted to place Ruiz, Bahamontes and Manolo Rodríguez, who finished second in the 1950 Vuelta a España, on an equal footing as co-leaders. However, the fast-track promotion of Bahamontes and Rodríguez caused a near-mutiny within the team, and as a result Ruiz was declared sole leader.

Bahamontes had to seek consolation in the huge headline that appeared in *L'Equipe* just before the start declaring him as the 'centre-forward' of the Spanish team'. Besides, he knew he had permission from Berrendero to race as freely as he wanted. Crucially for Bahamontes, Jesús Loroño, King of the Mountains the previous year, was missing through injury, while all-rounder Miguel Poblet had pulled out at his own request because of poor form.

There were many other top names missing from the Tour, too, including all the Italians. Their federation refused to enter following arguments with the Tour organisers when they tried to incorporate commercial publicity on their riders' clothing. Their decision not to start was made easier when Fausto Coppi, the 1949 and 1952 Tour winner, had had a freak training accident in June, fracturing his skull after a wheel came off a lorry in front of him. Only the French, whose 'A' team was led by 1953 winner Louison Bobet, looked as if they would provide serious opposition.

The Spanish were certainly protective of their riders before the Grand Depart in Amsterdam, the first time the race had started outside France in its history. The build-up featured a spectacular pre-race launch in central Amsterdam, with the presentation of six former winners, including the race's first champion in 1903, Maurice Garin, by now eighty-three, and Odiel Defraye, who won in 1912. Berrendero banned his squad from eating cherries at the presentation dinner for fear they would catch dysentery, though they were permitted to eat melons, oranges and bananas. However, Berrendero's request that the cooks at their hotel use 'the delicious local Dutch butter', as he called it, to fry the riders' food fell on deaf ears; to his annoyance, the Dutch chefs had already opted for olive oil, which they thought the Spaniards would prefer. Bahamontes seemed unconcerned about all the fuss to the point that he was already playing up to his role as the loose cannon in the team. 'Tell the fans "hello" from me,' he instructed one journalist, 'and that they should forgive me if I do something "mad" in the race.'

For the first half of the Tour, as it slowly wended its way

southwards, Bahamontes gave no indication that he had any acts of insanity planned. However, no sooner did the Tour reach the Pyrenees, on stage eleven, than he went on the rampage. It was a painfully early morning start at 8.15 bearing in mind the riders would get up three hours earlier to cram their bodies with the massive food intake required. Bahamontes was wide awake, though, and tried to forge the early break of the day along with the top French sprinter André Darrigade and three others. That move fizzled out, but on the descent of the Soulor pass Bahamontes was in the thick of the action again, forming part of an eight-strong breakaway group which included Charly Gaul. It was on the Aubisque, the first classified climb in the Tour's King of the Mountains competition that year, that Bahamontes finally shed a Tour pack for good for the first time. Initially chased by a Belgian, Richard Van Genechten, to the delight of the large numbers of Spanish fans who had crossed the nearby border, Bahamontes went clear. However, after reaching the summit of the Aubisque in first position, and with a forty-five-second advantage to boot, disaster struck. On a notoriously tricky descent made worse by fog, Bahamontes crashed and eventually struggled into the finish at Pau in thirty-second place, seven minutes down. Nonetheless, the Spanish press was jubilant. 'Bahamontes has confirmed that the great hopes we had in him were justified, although undoubtedly he did not take enough risks on the descent,' trumpeted *ABC* the next day, Its caveat was perhaps harsh considering how many riders have crashed coming down the Aubisque in the Tour's history. But it set the general tone for future press coverage: Bahamontes' descending skills would be called into question time and again.

In the Pyrenees the next day Bahamontes was back on the attack. Indeed, he came as close as he would in the whole of the 1954 Tour to a stage win: he lost by half a wheel in Luchon to the French 'discovery' of the race, Gilbert Bauvin, from a break of three. Before that, though, Bahamontes produced a typical 'yo-yoing' performance in which he pulled ahead on several occasions before falling back. He managed to cross in first place two of the Tour's best-known Pyrenean cols, the Tourmalet and the Peyresourde, with a third place on the Aspin in between. After crossing the summit of the Peyresourde with a one hundred-metre advantage over the Frenchman Jean Mallejac, yet again on the descent he was caught by the chasers, Mallejac and Bauvin. But though Bauvin proved to be the fastest at the finish in Luchon, Bahamontes had established a six-point advantage over Bobet in the King of the Mountains competition.

In a strategy set to repeat itself over the years, Bahamontes continued to rack up points in the King of the Mountains competition day after day by making an early attack then letting himself be swept up by the main pack, and then attacking again to gain more points. That was the tactic he used on stage fourteen from Toulouse to Millau, and again on stage fifteen, putting in a first-hour move with Frenchmen Rafael Geminiani and Robert Varnajo and taking second place on the Causse de Sauveterre climb. Finally on stage sixteen, on the Col de Pertuis and Col de la Republique, Bahamontes was again in the break, though he was not the first over the climb. His slightly less aggressive attitude as the race wore on led the Spanish press to speculate whether he was losing the form that had led him to shine in the Pyrenees. That was far from being the case.

On the first Alpine climb, la Romeyere, Bahamontes was on the move once more. This particular attack, though, thanks to what happened at the summit, would have a far greater long-term impact on cycling fans than he could have imagined. Ice cream breaks notwithstanding, what was particularly impressive was how Bahamontes battled throughout the Alps at the same consistently high level as he had during the Pyrenees, even if there were the same radical swings in performance within each stage. On stage eighteen, after scooping the points on the first two 'easy' climbs of the Laffrey and Bayard, where he outpowered Bobet, Bahamontes fell adrift on the Izoard. However, despite starting the climb in thirtieth place, he rode so hard that by the summit only Bobet managed to stay ahead of him, and that by a margin of just fifty-five seconds. Come the finish in Briançon, in any case, Bahamontes was in an unassailable position in the mountains classification with thirty-three points more than Bobet, who had all but won the Tour that day. Yet Bahamontes wanted more.

The final big day in the Alps included an early assault of the infamous Galibier, the highest climb that year, with a special prime of one hundred thousand francs for the first rider to reach the summit. Though the 1955 Vuelta a España winner Jean Dotto had taken off alone, Bahamontes refused to let him go clear. After overtaking the Frenchman, only a broken pedal on the descent prevented him from clinching his first Tour stage.

Even so, Bahamontes' achievements in his first Tour were enormous. 'A couple of years ago, this cyclist was just wearing alpargatas [in those days, Spain's cheap alternative to leather shoes],' pointed out ABC. 'This has been amazing progress.' Not only did Bahamontes – dubbed, for the first time that year 'The Eagle of Toledo' by one admiring French journalist – take the King of the Mountains title by a huge margin, he was first over the Tour's two legendary climbs, the Tourmalet and Galibier, as well as the Aubisque. Of the biggest climbs that year, only the Izoard escaped him, and only Bobet, the overall winner, could beat him there. In fact, on every Tour stage with a classified climb in it, Bahamontes had increased his points total, and of the twenty-five classified climbs he had been first over twelve of them. Over-exaggerating wildly, Bahamontes claimed at the finish in Paris that the mountains of France were 'nothing' in comparison with the steep slopes of the city of Toledo. 'We've got real climbs there, they are more difficult than any of the ones that they talk about here,' he said. 'All this talk about "cols", but none of them are as steep as Doctor Marañón Street in Toledo. The roads here in France are too good, too well-surfaced, they're like riding across a dancehall. If the roads weren't so smooth they'd never have dropped me on the descents and on the flat.'

Bahamontes ended the race with ninety-five points, nearly double those of Bobet. Such a startling breakthrough came with a hidden price, though. Just as when he took the King of the Mountains crown in the 1953 Volta a Catalunya, such fast-earned success meant Bahamontes risked becoming too focused on one objective so early in his career. By ignoring the greater prize of the overall title so often, he would be accused of deliberately losing time at certain points in his races, and as such wasting his talent.

As Bahamontes says, it was not until 1959 that he seriously thought about winning the Tour itself. Yet earlier on in his career, fighting for the general classification was not an unrealistic prospect. In the final time-trial of the 1954 Tour, for example, Bahamontes was the best-placed Spaniard, even beating the more experienced Ruiz by twenty-four seconds. That achievement was buried in all the excitement about Bahamontes' climbing prowess. However, with the benefit of hindsight, what more could he have done overall if he had decided to work on improving his time-trialling? Or if there had been more summit finishes than just the handful in the whole of the 1950s?

Much was made of Bahamontes' poor descending, and it was a major chink in his armour. But as was so often the case with Bahamontes he deliberately exploited this defect. 'I knew everybody thought I was lousy at going downhill,' he reveals, 'so I decided to make the most of that impression. Every time the race went down a mountain, while others were concentrating on going as fast as possible, I was concentrating on recovering as best I could and eating as much as I could. Every morning I'd get out a stage map, and mark the points where I should eat with a cross before I got caught. Then when it came to the next climb I'd get caught, but I'd have eaten some more food, my batteries were recharged, and I was ready to go on the attack again. But that wasn't something I was going to reveal to the press in case my rivals got wind of my tactics. That would have been like in that story [about a besieged fortress] where they [the defenders] send out a message, "Send us bullets, we're running out!" '

If Bahamontes' descending tactics brought mixed reactions, it was not thought he could improve much in one other key area, that of weight. One of the most frequently used strategies for improving performance in cycling is for a rider to slim down, but in Bahamontes' case that was not practical. In 1954, he finished the

Tour weighing sixty-six kilos, just one less than when he started. 'He is so thin,' *ABC* reported, 'and his cheekbones stick out so much that he is in serious danger of cutting himself each time he shaves.'

Back home, Bahamontes was showered with praise, with his first Tour de France title far outshining Ruiz's well-deserved, but hardly spectacular, eighteenth place overall. 'Bahamontes, a real discovery for the world of cycling, has confirmed beyond any doubt in this, his first stage race outside Spain, what we always knew about him,' claimed a report in *ABC* before the race had even reached Paris. A photograph of Bahamontes filled the whole front page of the paper. 'All that climbing is much, much easier for him than it is for the vast majority of cyclists,' the article continued, 'and never before has a King of the Mountains racked up such an impressive quantity of triumphs: [first on] three first category climbs – at the time, the top ranking for climbs in terms of difficulty – [first on] five second categories climbs and [first on] as many third categories as he cared to take. The name of Bahamontes, familiar to hundreds of millions of Europeans, generates more excitement and enthusiasm than any other Spanish bike rider. Hundreds of fans charge up to him, greet him, open their arms to him . . . *"Vive L'Espagne"*, one Frenchman, who wishes he was Spanish, shouts.'

It is not surprising, then, that even a fortnight after the event, Bahamontes' return to Spain was marked by a huge reception at Barcelona airport which lasted an entire afternoon. When he arrived in Toledo at the end of August, despite a low-key performance at the World Championships where he abandoned, an estimated twenty-five thousand people filled the Plaza del Generalísimo to cheer him. Met earlier by the mayor of Toledo with his car in Madrid, thousands of banner-waving Bahamontes supporters had crammed into open lorries so they could follow the local boy's journey home. Some waited up to fifteen kilometres away from the city so they could be guaranteed the best spot in the makeshift procession. Once in Toledo, rockets were fired and bunting rained down on Bahamontes. Speeches were made in his honour by the city's top brass before Bahamontes laid bouquets at the feet of the statue of the Virgin Mary in the local cathedral. The only upset came after Bahamontes was invited to kick off a local football match between Toledo and a side from Madrid. The Toledo club president gave him a bejewelled brooch, and Bahamontes promptly lost it. After a frantic search, a ten-year-old girl finally found it and, rather than making off with it, handed it over to Bahamontes, who duly re-pinned it to his chest. Nothing, it seemed, could go wrong for Spain's newest sports star that day. Bahamontes freely admits now: 'That year was the most emotional I ever got about the Tour de France, even more so than in 1959. The reaction in Spain really affected me.'

However, his success that year can not be allowed to cloud the implications of the ice cream incident. Not for the first time in his career, Bahamontes had shown a tendency to over-react to the most minor of events. It is not stretching a point to say that briefly Bahamontes had all but opted out of the race because of two broken spokes. He was leading comfortably on the climb but he still ended up losing eleven minutes by the finish. Such excessive sensitivity to even the smallest of misfortunes, coupled with a fragile ego, is not infrequent in top professional bike riders. Indeed, one team director I talked to likened one of his top riders to an expensive make of sports car: 'It goes wonderfully, but the smallest mechanical problem and the whole thing gets shot to hell.' However, with Bahamontes that extreme sensitivity seemed to be even closer to the surface than usual. What probably aggravated this particular character trait was that Bahamontes knew that even if he did fall wide of the mark on occasions, and even if he play-acted, his talent was so great he could still win prizes beyond the wildest dreams of a former teenage black marketeer and half-starved street urchin.

In fact Bahamontes seemed to pick up prizes even when he did not want them. In the 1950s the final stage is far from being the glorified criterium [exhibition race] it is now, in which only the sprinters are racing flat out. In 1954, when Bahamontes punctured late on, and lost a place to finish twenty-fifth overall, he was given the prize for 'Most Unfortunate Rider'. Then there were post-Tour criteriums, where the top riders would make more than they did in

the race itself. That was certainly true for Bahamontes after Daniel
Dousset, France's top agent for criterium contracts, took charge of
his contracts. Just as many riders do now, Bahamontes prioritised
criteriums over returning home straightaway. While he made five
hundred thousand francs [£9,000 in modern money] from his first
King of the Mountains title, much of it was distributed to his team-
mates. Where Bahamontes could really cash in was in the
post-Tour events, and he calculated he made seven hundred
thousand francs [£11,000] in 1954 alone. 'I made more money than
I would have done in five years as a professional,' Bahamontes
pointed out. 'A top pro in Spain would have made about five
thousand pesetas a month [£1,300] while I [as a rookie pro] was
making one thousand pesetas [£270] a month.'

The kudos from the King of the Mountains win was so good, in
fact, that when he crashed badly at a criterium in Belleville, France,
and the Spanish press got wind of it, Bahamontes had Dousset to
ring up the organisers of the forthcoming Barcelona criterium to
reassure them that even with a badly injured knee and elbow he
was still coming. It seemed not even Dousset could stop
Bahamontes from inside wheeler-dealing, though. A newspaper
later reported Bahamontes had 'sub-contracted' his place in several
French criteriums in 1954 to another Spaniard, Francisco Alomar,
so that Bahamontes could race in the Volta a Catalunya, where, of
course, he would be paid by the organisers as well.

As a further side-effect of his King of the Mountains success,
Bahamontes came into closer contact with some of General
Franco's most fervent supporters. One of these came at a formal
reception in honour of his victory with Doctor Enrique Pla y
Daniel, the Archbishop of Toledo and the first highly-placed figure
of the Spanish Catholic church to support Franco's uprising. Then,
straight after he had returned from his criterium campaign,
Bahamontes met General Moscardó, the Nationalist hero of the
Alcázar siege. In peacetime, Moscardó had become the chief of
Franco's personal *corps de garde* and as the sports delegate in
Franco's government, the most powerful figure in sport in the

country. According to media reports, their conversation rather improbably centred on how Bahamontes could improve in his track racing. Yet if Bahamontes was being sounded out by Moscardó for his potential as a sporting idol by the ruling regime, as seems more likely, there was no immediate external sign of it. That summer the Government-controlled media at least preached caution about Spain's new star. 'Bahamontes is the only Spaniard who can win the Tour de France,' *ABC* wrote, 'but he can mess it up, too. Moving fast [in sport] is a risky process, and Bahamontes is already receiving many laurels for him to sleep on. He has done nothing more than start.'

At least one other rider was blunt about Bahamontes' potential, and his potential limitations. As Tour winner Louison Bobet put it after the race: 'I have never seen such a great climber. Bahamontes can achieve a lot, if he stops clowning around.'

Chapter Four
The Gypsy Rider

It is a cold, misty, early spring morning in Orihuela, an elegant, slightly battered-looking spa town in southeast Spain, bisected both by the wide, shallow waters of the River Segura and lines of six-foot-high palm trees. Close to the centre is the town's casino, a gracefully appointed nineteenth-century building with spacious, high-ceilinged rooms, wall-length windows and well-varnished wooden floors. The silence is broken only by the clattering feet of a stray, bow-tied waiter. That morning Bernardo Ruiz, the 1948 Vuelta a España winner, and I are almost alone. Yet, despite his age, and the absence of other customers, to judge from the furtive way Ruiz keeps looking around to check we are not being overheard we could be plotting a bank robbery. The explanation for his behaviour finally arrives when Ruiz places his coffee down with the cautiously calculated movements of an eighty-something-year-old, then leans forward and all but hisses: 'Does Federico know you're doing a book on him? And does he know you're talking to me?' More than half a century has passed, but Ruiz is apparently still worried sick about the consequences of what he can tell a journalist about bike racing and Bahamontes in the 1950s. Old habits, it seems, die hard. For Federico Bahamontes' generation, the so-called law of *omerta* that has reigned for so long in cycling – about drugs, race-fixing, secret alliances and open treacheries, not to mention their real opinion of fellow riders – remains almost unbreakable.

Ruiz, a six-foot, muscular man, is a conundrum. He spills the beans on a lot of issues that cast Bahamontes in a poor light. At the same time, however, he still refuses to divulge a lot of what he knows about his old rival. He almost seems upset that the unwritten code of honour obliges him to stay silent about a fellow professional for whom (and this is being polite) he has scant sympathy. Along with Jesús Loroño, and occasionally Miguel Poblet, Ruiz was one of Bahamontes' biggest rivals in Spain. However, that rivalry is not the main reason for his lack of appreciation for the Eagle of Toledo. What appears to be mutual dislike, fuelled by accusations of betrayal and mistrust throughout their careers, is reinforced because Ruiz cannot comprehend what made Bahamontes tick as a person. Yet they would frequently find themselves thrown together in the same team, most notably in the national squad for major Tours. Indeed, for a year, in 1960, Ruiz was Bahamontes' sports director in the trade team Faema. To judge by our conversation, it was not a happy twelve-month period for either of them.

Interestingly, Bahamontes has no such problem with Ruiz or the rest of his contemporaries because he thinks they are too far beneath him. He has such a low opinion of them that he refuses point-blank to discuss them, once dismissing them all with the throwaway comment: 'How can I call them rivals, when none of them could beat me?' Ruiz, on the other hand, is cagey, and unhappy that he feels obliged to be so. The conversation is broken by silences, moments when he shakes his head as his voice trails off while muttering: 'The things I could tell you, the things I could say . . .' There is no getting past him, though, when he does not want to talk. Even when I promise that the book will be published first in English, he responds: 'Yes, but there are [Spanish] journalists who will read it.'

Even so, of the few Spanish riders still alive who witnessed Bahamontes' career close up, Ruiz's reminiscences are telling: without giving too much away, he depicts his former rival as a rider whose excessive individualism made him an isolated figure, incapable of asking for or receiving assistance at crucial times.

When I ask him if Bahamontes was someone who remembered favours done for him in the past, Ruiz stiffens visibly and finally booms out: 'Fede? He's never been grateful to anybody in his entire life.' As Ruiz sees it, 'He should have won [the 1957 Vuelta], but he didn't know how to position himself in the bunch to stop them wrecking his chances, and that's . . . why we always beat him.' And Ruiz later adds. 'He was a magnificent climber but he did not know how to use his own strength; he was out of control. One day he'd beat you, then the next he'd do nothing. I couldn't work out what was going on inside his head.'

Ruiz had plenty of opportunities to try to find out. According to Spanish Cycling Federation figures, there were just twenty-three fully-fledged Spanish professionals in 1954, and across the three categories immediately below them (*Primera aspirante/Segunda aspirante/Primera independiente*) there were only another thirty-eight. It was a small world, where the same old faces appeared time and again in races; one where friendships formed rapidly and rivalries could harden just as quickly. In the case of Ruiz and Bahamontes, things went wrong on a personal level almost from day one. Ruiz admits he was initially at fault, but Bahamontes' ability to take everything to extremes turned a minor row into a major one. 'I first met him in 1954, in the Tour of Asturias,' Ruiz remembers. 'He was fighting to beat Rik Van Looy in the overall, and I don't know why but I said something stupid. We had raced over [the climb of] Pajares the previous day and he'd done well. Then in the next day's time-trial, which started with a descent, he started off just before me. As we waited there on the line to start, I jokingly said to him, "Be careful, you'd better get out of the way on the downhill or I'll mount you from behind like you were a horse", basically meaning, "Either you get out of my way or I'm going to ride over the top of you", because I knew he was a bad descender. It was a bit foggy and when I finally saw him, about forty or fifty metres ahead of me on the descent, I shouted out and, maybe because he took fright at my shouting, he took a curve badly and ended up going off the road. At the finish he told everybody I'd pushed him off the road, which was a total lie. I hadn't touched him, but when I won the race overall I got booed by the crowd all because of his big mouth. It's funny now, but back then that was what would happen . . . Bahamontes was a great climber, but he would lose his self-control easily and end up paying the price. He was always a bit naive, too. In the Vuelta a España when I was his sports director and he abandoned [1960], he went off the rails completely, again.'

There were other reasons why they fell out. With such a small group of top professionals in Spain, it was not too hard for races to be fixed. However, as Ruiz explains, Bahamontes was reluctant to play the game, as he showed in the Volta a Catalunya in 1953 with his dramatic lone attack that upset the plans of his more conservative superiors. When deals were struck, Ruiz says, Bahamontes could all too often renege on them: he was too much of a loner and perhaps too distrustful to maintain 'honour among thieves'. 'Believe me, the number of things we did so that Fede could win races . . .' Ruiz says almost mournfully. 'But because of his character or whatever, he couldn't adapt. If something is agreed upon, then you have to stick to it. Within the teams, we'd agree before the race, "I'm going to do this, I'm going to do that, I'll let you sit on my wheel because if we break away you'll work for me afterwards, and so on". But once the start whistle blew, what can I say? Everything we'd agreed beforehand went down the pan.'

It is ironic that, according to Ruiz, one of the biggest problems Bahamontes caused his fellow professionals was not that he refused to buy and sell races, but that he was too taken with winning for them to trust him to keep his word. Indeed, Bahamontes remains contradictory on the subject today, sometimes admitting to having sold races, at other times denying it. 'With time, Federico wasn't so wild,' says Antonio Jiménez Quiles, who finished second in the Vuelta a España in 1955, aged just nineteen. 'At first he thought he was the King of Kings. Later, he got taken down a peg or two and he became much more calculating. But he was always a really individual guy, always separate from the rest.

Antonio Jiménez Quiles and Bahamontes became acquainted in

1955 when the Vuelta a España returned after a five-year absence. However, at a time of severe political repression, prison camps and economic misery, that year's Vuelta a España was hardly a showpiece event. 'It was bloody miserable,' says Ian Brown, who rode for the Great Britain team. 'There were all these guys standing around with guns and helmets, nobody looked happy. When we flew into Spain, we did some training beforehand and went past a massive concrete building, maybe half a kilometre long, and there was a long line of guys all chained together. I asked a Spanish rider we were training with, "What's that?", and he said, "You didn't see anything, it's political". We started off in Bilbao and went down towards Barcelona, and the roads were terrible all the way. I got four punctures in one day.'

After his success in the Tour de France the year before, Bahamontes was in Spain's national 'A' team. But according to Jiménez Quiles and Ruiz, the idea of riders working for each other in the national selection was risible. 'There was never a friendly atmosphere,' Ruiz recalls. 'We were all fighting each other every day . . . and everyone would have problems, to a greater or lesser extent, with all the rest.' Jiménez Quiles says: 'All the teams were the same – a bunch of guys flung together, and that was as far as it got. You ate together, you slept together, then you got on your bike and it was a case of "last one to the finish is a poof". It wasn't like these days where you have a single leader and some cohesion.' Jiménez Quiles recalls that he was the only Andalusian rider at the 1955 Vuelta in a mixed team of Catalans and riders from Aragon. 'All the Catalans would sit in one table in their fine track suits and with their nice food, and I'd be all by myself at another,' he says. 'During the race, I got no help from them whatsoever. I ended up paying a guy from another team to give me his bike if I ended up crashing.' Another point of assistance was Bahamontes himself, but at a price. According to Jiménez Quiles, throughout his career Bahamontes 'had an entire shop in his suitcase. He would sell gears, spokes, rims, inner tubes, the lot. He'd get them from France and sell them over here to the rest of us. You could get two types of inner tubes back then, the ones that were fresh out of the factory, and which would lose their tread after you'd ridden about two hundred kilometres. Then there were the ones which had been kept hung up for a year and dried out properly, and they had really good treads. Bahamontes would charge you a one hundred per cent mark-up on those. He would only take cash, no credit.' Somewhat uncomfortably to modern ears, Quiles adds: 'He was a right gypsy.' And he was not the only one to give Bahamontes that name: gypsy (el Gitano) was the nickname by which the entire peloton eventually came to know Bahamontes. Moreover, Bahamontes does not appear to object to it. The late Miguel Poblet, another of Bahamontes' rivals in the 1950s, and who wore a toupé, once recounted: 'When I ring Bahamontes up, I'll say, "Hey, gypsy, how's it going?" and he'll answer back, "Hey, wiggy, you ok?"' Given the degree of animosity in Spain towards that ethnic group, then and now, the nickname seems sadly apt for a loner like Bahamontes.

While Jiménez Quiles was isolated within his second-string regional team, yet still managed to finish runner-up to France's Jean Dotto, Bahamontes had a similarly miserable time in Spain's 'A' team, and ended up twenty-first. Though a breakaway on stage one with Loroño looked promising, things began to go wrong for Bahamontes almost as soon as the Vuelta started. On stage five to Lerida, Bahamontes' left knee starting to give him grief. Calcium injections were little help, not surprisingly since their only effect is long-term strengthening of the bones. However, in those days the sport's medics were often little more than quacks, and riders would be given the most bizarre substances. By the rest day in Barcelona, there were rumours that Bahamontes would not only be unable to finish, but that the Tour de France was out of the question, too. However, Bahamontes' Barcelona-based professional team, La Solera-Cacaolat, came to the rescue by hiring a doctor, Joaquim Cabot, specifically to treat their star rider. Cabot confirmed that Bahamontes' knee injury was due to a twisted tendon, but was unable to identify the cause. Bahamontes initially claimed it was due to being kicked by a horse in his youth. Nonetheless, Cabot said he could continue racing. On the stage from Barcelona to

Tortosa, Bahamontes was back in action, trying to get in several breaks. It was not the best of ideas. On the stage to Cuenca, Bahamontes was already in trouble, and when he got off the bike to greet his mother as the race reached Madrid, reporters noted he was limping again.

Meanwhile, the 'A' team was falling apart as a squad with Loroño bellowing for the benefit of the journalists: 'Team-mates? Where are my team-mates?' as he crossed the finish line at Lerida, after he had apparently been abandoned to his fate when he was dropped. Asked by a reporter in Barcelona why there were problems inside the team, Loroño answered testily: 'Because we all want to win and only one of us can.' According to Chico Pérez's *Historia de la Vuelta*, Loroño added elsewhere: 'We've declared war all right, but it's a war between us team-mates.' Bahamontes was quoted by the newspaper *El Correo Catalan*, as saying: 'We're all fed up with Loroño and with what he says.' So much for team spirit.

The disunity in the top team contrasted with the success of the regional Spanish racers, one of whom, Rene Marigil, even took the yellow jersey for a couple of stages before Dotto moved into the lead. By the time the race reached Madrid Jiménez Quiles was in the top three overall, and Loroño was reduced to cheap criticism. He claimed that the reason for the top riders' relatively poor performance was because the 'B' [regional] teams are all watching the 'A' team like hawks, before hastily rectifying that with: 'I mean, everybody is watching us.' With three stages left, the press held out little hope for the best-placed Spaniards, with *ABC* asking: 'What kind of support can Marigil count on? The truth is, very little. A lack of agreement between the riders of the "A" team has had fatal consequences. With a few exceptions, each rider has fought the race as an individual, not as a team. The fact that Loroño was in yellow meant that Bahamontes did not make too big an effort and Poblet – after racing through his region – decided to pull out altogether. The second-level [regionals] have given our top men a lesson. The "A" team had the chance to win stages and make money and instead they've all attacked at the wrong time or without a clear aim.'

It was not only the riders in the Vuelta who had problems. The race co-director, Luis Bergareche, was badly injured when he fell out of a fourth-floor window in his hotel, plunging through a canopy and landing on a taxi bonnet. 'A' team trainer Julián Berrendero, meanwhile, received a public warning from the race organisers for 'talking to the press and not to his team'. Spanish hopes of a last-minute turnaround in fortunes sank even further when Marigil pulled out injured. Not even treatment with hydrocaine, a cocaine-based medication, could help him.

As for Bahamontes, he had tried to get over Leones, the climb in that year's Vuelta closest to Toledo, at the head of the field but was beaten to the punch by an Italian rider. Then, on the stage to Valladolid, to add to his misery he rode for the last hour on a spectator's bike after lending his own to Loroño, who had punctured twice. It was a rare moment of fraternity between two riders normally at daggers drawn. To cap it all, later on the same stage Bahamontes fell and hurt his elbow and shoulder. His knee was also playing up again, increasingly seriously and when it was announced with three days of the Vuelta a España to go that Bahamontes would not be doing the Tour de France, nobody was particularly surprised.

It has almost become a party trick. Bahamontes grabs your hand and puts it on the side of his knee, saying: 'Feel that?' And what you detect beneath his trousers is a lumpy protrusion roughly the size of a twenty pence piece. That was how he reacted in 1993 when I first interviewed him and asked him why there had been such a lean period in the Tour de France between his first King of the Mountains title in 1954 and the second in 1958. When I asked the same question in 2008, more because I suspected I would get the same response than because I was interested in the answer, out shot his hand again to provide the same explanation. 'That injury cost me a ride at the Tour in 1955 and I thought it would cost me my career,' Bahamontes says. 'It was so bad I could hardly walk, let alone ride my bike.' Bahamontes traced the root of the problem, a partly dried-out meniscus (the disks of cartilage that cushion the knee) to a badly-aligned shoe plate. It was just a few millimetres out of place, but that was enough for it to act as the metaphorical snowball that, eventually, provokes an avalanche. 'It altered the position of my foot, which in turn meant the angle of my leg was out of kilter every time I pedalled,' he says. 'And that caused some tissue in the knee joint to rub together. The injury ended up leaving me completely lame. I tried walking with Fermina half-supporting me and after fifty metres it was so painful I collapsed. I couldn't get on my bike, and as I couldn't get on my bike, I couldn't race. The thought of an operation really scared me. That and not being able to race.'

Such insecurity about a career-threatening injury is only to be expected, particularly as Bahamontes could not forget the abject poverty of his childhood and beyond. If Bahamontes wanted to see the consequences of being out of a job, he only had to look around at the pinched faces and ragged clothing that predominated in Spain then. Bahamontes was on the horns of a simple dilemma: racing was his ticket to financial security, but racing hard with an injured knee would only aggravate the problem.

In fact, things had started going sour for Bahamontes almost as soon as he stepped off the podium in Paris in 1954. After injuring his hip in a post-Tour criterium, then abandoning during the World Championship following a lacklustre performance, Bahamontes pulled out of the Volta a Catalunya with stomach problems. He blamed the water he drank from a fountain in the town of Mataró, but there were rumours he had overdone it on the post-Tour celebrations and was under-prepared.

The next setback was financial, and much closer to home: it involved Toledo's main cycling club and their star rider. According to a lengthy letter sent by the club to the newspaper *ABC*, Bahamontes and fellow Spanish professional, Mariano Corrales, had agreed to take part in a criterium during the city's week-long fiesta in October. But, the letter went on, just a few hours before the race was due to take place Bahamontes and Corrales turned up in the club's offices, demanding 'start money' ['appearance money' in cycling jargon], which was refused. The organisers wrote that since the race was funded by the town council, they had reminded

Bahamontes it was being run on a shoestring. They even claimed that Bahamontes had promised to race for free. Bahamontes and Corrales refused to take part a second time, and the start was delayed by twenty minutes before the race finally got under way without them. However, when the two turned up at the finish and demanded payment a third time, the organisers reacted by explaining over the loudspeaker system why the local hero was not in the peloton. Both riders were duly booed and wolf-whistled by the crowd in stark contrast to the ecstatic welcome Bahamontes had received just a few months before. Bahamontes says he has no recollection of any of this happening, but whatever the truth he did not come out of the affair well. 'Bahamontes has lost popularity and was whistled at by people from his own city,' a semi-humourous column in *ABC* reported in early December, 'the problem being they have yet to see their hero turn a single pedal stroke. They have only read about the Aubisque in the newspapers.'

The next mini-scandal was physical, rather than financial, and blew up when Bahamontes allegedly lashed out at Miguel Poblet after the first stage of an early-season race, the Tour of Andalusia in 1955. As Poblet recalled: 'We were in a break together and the bunch was on the point of catching us with about three kilometres to go, and I said to Federico, "I'm not going to work with you because we're going to be caught and I'll have to sprint". Well I won, and he got second or third, just a little behind me, and he was pissed off because I hadn't worked with him in the last kilometre. So he hit me with his bike pump. That's his nerves for you. He was very nervous, very temperamental, but it didn't go any further. The next day we didn't even remember what had happened.' The Catalan laughed away the incident, but there was at least one newspaper report that the injury was so bad Poblet had to abandon and could not train for several days. Poblet's sports director told *ABC*'s cycling correspondent that his rider had been kicked in the stomach by Bahamontes, 'in front of everybody, and I believe him'. Bahamontes, the sports director continued, was annoyed because Poblet had chased him down three or four times close to the finish and Bahamontes' attempts to block his path by zig-zagging across the road failed. Bahamontes' recollection of events is very different: 'He said I kicked him in the nuts but I never touched him. If I had kicked him there, how would he have been able to ride his bike?'

Yet amid the controversies, awards for Bahamontes' 1954 Tour success continued to roll in. The most important was the Baron de Guell Cup from the Ministry of Sports, one of biggest prizes in Spain for sporting achievements. The Spanish Cycling Federation named him their 'rider of the year'. In late October, aged just twenty-seven, his first biography was published, costing 1.5 pesetas [fifty pence] a copy.

And in some ways, the 1955 racing season had started well for Bahamontes. He began it by beating future Vuelta winner Jean Dotto's record for the hill climb held on the infamously steep Mont Faron, just outside Toulouse, in February. He clocked the fastest time at both intermediate checkpoints, finishing the quickest by fifteen seconds. Over time he would prove that when it came to single-climb races he was all but invincible. 'It wasn't as tough as they said,' Bahamontes remarked afterwards, 'but now I have to win a race on the flat because if I don't I'll end up being considered a climbing specialist.' Dotto stated emphatically: 'There is nothing to do against Bahamontes in the mountains. He is simply the best of all us.' As if to confirm Dotto's words, Bahamontes then won the GP Monte Carlo despite not starting the race until the peloton was already out of sight. He had gone for a walk along the seafront and had not realised the race had begun.

With the knee injury threatening his embryonic career, Bahamontes sought emergency medical treatment after the Vuelta a España in 1955. 'According to the doctor I saw in Madrid, López Quiles, I had to have the knee treated, obviously,' he says. 'My knee swelled up and they drained the wound every few days. But thank goodness he said I didn't need an operation. Just a lot of rest. However, Bahamontes did not follow the medical advice. Instead after the Vuelta, he embarked on a lengthy campaign to prove his form ahead of the Tour de France, recording an impressive run of wins, including the Tour of Asturias and the Bicicleta Eibarresa stage races, and the Vuelta a los Puertos one-day event. It all seemed to be going well, and when the Federation doctor carried out a medical examination immediately before the Tour, the newspapers were able to report that 'several X-rays' indicated the knee was completely cured and there was no bone damage whatsoever. On 24 June, *ABC* reported that Bahamontes had confirmed again that he was 'ready to take part in the Tour'. With a week to go he was named on the official list of participants. However, after placing an unremarkable nineteenth in the National Championships in Barcelona on 29 June, Bahamontes and his team-mates were given another medical. This time the result was different and Bahamontes was substituted by Antonio Gelabert, the new national champion. To describe this as a bombshell is no exaggeration. Bahamontes had won the Tour of Asturias less than a fortnight before, but the Federation's official report could not have been more damning. According to *ABC*, a Federation communique stated: 'Having given all the riders their check-up, we have confirmed [their physical fitness] with the exception of Federico Martín Bahamontes, who is suffering subjective pains in his left knee, and we therefore believe his participation in the Tour is not recommendable, given that possibly he will not perform well.' Calling Bahamontes' injury 'subjective' was like a green light to the press for some ferocious criticism of the Eagle of Toledo and they went at it with gusto. 'Our trump card of the Tour, Bahamontes, has gone up in smoke,' said *El Mundo Deportivo* before displaying the blackest of humour and claiming: 'We hope that our explanation why this has happened – our man from Toledo has commited suicide – goes up in smoke, too, and that he gets well soon and that the phase he is going through is as brief as possible. If the official reason – "doctor's orders" – sounds odd given his statements of a few days earlier, we don't want to go into the real causes. My opinion is that Bahamontes, the real, great Bahamontes whose racing [was so spectacular it] caused Europe to grind to a halt last year, has been a victim of the "frivolous" Bahamontes. He saw money, contracts and laurels, and instead of taking care of himself and his future, he has let himself be worshipped, forgetting that riding a bike is such a tough sport.'

Having thrown Bahamontes to the wolves, the Federation then attempted belatedly to try and repair the damage to Bahamontes' image. 'His knee is suffering from malaise,' Federation president Alejandro del Caz claimed, 'and that's not what he wants, and neither do we.' With the Tour de France lost and his reputation for unreliability considerably reinforced, Bahamontes' knee finally received the rest it needed. When he returned in early August he was forced to pull out of the Vuelta a Galicia stage race, which caused a minor controversy because his team had no idea why he had abandoned, and the organisers insisted his team-mates had to quit as well. But Bahamontes bounced back in September when he took two stages of the Volta a Catalunya. By October it was business as usual as he planned the season ahead. It was typical Bahamontes. Just as he could swing unpredictably from feeling upbeat to exuding total gloom, on the few occasions he was injured seriously in his career he appeared equally capable of regaining his race condition in record time.

His knee, though, still clicks when he walks. And ever since 1955 he has been grabbing visitors' hands and getting them to feel the twenty-pence-sized hole that marks his old war wound.

Chapter Five
Pointing the Finger

If Federico Martín Bahamontes' career was put on hold by injuries during the summer of 1955, the following year it was on an upward swing again and he had chances of victory in all three major Tours. Yet he failed in all of them. Each time Bahamontes pointed the finger at something or somebody else being responsible, but never at himself. Then as now, self-criticism is something the Eagle of Toledo rarely indulges in.

It has been argued that 1956 represented Bahamontes' best chance of winning the Vuelta a España. What the race highlighted again was that Bahamontes was no team player. According to Bernardo Ruiz, as early as 1955 his team-mates had discovered that Bahamontes was too much of an individualist when it came to making deals, even when he would have benefited from them.

'Bahamontes was a gentle person,' says Brian Robinson, the Briton who finished eighth in that year's Vuelta, 'except when he was shouting at his team-mates or he got his hackles up with his team director. He could be very fiery then. When they [the Spanish team] did start arguing they would go on shouting for ever. They couldn't agree on anything. Just getting them to agree a menu for dinner would have been difficult enough.'

Robinson is the British cyclist who knew Bahamontes and the Spanish the best. He first came across Bahamontes in 1956 on the Vuelta, and a year later they were nominally team-mates in the St. Raphael-Geminiani squad, though Bahamontes barely raced for them. Their careers would run parallel until Robinson retired in 1963. 'Bahamontes was a friendly, bubbly guy, I don't think I ever saw him down,' recalls Robinson, now in his early eighties. 'We'd talk in a kind of French, though his was a bit of a patois and he mangled Spanish and French together. If he had a puncture, a *crevaison*, he'd yell out, *"Je clavais! Je clavais!"'*

Robinson also travelled around Spain with Bahamontes, which gave him an insight into how widely appreciated he was on home soil. 'I once did a week's criteriums with him, Anquetil, Darrigade and various other local Spaniards. First we were riding down in Benidorm – which was just a fishing quay in those days and we spent the whole evening riding over cobbles – and then all across Andalusia, mostly on what seemed like football fields. There were good crowds and Fede was hugely popular. We stayed in the best hotels and got good money, paid on the nail, too. They couldn't muck around with the big names. Particularly Fede. They even did special flamenco dancing in these dives every evening, with the words in the songs all about Bahamontes.'

However, if Robinson had no objections to riding alongside Bahamontes in exhibition races he would try and steer clear of him when it came to serious road-racing. 'We'd be friendly enough and if there was a gap in the bunch you'd shove him in it, no problem. He'd remember favours, and in criteriums it was all about putting on a show with as little effort as possible. You all pitched in. When it came to breaks, too, he'd work. At least I don't remember him ever "swinging a leg". But the problem was that the Spanish were more erratic than other nations in the peloton, tossing their bikes about, because they were more impulsive. They weren't as steady as others. [Miguel] Poblet was good because he had track experience, and [Jesús] Loroño was solid enough; otherwise you always had to be careful if you were riding behind a Spaniard. If that Spaniard was Bahamontes, "who was always switching about", you had to be doubly careful.'

Even though he could not speak any Spanish, Robinson had no problem appreciating their different personalities. He got on so well with Poblet, in fact, that he assisted him to his first Milan-San Remo win in 1957 by leading him out despite being on a different team. 'The team manager had said we should help him, it was something to do with us having the same bike company,' Robinson recalls. Robinson still finished third, at the time the best result in a major Classic by a Briton since the nineteenth century. 'Loroño was calm as anything, and Poblet could get upset,' Robinson says. 'But Fede was definitely the most excitable of them all, he couldn't keep still. He always had very fixed ideas, too. Once he got an idea, you couldn't change his mind.'

To the rest of the cycling community, the Spanish stood out for reasons other than their poor bike-handling and constant arguing, not least their collective lack of money. Unofficially the Spanish were rated fourth in the world behind the Italians, French and Belgians, which was an amazing achievement considering it was just five years since they had returned to the international scene. But their finances placed them a lot further down the list. 'The Spanish were always a bit ramshackle as a national squad,' says Robinson. 'Normally a team would have its own bikes, but the Spanish would turn up and take the yellow Tour bikes the organisers would provide if you couldn't afford your own.' Despite their 'low-budget' look, Robinson knew Bahamontes was deadly in the mountains, and had to be respected. 'He used to go' – and Robinson makes a highly expressive sound to describe the noise of Bahamontes' pedals turning at high speed – 'tsch-tsch-tsch-tsch and get a hundred metres, have a little look back at us, stay there, then go tsch.-tsch-tsch-tsch again, really pedalling away on the low gears, get another hundred metres. Then he'd be gone. He'd just ride away. He wouldn't have won the prize for elegance in his riding. He had that funny position, more of a sitting position, with his arms looking so stiff holding the bars close up. But if he came to a race you'd know that he could drop me, Geminiani, Anquetil, the good boys if you like, on the climbs. He had the edge on all of us. When he put his mind to it.'

Spain's ten-man 'A' team for the Vuelta a España in 1956 was designed to put behind them the misfortunes of the previous season. That was the theory. In practice, the squabbling began before a pedal was turned in anger. Loroño was furious that Luis Puig, the team's sports director, had decided Salvador Botella was to fight for the overall while he and Bahamontes would only go for the King of the Mountains competition. 'Botella has no right to be the boss,' Loroño stated before the race left Bilbao. 'I've just won the Bicicleta Eibarresa [stage race], yet that doesn't seem to interest my sports director. I can't stand that. I'm the strongest and I should be the boss.'

Robinson was there with fellow Britons Tony Hoar and Ian Steel thanks to an invitation from manager Phillipe Louviot to ride under a flag of convenience for the Swiss team. It was not a luxurious experience for any of the riders with little support from the organisers or teams. After each stage the peloton would grab their suitcases from the army jeeps which were acting as support vehicles, balancing their bags on the handlebars, and head off to low-budget *pensiones* anything up to twenty kilometres away. 'The race was a bit of a shambles,' Robinson recalls, 'and the living conditions were so bad in Spain generally that I came back with dysentery. I was passing blood and spent six weeks off the bike. I don't remember ever getting any prize money, either. I remember you could get a made-to-measure suit of English Worcester completed for you in a night for a pound. So the guy who made it couldn't have earned much. And the food was really poor. It was pre-refrigeration days and all we got was eggs or a scrawny chicken that had been running around in the wilderness, no red meat and no fish unless you were by the sea. And I can't remember once seeing butter.'

Even in 1959, when he next rode the Vuelta, Robinson says it was much like the infamous *Monty Python* sketch where the cafe menu offered nothing but spam. 'They kept on giving us eggs and more eggs, and that got to some people. There was one hotel run by nuns and we were all seated round the dinner table when they came out with a great platter of eggs, and [Raphael] Geminiani suddenly shouted out, "I'm sick of bloody *huevos!*" and threw the whole thing, bang!, against the wall.' It was not easy to look for alternatives, either. 'There'd be soldiers at every crossroads, and when we tried to snaffle some grapes once from a field, one of them started loading up his gun, putting the cartridges in, and making like he'd shoot us. We got out of there in a hurry.' Nutrition was such an issue in the 1956 Vuelta that the French team pulled out with food poisoning after claiming the lunchtime sandwiches provided were going rotten. The organisers responded by saying that the official responsible had given the team the wrong batch by mistake when he grabbed them from the back seat of the car. Assuming they were not lying, it is unclear for whom the dodgy *bocadillos* had been intended. But if the British and French were unhappy, nobody knew about the lack of food in Spain better than the Spanish themselves. 'The Vuelta a España and the Tour de France were light years apart,' says Ruiz, 'right down to the food. I used to say to my team-mates when we did the Tour that even if we were at the back of the peloton it was better to be in France than in Spain, if only because we'd get good stuff to eat. You'd go into the hotel dining room after each Tour stage and you could have what you wanted – meat, jam, butter, bread. Here in Spain, we had nothing.'

If the food was dire, Robinson says the roads were equally poor. 'You'd see these women with baskets of stones on their heads, trying to repair them. But they had no proper surface. The only roads with macadam on them were on the coasts and that was very poor quality. When it snowed on one stage, they just cancelled it straightaway and made us go on trains, sitting on wooden slatted seats just like in the utility trains we'd had back home. With no toilets, the sanitary gutters ran through the middle of the roads, too, and it wasn't pleasant riding through all that.' Punctures and crashes were frequent on what were little more than cart-tracks. As a result, solid back-up from the team or even a hand from a friendly rival was crucial. However, Bahamontes' lack of nego-tiating skills and preference for going it alone meant, just when he needed them most, he was guaranteed neither.

The high point of Bahamontes' 1956 Vuelta came when he was just eight seconds behind leader Angelo Conterno of Italy after stage fourteen. With only three days' racing left he should have been poised for his first major Tour win. In fact, he soon found himself battling merely to survive, and battling with his team-mates, too. The first backwards step came with a major crash on stage fifteen, caused by the ruts in an unsurfaced road, which left Bahamontes with thigh and knee injuries as well as a broken set of handlebars. Loroño then opened up a minute's gap on the main pack by the finish in Bilbao and put extra pressure on Bahamontes' second place. The next morning, as rain fell in Bilbao and mist closed in, a heavily anesthetised Bahamontes set off for Vitoria on stage sixteen. A puncture early on did not cause him any undue problems, but another on the climb of La Herrera most certainly did. Though Ruiz and three other Spaniards dropped back to assist him, by the time they regained the peloton following a furious pursuit Conterno and the rest of the the Italian team had raced away. At the summit of La Herrera, Loroño and Conterno had established an advantage of ninety seconds over Bahamontes; by the finish in Vitoria, after two further punctures, it had stretched to more than three minutes. Bahamontes had dropped to fourth overall and was nearly four minutes back. With one stage left, and in the space of two days, Bahamontes had almost slid out of contention.

Some claim that Bahamontes' injuries were the main reason he was so suddenly out of the running. But a key Spanish team-mate has told me that Bahamontes lost the Vuelta a España that year because of an internal conflict: he refused to go along with plans to break a pact to keep Conterno in yellow. This version of events might sound implausible, but there are three facts in the team-mate's favour. Firstly, though Bahamontes was three and a half minutes down overall, with a mountain stage still to come, the gap was not unbridgeable. Secondly, though injured on stage fifteen, Bahamontes had still managed to drop the entire field on the first climb of Urkiola, so he was in good form. Thirdly, and most significantly, after stage sixteen had finished in Vitoria a rumour started up in the team hotels that Conterno, the race leader, had fallen seriously ill with bronchitis. So maybe there was still something to play for. The questions remained, though: was Bahamontes interested in playing and did he know how to?

According to the team-mate, with a first Vuelta a España victory at stake, that evening word came that the Italians had requested that Conterno be allowed to keep his lead on the final day and other reports say they were willing to make cash payments to those who agreed. It has been claimed members of the Spanish team promised that they would not challenge the Italian. The Belgians, who were to provide Conterno with invaluable assistance the next day, certainly agreed. However, there were wheels within wheels. Despite Loroño being the best-placed Spanish rider, in second spot, the would-be pact-breakers within the Spanish team wanted Bahamontes to go on the attack, and wreck all the previous arrangements to keep Conterno in yellow. 'In Vitoria all the teams had made agreements about who would win the stage, stay second, or keep the general classification as it stood,' the team member told me. Bahamontes, he claims, 'initially agreed to break the pact, but as he'd actually got quite a good placing overall he changed his mind and that annoyed a lot of people.'

Bahamontes version of events is far less convoluted: he attempted to attack on the following stage, but failed to get away because Conterno first held onto his shorts, and then because Conterno received 'external assistance.' Ultimately, the row that took place between Bahamontes and the rest of the Spanish team in Vitoria lacked any relevance since Conterno was helped on the last stage by the Belgians who pushed him up and over the Sollube, the last climb of the race. Conterno was given a thirty-second penalty for the obvious cheating, but still won the race from Loroño by thirteen seconds. 'Conterno received all kind of assistance,' Loroño claimed later. 'He rode up the Sollube without even realising he was going uphill.' And Bahamontes? He had offered Loroño some limited support on the Sollube, but it was not the devastating solo move that others had been hoping he would make. If Bahamontes' foibles had provoked antipathy among his team-mates before, he was now in danger of becoming permanently isolated.

To modern sensibilities, such overt wheeler-dealing may seem shocking. But in a Spain suffering its worst economic recession of the century the pressure to make a fast buck was enormous. Though the money earned from cycling was often comparable to top football players in Spain, there was a key difference betweeen the two sports: no rider was guaranteed a salary from his team sponsor. Until the very end of the decade Spanish team sponsors rarely paid their riders anything except perhaps a few bonuses for victories, making prize money the only certain income. Local clubs would sometimes provide their professional riders with a basic subsidy which Bahamontes says was around one thousand pesetas [£300 in today's money] a month in the early 1950s. Others might come under the wing of directors like Santiago Mostajo, who in 1954 was paying his riders five hundred pesetas [£120] a month, though that was not enough to live on.

'It was simple: whenever I went to a race in Bilbao, say,' explains Ruiz, 'I'd have to win, otherwise I wouldn't eat dinner that night. Then I'd go to Mallorca, on the other side of Spain, and it would be the same – first or second, or no food. I'd make damn sure I won, too, because if you didn't you wouldn't get a hotel to sleep in that night, either. You'd fight and fight with the riders to win, then fight and fight with the organisers to get them to pay for your hotel.' It is therefore not surprising that the top riders were so frequently at odds when their whole livelihoods depended on winning.

'Given how much the train cost, you'd ride from Barcelona up to the Basque Country, seven or eight hundred kilometres at a time, ten or twelve of you in a line, praying the police wouldn't stop you because you'd be fined for riding in a group [which was considered dangerous to other traffic],' says Ruiz. 'If it rained you'd sleep wherever it caught you. You'd have a masseur lined up in Madrid or whatever, stop there, get a massage and a bit of kip, then go on.' Under such circumstances it seems logical that riders would work together to ensure certain results were fixed, if only to ensure a minimum income. But Bahamontes did not want to pitch in with the rest of his contemporaries. Instead he 'moved alone', as he liked to say. For that, at least initially, he paid a high price.

If Bahamontes was proving to be cycling's equivalent of Greta Garbo, it is not an unusual trait among climbers. In more modern times Scotland's Robert Millar also cut a lonely path in the peloton, while Charly Gaul became a notorious recluse after he retired, living alone in a wood with his shotguns and his dog, the crampons he invariably wore on his shoes the only reminder of his past. As a racer, though, Gaul was the complete opposite to Bahamontes in many ways: while Bahamontes was most effective in warm weather, Gaul seemed to come alive whenever the temperature dropped and the heavens opened. It was his ability to blast away in the coldest, most miserable of conditions that enabled Gaul to win both the 1956 Giro and the 1958 Tour. He is most famous in France for the attack in a rainstorm across the Chartreuse mountains that regained fourteen minutes on race leader Geminiani. Only the national team system, which put the rider from little Luxembourg at a distinct disadvantage, probably prevented him from winning more.

There could be no doubting Gaul's genius at breaking away whenever the roads steepened. Geminiani called the former abattoir worker 'a murderous climber'. French writer Antonie Blondin, perhaps the greatest of cycling journalists, described him as 'Mozart on two wheels'. 'When we raced we were irreconcilable,' Bahamontes told me when Gaul died in 2005. 'Going uphill even he admitted I was better, but when it rained he was impossible to beat.' But for all his affinity to Gaul, Bahamontes was kept at a distance like everybody else. 'Charly was friendly enough,' recalls Robinson, 'but you could never get close to him, never really get to know him.' And where Bahamontes was outspoken and fiery, Gaul was gloomy and withdrawn. 'He gives the impression that an evil deity has forced him into a cursed profession,' commented one writer.

Team-mates had the same problem with trying to get to know Bahamontes, which meant he received scant sympathy when things went wrong as they so often did in 1950s stage racing. It was a risky policy on Bahamontes' part. As his knee injury proved the year before, nobody could be sure they would not need a helping hand. In Bahamontes' case, his physiognomy meant he had to depend on team-mates. According to Ruiz: 'Bahamontes always had one or two days where he'd have a sudden physical crisis, and depending on the terrain he'd either be able to get over that crisis or not.' Known as 'the bonk' in British cycling circles, this sudden loss of energy is due to a rapid depletion of glycogen stores in the muscles. In Spanish it is called *una crisis* or, more poetically, *una visita del hombre del mazo*, a visit by the man with a mace. 'On the stage to Vitoria [in the 1956 Vuelta] he started to claim his brakes weren't working properly and he had punctures,' says Ruiz. 'That was why he had to stop on La Herrera, not for punctures. I had to stay with him to help him get there, using whatever means necessary, but I'm not going to tell you how.' Another member of Bahamontes' team is not so reticent on how this was probably achieved. 'He'd jam his arm between your elbow and you'd drag him alongside you,' says Jiménez Quiles.

Like so many climbers, Bahamontes lacked the technical skills for weaving his way through the bunch and relied on a 'sherpa' to guide him. He would also need help regaining time lost on the downhill sections. 'He and Charly Gaul had this thing in their legs so that whenever we got to the mountains it was "Goodbye boys, we're off now",' says Robinson. 'But Bahamontes was a bad descender, even worse than Gaul. And they'd both trail around at the back quite a lot. I can't remember Bahamontes doing a turn on the front. That's not the way to race and that limited the damage both could do.'

Eighty-three riders started stage eighteen of the Giro d'Italia in 1956; forty-two finished. One photograph sums up what they had to endure that day. It shows the previous year's winner, the Italian Fiorenzo Magni, halfway up one of the stage's five major cols. At that point it is snowing lightly. But in weather conditions still rated as the most extreme in the race's history, Magni will also have to battle through hailstorms, torrential rain and blizzards for nine hours and two hundred and forty-two kilometres. 'This day surpassed anything seen before in terms of pain, suffering and difficulty,' wrote the former Tour organiser Jacques Goddet. With behaviour that seems to border on the lunatic, Magni – who has been riding with a broken collarbone since stage twelve – has the end of one length of inner tube from his tyres clenched between his teeth and the other wrapped around his handlebars. He is trying to use the miniscule additional leverage he receives by pulling with the inner tube both to keep the front half of his bike as high out of the snow as possible and reduce the pain in his shoulder to a minimum.

For Magni to have reached the point where he is reduced to such painful measures just to keep going epitomises the extremes to which the participants were pushed on this stage. The exit of Niño de Filippis, the provisional leader, was one of the most memorable: with his fingers glued around the handlebars with cold, and having ridden himself to a standstill, he and his bike simply keeled over in unison. Magni, however, made it through. He finished third, just twelve minutes down on stage winner Charly Gaul, who also moved into the race lead. Bahamontes would have moved into top spot overall had he stayed with Magni. But around fifty kilometres from the finish, and the final ascent to the Bondone, Bahamontes abandoned. He then had to make his way through snow and freezing fog to the nearest farmhouse to seek shelter. 'It was impossible to race. There had been landslides and stones as big as a cupboard were all over the road,' Bahamontes recalls. 'Charly Gaul ended up partially deformed by the cold and I had frostbite in my hands and feet. I couldn't use them properly for a month.'

As winds reached speeds of 70 k.p.h., riders plunged their hands into bowls of warm water supplied by nearby inhabitants or downed glass after glass of brandy to try and regain some energy. Gaul was reduced to descending at a snail's pace because his fingers could not pull on the brakes. When he reached the finish he was trembling so violently his clothes had to be cut from him. 'I'd never known such bad weather. It was really frightening,' Bahamontes continues. 'We just stopped wherever we could, two here, six there, wherever you were you abandoned.' Bahamontes asserts that 'nobody got to the top on a bike', which is untrue of Gaul. However, his claims that a large number of the 'finishers' that day reached the line by car, has been corroborated. 'Me and [fellow

Spaniard] Jesús Galdeano sneaked into somebody's house and put on some pajamas we saw lying about,' he says. 'Finally we were picked up by a lorry. We all quit. Anybody who says the opposite is lying because then they came by the hotels the next day asking who wanted to finish the Giro. But I hadn't reached the finish line so I wasn't starting.'

While he now says it was the extreme cold that caused him to abandon, in a profile of Bahamontes' career cycling historian Javier Bodegas claims that was not the case. Rather, Bahamontes roundly blamed his sports director at the Girardengo-ICEP team for his race's premature end, saying he had sold out to Gaul and had deliberately driven ahead of Bahamontes in his team car on the ascent of the Bondone. There were also reports that when Bahamontes saw what had happened to De Filippis, falling like a deadweight on to the road, he was so frightened he stopped instantly. Whatever really happened, Bahamontes would surely have led the Giro had he finished the stage, and then gone on to become the first Spanish winner. He had started just six minutes down on the leader and ten minutes ahead of Gaul. Instead, Gaul, his face wrinkled with cold, his hands and feet blue, gained a seven-minute advantage on his nearest pursuer, Alessandro Fantini. 'Charly has the skin of a hippo,' remarked Geminiani; *El Mundo Deportivo* called the stage 'a hecatomb', slaughter on a large scale.

Gaul's epic ride also brought him the record for overturning the largest overall disadvantage in the Giro to take the leader's jersey. It is a feat that, more than half a century on, no one has matched. Meanwhile, Spain's first winner of the Giro was not Federico Bahamontes in 1956, but Miguel Indurain in 1992.

'There is always the Tour,' *El Mundo Deportivo*'s editorial reflected after Bahamontes' exit from the Giro. But it was not as straight-forward as that. Initially Bahamontes did not want to go to France; once there, he did not want the Tour to finish. 'If the 1956 Tour had lasted another week I'd have won it,' Bahamontes now claims. 'I lost nearly fifty-six minutes in the first two stages and every day I was pulling back time to the point where I finished fourth.'

Before the race, Bahamontes had suffered from sinusitis and stomach problems. 'My stomach swelled up,' he says, 'and it was so bad I had to cut my shorts open at the waist. That was when I started to use braces regularly. Fortunately the Tour doctor [Pierre Dumas] understood me well and gave me pills with carbon to get rid of all the extra gas and that sorted me out. In fact every day I was getting better and better and everybody was waiting to see if I would win.'

Robinson has one word to describe the 1956 Tour, won by outsider Roger Walkowiak, and that is 'odd'. He says: 'Each day was like a blank sheet of paper. You had no idea what was going to happen. Breaks would go, but nobody really controlled anything.' The absence of Louison Bobet, winner of the three previous Tours, following a painful operation on a testicle, left a vacuum that no one was able to fill. In its post-race analysis, *L'Equipe* commented: 'The Tour had a new appearance this year. No Bobet, because of his operation, and no [Jean] Robic because of an accident. Charly Gaul should have been the number one favourite, but he became overly involved in a fruitless combat with Stan Ockers for the overall and Federico Martín Bahamontes for the King of the Mountains competition. Overall, the Tour lacked panache, particularly given "Walko" did not win a single stage.'

Bahamontes recalls: 'I was in the same breaks as Walkowiak, but as he was ahead of me in the overall I couldn't win. Still, which other rider apart from me could have been fifty minutes down and end up fourth, at ten minutes overall? I'm sure the Tour de France has never seen such a huge comeback. Everybody thought I could win.' However, the race was simply not long enough for Bahamontes.

Things also did not go his way in the King of the Mountains competition. His tactic of attacking on the mountains, and then waiting for the pack, fell foul of a Tour that ran out of control and where breakaways were coming from unlikely scenarios. Bahamontes' strategy depended on a stage developing predictably, and the 1956 Tour was anything but that. *L'Equipe* went so far as to describe it as 'hair-raising'.

Though in poor physical condition early on, Bahamontes started to improve on stage four to Rouen, where he took third place in a short individual race against the clock, thereby proving that his time-trialling was better than people thought. However, as he points out: 'Even though the differences were not huge at that point overall, certainly not to start worrying about losing the race, we then lost a lot of morale in the next stage, when five of the Spanish crashed.' To make matters worse, on stage seven to Angers, a thirty-one-man attack, including Walkowiak, gained eighteen minutes on all the favourites. Another significant move on stage ten added nearly a quarter of an hour on the bunch. Bahamontes, significantly, was not part of either of them.

After the first stage in the Pyrenees, Bahamontes found himself lying thirty-fifth overall, nearly fifty minutes behind race leader André Darrigade. Just the sight of Darrigade, a sprinter, donning yellow after a day that should have been reserved for the climbers confirmed Robinson's assessment that this Tour de France was indeed 'odd'. On paper the time gaps for riders like Bahamontes seemed insurmountable. Or as Bahamontes once rather poetically put it: 'They were as big as the distances between continents, and we had to row our boats day and night to try and arrive with enough time to conquer them.' However, that was only on paper. On the road Bahamontes pulled back four minutes on the second stage in the Pyrenees. Then he regained seventeen minutes in a five-rider break on a flat stage between Toulouse and Montpellier. 'My boat,' as he put it, 'could see land in sight on the continent ahead.'

Suddenly back in the top twenty at a mere twenty-one minutes nineteen seconds behind new leader Jean Adriaenssens of Belgium, Bahamontes progress had not gone unnoticed. The prestigious *Miroir-Sprint* magazine published an article entitled: 'And if Bahamontes were to win?' He pulled back another seven minutes on stage sixteen, another flattish day, and moved into thirteenth place overall. André Leducq, a Tour winner twice in the early 1930s and a team director in the 1950s, was quoted as saying: 'If he climbs as well as he did two years ago, Toledo may light up again . . . he's only eighteen minutes down and it wouldn't take a miracle for him to pull them back.' Bahamontes put it even more graphically. 'As I waited in the team hotel I couldn't stop ticking the minutes off for the next day's start in the Alps. I was sure that Fermina would light a candle for me when she heard it was getting so close . . . because what were eighteen minutes to a climber of my class?' Bahamontes, usually one of the most pragmatic individuals in the world, even went so far as to say: 'I will buy her a garage . . . she will no longer have to worry about the future. She is everything to me.'

But for all the emotionally hyped-up, gung-ho image Bahamontes presents of himself, it was not quite as straightforward as that. It was only logical that the closer he got to the yellow jersey, the nicer the things the press said about him, the less likely the rest of the pack were to let him go. Yet another massive break on a stage through the Alps to Turin enabled him to shave seven more minutes off the race leader's advantage, and move into ninth overall. At the same time, Walkowiak was proving a much trickier customer to shake off than everyone had anticipated. 'We never gambled on him being so dangerous, and we never raced together against him,' said Bahamontes. 'Still there was one big day in the Alps to go [the two hundred and fifty kilometres from Turin to Grenoble] and for sure Walkowiak wasn't sleeping easy in his bed the night before.'

The next day, Bahamontes attacked from the gun, taking Gaul with him. But he was predictably dropped on the descent of the mammoth Alpine pass, the Croix de Fer. Bahamontes finished in a three-man chasing group behind Gaul and moved up to sixth. However, it looked as though his poor downhill racing would cost him at least a place on the podium. It was during this stage that one of the most persistent of the Bahamontes myths emerged: that he threw his bike down a ravine in frustration at not being able to chase down Gaul. Bahamontes, however, denies its veracity. 'If I'd been able to stay with Gaul, everything would have changed,' he says. 'I'd have made up at least seven minutes on Walkowiak, but once again my descending skills let me down. Instead, Walkowiak got his moment of glory by making it into two breakaways on days when the big names forgot about him. He will always be remembered as the least deserving winner of the Tour de France.'

Though 'winning *a la* Walkowiak' has now entered cycling terminology as meaning 'to win from a flukey breakaway attack', not everybody agreed with Bahamontes' cold assessment. 'Little Walkowiak has beaten the biggest stars, so that makes him a "big star", too,' *L'Equipe* argued. 'Maybe there were no great names in this race, but it was still a great Tour.'

One reason Gaul was not overly prepared to form an alliance with Bahamontes in the Alps had nothing to do with the overall classification. While Bahamontes had not made the King of the Mountains jersey a specific objective, with three days left there was just one point separating the pair at the top of the ranking. As a result, on the second last stage with classified climbs, when Gaul and Bahamontes *did* get away together ahead of Walkowiak, there was anything but mutual collaboration. However, Gaul's refusal to do more than mark Bahamontes, and grab some more mountain points in the process, ended with the Spaniard gaining only another ninety seconds on Walkowiak overall. 'The King of the Mountains was decided on the eve of the race's arrival in Paris,' Bahamontes says, 'and Gaul formed an alliance with other riders so that I would not score any points.' In other words Bahamontes was outwitted. He ended up fourth in the overall classification and second in the King of the Mountains. But he was bullish enough to swear blind to anyone who would listen in the Parc des Princes, where the Tour finished, that in 1957 he would win the race.

Bahamontes' season petered out after that, so that 1956 became the only year of his career that Bahamontes finished with no victories at all. He dodged the Spanish Nationals because he was 'resting up for the World Championships', then abandoned them, claiming that the course did not suit him, though not before courting controversy by refusing to travel on the Spanish Federation's specially chartered flight. Finally, he again bypassed the Volta a Catalunya in favour of more profitable criteriums in France.

The highpoint of his year, in fact, had nothing to do with bikes. On 3 November Bahamontes married his longstanding girlfriend, Fermina Aguilar Sanchez. Like her new husband, Fermina had been working in the market in Toledo when they met. One of Federico's main charms for her, she informed the press, was that he 'always behaved like a real gentleman'. For example, she said: 'When we go out riding our bikes, he never overtakes me, not even on a climb.' A glance at the witness list – the Mayor of Toledo, the head of the Spanish Cycling Federation Alejandro del Caz, as well as his close business associate Evaristo Murtra – and the location (Toledo Cathedral) made it clear that socially Bahamontes was an established figure. In sporting terms, though, with three successive near-misses in the Grand Tours, his position was far less stable. Rather than mark a high point in the career of a young professional, 1956 established a pattern of unpredictability, isolation and blame games in Bahamontes' performances that was to dog the whole of his career.

Chapter Six
Loroño v Bahamontes –
A Knife in the Table

Federico Martín Bahamontes seems to have fallen out with a large number of members of the Spanish peloton at one time or another. The most spectacular and longest-running dispute was with Jesús Loroño. It turned into an eight-year duel which tapped directly into some of the most important divisions within Spanish society of the time and is still referred to as the most intense rivalry between two individual athletes in the history of sport in the country.

'Bahamontes versus Loroño is something that is hard to understand now, but at the time it was so serious it split Spain down the middle,' Josu Loroño, son of the father, confirms between mouthfuls of croissant one rainy spring Sunday morning in a bar near Bilbao. 'It got to the point where there were families I knew who wouldn't talk to one another because they were either *Bahamontistas* or *Loroñistas*. But I truly believe that just as Loroño wouldn't have been so good without Bahamontes, so Bahamontes wouldn't have been so good without Loroño. They were rivals, but they needed each other, too.'

Jesús Loroño stopped racing in 1962 and died almost two decades ago, but he remains a star of the sport in the Basque Country, the heartland of cycling in Spain. If Loroño is less famous internationally than Bahamontes or Miguel Poblet it is because he rarely raced abroad; when he did, though, he usually won as he showed in the Tour de France in 1953. Born in 1925 into a farming family in the village of Lattabetzu, close to Bilbao, Loroño's first job at eleven was digging trenches in the 'Iron Belt', a line of fortifications built to defend the city in the first year of the Civil War. Five of his eight brothers and sisters were imprisoned in labour camps after the Basque Country fell to the Nationalists in July 1937, but Loroño earned his living as a woodcutter. He became one of the region's top amateur cyclists, despite only being able to train at night (his mother used to threaten to take his woodcutter's axe to his bike in case he fell ill from sweating so heavily while out in the dark, cold Basque winters). Nonetheless, like so many Spaniards in the 1940s he thought his best option was to emigrate, in his case to Chile with one of his brothers. Before he could head to South America, however, Loroño had to fulfil his military service. As it happened, his commanding officer was a cycling fan who not only encouraged Loroño to train, but persuaded him to enter his first major race, the Subida a Naranco hill-climb in Asturias. Loroño won, netting the considerable sum of seven thousand pesetas (£3,500), and beat all the established domestic stars of the time. As a result he opted to stay in Spain and start a professional career in which he won the Vuelta a España and Volta a Catalunya as well as a King of the Mountains title in the Tour de France. He became Bahamontes' deadliest rival and even when they had both retired the mutual antagonism never really died down.

'Fede was and sometimes is like a child,' Loroño told one of Spain's top cycling reporters, Josu Garai, shortly before he died in 1994. 'I was stronger than him time-trialling, and he never beat me, not on the flat, not on the climbs, not even in hill-climbs which suited him perfectly because you started the climb "cold". Well, he only beat me once, and that was in a sprint I messed up. But he refused to recognise my triumphs.'

In the public's eyes, particularly in a cycling heartland like the Basque Country, Loroño's most important success was winning the toughest mountain stage en route to the King of the Mountains jersey in the 1953 Tour. 'My father told me his King of the Mountains jersey had a huge impact,' says Josu, once a cycling journalist, and now a councillor for the Basque Nationalist Party in Getxo, a dormitory town of Bilbao. 'When he came back from France that year the celebrations were far bigger than when he won the Vuelta. The reason was that for the Basques and for Spain, France in the 1950s was like another planet. Even twenty years later when I was growing up in the 1970s you went across the border to buy things that you just couldn't get in Spain. As late as the 1980s, when I was a journalist covering the Tour de France I remember the telecommunications in France were light years ahead. So just imagine when some kid like my father goes over the border in the 1950s and beats the French at their own game.'

However, Loroño was unable to defend his King of the Moutains title in 1954. And who should take it but Bahamontes. 'My father couldn't go because he was laid up in hospital for three months after crashing in the GP Eibar when he collided with a motorbike coming the wrong way. Jacques Goddet [the Tour director] had called my father his favourite [to win the Tour outright] that year, and that was his biggest regret: not being able to go to the Tour that year, far more so than in 1959.' Josu says the antagonism between Bahamontes and his father did not get serious until the 1955 Vuelta. But the fact Bahamontes had identical aims for the 1954 Tour as Loroño had the year before, and succeeded in claiming the King of the Mountains jersey while its previous owner lay in a hospital bed, all added greatly to the grist of the pair's rivalry.

Sport apart, there was also a major social divide between the two. For the Basques, Loroño was a well-built, no-nonsense, working-class hero from Bilbao's industrial and agricultural hinterland, who was taking on the more eccentric, erratic wisp of a climber from some dusty city down south. Certainly their personalities could not have been more different. Loroño was dour, pragmatic, straightforward and a direct kind of talker. Bahamontes, on the other hand, was far more Quixotic. Or as *El País* described him at the age of eighty: 'Affable, unique, contradictory, ultra-individualist and daring . . . as agile as an adolescent and as restless as a hyperactive child.' The biggest difference, though, was political.

Loroño's family were diehard Basque separatists, whereas Bahamontes, from authoritarian, central Spain, was so popular with Franco he even met him personally at least once. As a result cycling's two leading figures came to symbolise one of the most damaging, deep-rooted divisions within Franco's Spain: the Basque Country versus Madrid.

If the 'Basque question' remains an important issue in Spanish politics even today, it was one of Franco's biggest headaches during his forty-year dictatorship. Of the eleven states of emergency Franco had to declare in Spain, six were in the Basque regions of Vizcaya and Guipuizcoa. Until a definitive ceasefire was declared in October 2011, the fifty-year drive by Basque terrorist group E.T.A. for an independent Euskal Herria was one of western Europe's most deeply ingrained and bloodiest conflicts. E.T.A.'s existence has historical links to the repression that followed the Civil War when the Basques were on the losing side. Despite being one of the most religious areas of Spain, which should in theory have placed them alongside Franco in the war, the political strength of the Basque separatist movement was such that two of the three Basque Country regions, Guipuizcoa and Vizcaya remained loyal to the Republic. Though they were cut off from the rest of Republican Spain from the earliest days of the war, the Basques held out for almost a year in Vizcaya. They pinned down a large number of Franco's troops and eased the military pressure on the main Republican strongholds. If their spirited resistance during and after the Civil War was not enough to make the Basque Country unpopular with the ruling regime and its supporters, the differences between Spain's most northerly region and the rest of the peninsula were far more extensive than whether the Basque *ikurriña* flag replaced the Spanish tricolor over the town halls of San Sebastian and Bilbao.

Those differences certainly outweigh any similarities. Take economics, for example: for decades many of Spain's traditional 'heavy' industries like mining, ironworks or shipbuilding were concentrated in the Basque region. That meant the Basques were far better off than the agricultural centre and south. Half a century ago, John Hooper said in his book *The Spaniards:* 'To visit the Basque Country is to take a trip in time back to the industrial North of Europe earlier this century. Its belching smokestacks, grimy buildings and dogged, pasty-faced inhabitants are the very stuff of Lowry paintings.' That was a far cry from the austere Castillian fortress towns like Toledo and the rugged, dry sierras of Teruel and Extremadura or the semi-deserts of Andalusia.

But the Basque Country had cultural and legal differences as well as its own language, Euskera. Deep into the twentieth century the Basques retained their traditional right to veto Spanish law and numerous other economic and social privileges. These *fueros* created envy and resentment between the Basque Country and the rest of the country and Franco banned them as soon as he gained power.

Sport, meanwhile, has always been vastly more popular in the Basque Country than in the rest of Spain. But the political implications of sport have always been close to the surface in the north. For reasons no one can quite fathom that has been particularly true of cycling. It was not just a question of one team versus another or one individual versus another: entire races could fall foul of the political tensions. After Basque separatist violence caused the Vuelta a España's final stages to be all but cancelled in 1978, Spain's biggest race did not return to the region until 2011. The fears that the race might be subject to terrorist attacks was no exaggeration: in 2005 E.T.A. threatened to attack it with rocket-launchers.

It was, therefore, only natural that the Loroño versus Bahamontes rivalry intermingled with the Basque Country versus Madrid conflict. For central Spain the fact Bahamontes came from the town of Toledo just outside Madrid, combined with their ingrained dislike of the Basques, automatically made him their champion. Bahamontes might have been a shade temperamental at times, but he was clearly capable of taking on Loroño and the Basques and that was largely all that mattered. Josu Loroño is convinced that

Spain's backward economic circumstances, as well as the political situation, fanned the flames of the rivalry. 'They fought each other during a crucial period for Spain – the post-Civil War era, a time of extreme [political] repression. Society's only safety valve was sport. It was the opium of the people.'

Other countries had damaging rivalries between their top cyclists, particularly France, and in 1958 and 1959 Bahamontes would take full advantage of that. However, as Josu points out, none of those rivalries had the breadth of Bahamontes versus Loroño, which had social, political, economic and sporting conflict rolled into one. Loroño's son believes the closest example would be that between Coppi and Bartali which divided Italy in the 1940s and early 1950s. But, in comparison, Loroño versus Bahamontes was wilder and less stage-managed than the elegant face-off between their Italian equivalents. It is hard, for instance, to imagine the genteel Bartali slamming his dinner knife into the table in front of Coppi if the two of them had raced in the same team. That is apparently what Loroño did as a 'conversation opener' when he was once having dinner with Charly Gaul and Bahamontes during a Giro d'Italia. The 'knife in the table' anecdote, more reminiscent of a bad Western than cycling, has never been confirmed. But that was the whole point of Bahamontes versus Loroño: it was a conflict with its own laws of engagement that went beyond everyday reality. Whatever outrageous stories the press made up about them, no one could prove that they were not true. 'Nowadays when you can see the whole stage of the Tour de France on television their rivalry couldn't have got so big,' Josu Loroño comments. 'Back then, though, when the only way people could get information was by going to the bar or shop that had the only radio in their street or village, it was far easier for journalists to make things up – not necessarily lie, but to imagine stuff, fantasise, exaggerate. Actually, the press and the fans were behind quite a few of their so-called disputes. Neither of them complained, though.'

Quite apart from the mutual dislike there was also fear in the case of Bahamontes. Josu claims that Bahamontes was sometimes so terrified of his father during their racing careers that he would hide in his hotel room to avoid him. As for Jesús Loroño, he considered Bahamontes to be 'mentally weak . . . sitting in his room saying, [and Josu puts on a fake falsetto] "Loroño wants to hit me, I'm not coming out, Loroño wants to hit me".' Yet the two were not always on such bad terms. Josu Loroño first encountered Bahamontes at the restaurant in Bilbao which his father opened after retiring, and where Bahamontes would sometimes drop in for a meal if he was in town. There were even times, he claims, when Bahamontes spent a few days as Loroño's house guest. However, media-wise, any examples of friendliness between Loroño and Bahamontes were brushed under the carpet for the simple reason that the rivalry was a newspaper reporter's dream.

And Bahamontes and Loroño fulfilled their roles to perfection: they cheerfully traded insults, refused to work together on the national team, and accused each other of betrayal, cheating and foul play. When it exploded it was pure dynamite. Physical aggression among cycling fans has traditionally been all but non-existent. Bahamontes versus Loroño, though, was the exception that proved the rule. When Bahamontes was selected for the Tour and Loroño was dropped, his fans threw stones at the national trainer's shop in Bilbao, spat at his wife and sent hate mail. On at least one occasion they tried to beat him up. In turn, contemporary photographs show Bahamontes' supporters parading in the streets wearing shirts with the words 'R.I.P. Loroño' stitched in black ribbons on the front. Josu recalls: 'With time, it got very complicated and more divisive, not less. Families would be split down the middle because Loroño had "rebel" supporters in the rest of Spain and Bahamontes had some in the Basque Country. For example, there was a well-known sports writer, Francisco G. Ubieta, who wrote for the *La Gaceta del Norte* newspaper here in the north. He was a sympathiser of the Franco regime, but at the same time he was a real Loroño fan.'

However, over time, as happens with most conflicts, the original reasons for their falling-out became forgotten and the rivalry became self-perpetuating. But did it ever, to Josu's knowledge, get seriously violent between the two? 'Well,' he replies '[they say] there was the time that they hit each other with bike pumps, and what I have heard is that once he grabbed Bahamontes by the throat. That's what they say, anyway . . . and then there was the time Bahamontes refused to come out of the room because he was scared my father would hit him. Some kind of row, I imagine.'

What really separated Loroño and Bahamontes was that they could not have been more different as people and were therefore almost doomed to rub each other up the wrong way. Bahamontes refuses to discuss Loroño. 'What's the point, if nobody's heard of him in France or Italy?' Loroño was equally contemptuous of his rival. 'Bernardo Ruiz has told him more than once, "Loroño beat you fairly",' Loroño said in 1994, 'and it's about time Bahamontes recognised it.'

'They had very different personalities,' Josu Loroño says. 'One of them was what we would call madness personified, the other would always play it straight down the line. Perhaps my father was a bit too stiff-necked at times, but in any case he was the complete opposite to Bahamontes. My father was the kind of guy who when he said something was "A" it was "A" even if he was wrong.' Loroño adds later 'He went so far as to say Bahamontes was weak – mentally weak – that he had no character.' And Josu says Bahamontes had a second problem with Loroño: 'Bahamontes suffered from Loroñitis: when he saw my father he used to shit himself. My father dominated his mind.'

Not only was 1957 the year that Bahamontes' conflict with Loroño reached its peak, he was also in serious trouble with his latest team. Bahamontes had quit Faema, Spain's most prestigious squad, for whom he had barely raced in 1956, for a much smaller one, Mobylette. He had been convinced that he was the victim of a persecution campaign at Faema, only to find exactly the same problems with Mobylette. 'I left Faema because I was supposed to be leader and the mechanic was puncturing every wheel I had.' But when he moved to Mobylette he alleges that Loroño only won the Volta a Catalunya 'because they paid off everybody else, including my team. The director I had was bought off by Miguel Torrello, the Faema boss,' he says, 'and then when I punctured five or six times on one stage, I can remember the Faema trainer laughing about what had happened.'

It would be easy to write Bahamontes off as being paranoid, but there were incidents that suggested he was the victim of a loosely organised conspiracy. The Volta a Catalunya of 1955 was a case in point. On stage six, Jiménez Quiles was in a break with Loroño and Bahamontes, and he says the Basque rider did everything to convince him to work against Bahamontes. 'I got into a move with the two of them with about twenty kilometres to go and they started making long, long drives on the front, much bigger than the ones they do nowadays,' says Jiménez Quiles. 'It looked like they were trying to wipe each other out. Finally I got away ahead of both of them and my director came up to me on a descent and told me to stop because Loroño had dropped Bahamontes. When Loroño caught up he persuaded me that I should work with him and let him win, purely because Bahamontes was behind, and he wanted to beat him so badly, and so I did. Jesús gave me the trophies and all the prizes from that stage – the trophies are over there in that cabinet if you want to look at them – because he said they belonged to me anyway. All he cared about was beating Bahamontes.'

Things were no better in the national team. 'Fede had more enemies in the national team for the Vuelta a España in 1957 than out of it,' Bernardo Ruiz recalls. 'The line-up consisted of all my team-mates who I had recruited to get on the squad. Then they kicked me out to make way for Bahamontes because I was apparently past my sell-by date at thirty-three. So there he was, alone in a team and surrounded by all my team-mates.' At this point the simplest solution would have been for Bahamontes to get out his wallet and buy himself some allies. But Bahamontes' refusal to do so, perhaps because a man who had endured such poverty in his early years might be reluctant to pay for loyalty, let him down dearly. 'The entire team was effectively my Faema squad and Bahamontes wouldn't spend anything to gain the team's sympathy. He was a magnificent rider, but that was a very serious defect,' Ruiz says, particularly since it was considered almost normal at the time to buy and sell races.

By 1957, Bahamontes' enemies had two natural magnets in Ruiz and Loroño. Just like the bulk of the country, the Spanish peloton divided into *Loroñistas* and *Bahamontistas*. Barring a very few key Bahamontes *domestiques*, like Julio San Emeterio, and a handful of notable 'neutrals' such as Miguel Poblet, Loroño had far more supporters in the bunch. These included Ruiz and his young ally Salvador Botella, already the winner of the Volta a Catalunya back in 1953. One catalyst in the Loroño-Bahamontes rivalry was Spain's team trainer, Luis Puig. An avuncular type given to bland, meaningless statements of goodwill that proved ideal for a political career that eventually led to him becoming president of the U.C.I., cycling's governing body, Puig was totally incapable of handling his two top riders. Instead, Puig relied excessively on Ruiz, who, unbeknown to him, was in the Loroño camp, and then promptly washed his hands of any major conflict. It took the Spanish Federation two years, and a huge scandal in the Tour de France, to realise that with Loroño and Bahamontes, someone willing to bang heads together would be far more appropriate for the job.

Meanwhile, the Loroño-Bahamontes conflict continued unabated to the point where their *domestiques* lined up and took pot shots at their leaders as well, even 30 years after the event. 'Bahamontes is the kind of bloke that if somebody he dislikes goes on an attack he goes after him even if it's flat and he [Bahamontes] is chasing all by himself ,' Jesús Galdeano, one of Loroño's most loyal supporters, told *El Mundo* in the 1980s. 'He doesn't believe in his own possibilities. He wins in the mountains and gets half an hour, then he loses half an hour on the flat and blames everybody else.' Poblet, a rival but also a friend of Bahamontes, said: 'Fede wasn't a bad guy. He didn't kill anybody. He was always a happy sort, but he behaved differently to most other people. His personality was different. He was wilful, too: when he wanted to do something he'd do it whether it was right or wrong. I can remember we were in the same team, with Charly Gaul, in a Tour of Italy [1958] and there was a stage finish with a ten-kilometre climb just before, then a descent, then a few kilometres of flat. And I said to him, "Don't attack before the climb, wait until there are a couple of kilometres to go, I'll watch your back, and then if I can, I'll win the sprint from the group behind". Then what does he do? He attacks right at the start of the climb, gets a minute or a minute and a half, then gets caught on the descent by Anquetil and the rest. Fortunately I won the sprint, but he finished dead last when he could have won. Loroño was much straighter, at least with me. But Bahamontes would tell you one thing and then the next day he'd go and do another.' Jiménez Quiles adds: 'In any case, what did he expect? Those days if you were in front and you saw a team-mate attack, you'd know it was up to you to go after him.'

Ironically, Bahamontes' 1957 season got off to a flying start when he outsprinted Loroño for victory in a Tour of the Levante stage – the one Loroño said he messed up – and then took his second win in three years in the Mont Faron hill-climb in France. The Vuelta a España started equally well, too, despite Loroño gaining a couple of minutes' advantage from a break on stage one. Forty-eight hours later Bahamontes bounced back with a vengeance to claim his first stage win and the leader's jersey after a solo attack in the mountains of Asturias. Loroño, on the other hand, was at nearly thirteen minutes, tenth overall and itching to counter-attack for all that he and Bahamontes were in the same squad. Ruiz, meanwhile, exiled to a regional squad but with his usual Faema team-mates filling out the Spanish 'A' team, was watching and waiting in the wings. Knowing that Bahamontes hated the cold, Loroño took advantage of a snowstorm en route to León on stage four to move ahead. However, with the weather conditions becoming worse on the Pajares pass the organisers decided to suspend the stage. Loroño was so furious at his misfortune that he continued pedalling uphill and had to be forcibly removed from his bike.

Bahamontes lost the lead briefly in Madrid to another team-mate, Botella, a close ally of Ruiz's. This was the first time that Bahamontes was indisputably let down by his team, and in particular Puig who failed to inform him of the sizable gap that Botella and other breakaways had gained. When Bahamontes found out, it was only thanks to the race organisers, not his team. He counter-attacked almost instantly, though not before having a shouting match with Puig for failing to tell him earlier. Just to complicate matters, when Bahamontes punctured the next day on the Navacerrada climb on a stage around the sierras of Madrid, Loroño voluntarily gave him a spare wheel. Though it was in both their interests that Botella did not gain too much time, Loroño later regretted this, telling the *La Gaceta del Norte* newspaper: 'I was the idiot who saved Bahamontes in Navacerrada.'

Bahamontes was determined not to let the race slip through his fingers, and bounced back brilliantly two days later when he asked for and received support from the French in a break on the way to Cuenca. By allowing Roger Walkowiak and his compatriot Gilbert Bauvin to take first and second places, Bahamontes moved back into yellow. Loroño, meanwhile, had dropped to eleventh and was nearly sixteen minutes behind. Puig confirmed to the press that Bahamontes would be the team leader from now on while Loroño went for the King of the Mountains. All went well on the long drop down from the tablelands of Cuenca to the coast at Valencia, but the next day on the coast road to Tortosa, Bahamontes was to discover just how friendless he was.

'I whispered in Loroño's ear, "Come with me",' is how Ruiz explains the start of the mass attack in which Bahamontes lost twenty-one minutes and the yellow jersey to his arch-rival. Poetically appealing though Ruiz's recollection of events is, the truth is slightly more mundane. Ruiz and two other riders powered up the coast road in the first hour, and when they had opened a twenty-second gap Loroño came across with four others. Then the race was on. But there was no doubt who the move was directed against. Another 1950s Spanish professional, Luis Otaño, recalls Loroño telling him: 'During the break Ruiz was yelling, "Go, go, Jesús, Bahamontes is dropped and you're going to win the Vuelta. You're better than him, fuck it, go, ride!"' Moreover, it was

rumoured that Bahamontes' team-mates participated in the conspiracy. Some reports claimed that rather than help their stranded
leader, they went as far as holding on to his shorts to prevent him
counter-attacking. Certainly he received little support. 'With
Loroño ahead, and with all my Faema team-mates and friends in
the national squad behind, nobody would work for Bahamontes,'
Ruiz recounts with a hint of smugness. 'Bahamontes was the
leader, he could have won that Vuelta, he should have won it, but
he didn't know how to win over his team-mates.' Evaristo Murtra,
Bahamontes' 'godfather', who was following the race, confirmed:
'He had no support whatsoever. Nobody wanted to help him, and
the last anybody saw of Puig was when the break had gained two
minutes, and he shot past in his jeep indicating with his hands to the
riders that they should take it easy and not work to bring back
Loroño's break.'

Ruiz says: 'So we reached Tortosa miles ahead, [Italian Bruno]
Tognacini gets the stage, Loroño got first overall, I moved into
second and Tognacini third, and that's when the scandals started.
Even the Federation had to intervene.' It was a brutal, barefaced
betrayal, but even fifty-five years on, Ruiz has no regrets. 'Fede says
that we robbed him of that Vuelta. But he was vulnerable, he let
himself lose it. And the ones who knew how to race, well, just like
in this Vuelta, we beat him.' As for Loroño, he claimed to be
surprised at his success, but equally pitiless. 'I never thought I'd get
the yellow jersey,' he says. 'From two-thirds of the way through
the stage it was pretty clear what was happening. But if
Bahamontes couldn't do anything then it was because he couldn't.'

Somewhere in Bahamontes' office, amid all the rows of photograph albums and collections of newspaper cuttings, lurks a piece
of paper that allegedly explains why he did not win the Vuelta in
1957. Given that at one point Bahamontes had an advantage of
nearly sixteen minutes over Loroño it seems almost more difficult
for Bahamontes to have lost the race than to have won it. However,
that was what happened.

Bahamontes' hand thrums on one knee and a ferocious glare

comes over his face as he gives his explanation for snatching defeat from the jaws of victory. He says he was 'robbed' by a government telegram, received while in Valencia, instructing him to throw the race in favour of Loroño. In the middle of a military dictatorship there was no ignoring an official communication. That the rider who benefited happened to be his sworn enemy only added insult to injury. According to Bahamontes the instructions came from 'above', which is how Spaniards refer to the higher echelons of power. At the very least, Bahamontes says, it was the Minister of Sport José Antonio Elola who put his name to the telegram.

Whoever decreed that Bahamontes should lose, if, indeed, such a decree was made at all, the logic behind the decision would have been purely political: Loroño was Basque, the Vuelta was Basque-run, and Euskadi was the most troublesome region Franco had to deal with. Rather than let someone from the Madrid area win, Bahamontes believes that Franco's henchmen let the Basques get one over the centre of Spain to satisfy local pride. In some ways it was like the Roman emperors who kept the noisiest parts of the populace happy with 'bread and circuses'.

It is an extraordinary claim to make, but Bahamontes says he still has a telegram from the Ministry of Sport to prove it. He has certainly kept others, like the telegram from Toledo town hall promising him some prime building land in the city after the Tour victory in 1959, which he is always quick to locate in a photograph album for anyone curious enough to want to see it. Yet when asked if it is possible to see the document that proves he lost the Vuelta as a result of political maneuvering, he says 'sure, sure', half-gets out of his seat, looks around and then slumps down again, as if he cannot be bothered. Or maybe he knows that the telegram cannot be found.

Even so, he is still adamant about his side of the story. 'It was all because of a telegram from José Antonio Elola telling me that even though I was leader Loroño had to win,' Bahamontes says now. 'I'm convinced Puig had a part to play in that, too, because Elola was staying in Puig's chalet at the time as a guest. In any case, the telegram said I had to settle for second and the King of the

Mountains, and let Loroño win because he was Basque and the race was Basque. I had to take it or leave it.' When interviewed a month after the Vuelta Bahamontes claimed: 'I didn't move because Loroño was ahead.'

The press was equally confused by what happened on the stage to Tortosa. 'I've been told Bahamontes was under orders not to [counter-] attack,' commented *El Mundo Deportivo*'s correspondent, 'and I admit it may be true. I can't understand what happened, though, and why a rider who fought so hard to get the jersey in Madrid was so prepared to sit back and let it go out of his reach so calmly. Isn't there one of Aesop's fables where somebody spends years and years putting together a fortune, then calmly throws it all down a mineshaft? That's what Bahamontes did yesterday with his yellow jersey.'

He was not the only reporter who suspected a possible government connection to the race's outcome. In the cycling gossip section of *La Región*, an Oviedo newspaper, an anonymous journalist going only by the name of 'Ricardo' wrote a one-line reference to the Tortosa stage, saying: 'Is this sport? Let us salute our "comrade" Elola for this case.' The correspondent of the pro-Loroño *La Gaceta del Norte* took a completely different and far-fetched point of view, running a story headlined: 'Puig-Bahamontes conspiracy against Loroño.' *L'Equipe* seems to have had a clearer idea of what Loroño's attack represented. They ran a one-word headline for their Vuelta coverage the next day: 'Heresy'.

Regardless of whether he messed up the race of his own volition or was annoyed because he had been told to throw it, newspaper reports claimed that Bahamontes spent most of that night's meal in the team hotel in Tortosa flinging insults at all and sundry. Finally, Loroño grabbed Bahamontes and demanded to know what his problem was. At that point Bahamontes apparently fled to his room, asking that his food be sent up and refusing to come down while Loroño was around.

Though one journalist claimed that 'the Valencia-Tortosa stage was the execution wall for Bahamontes, and Loroño and Luis Puig were the ones firing the rifles', in fact things were not much better between team director and Loroño. While no friend of Bahamontes, and after failing to ensure the support of his team-mates, it later emerged Puig had sat even more firmly on the fence by trying to stop Loroño from attacking, too. 'Puig kept blocking the road with his car, telling Loroño he had to sit up,' Josu Loroño recalls, 'but my father would dodge past, saying he was having none of it. Puig even shouted at him to stop at one point, and my father yelled back, "Not even if the Civil Guard come and get me!" And in those days, that was quite something to say about the *Guardia Civil*.'

The following day's stage between Barcelona and Zaragoza went calmly enough until ten kilometres to go when the Loroño-Bahamontes war broke out again. Bahamontes went on the attack and Loroño, who had been waiting for the move, immediately chased him down. Still riding a few metres ahead of the bunch, the two then began arguing with each other at the tops of their voices. Their row enabled a number of top foreign riders to take advantage and go clear. Indeed, by Zaragoza the leaders had gained a minute's lead on the Bahamontes-Loroño group. Neither seemed to care. Loroño then continued to claim to all and sundry that Bahamontes had been attacking him 'non-stop' since Barcelona, and 'that was how he paid me back for the help I gave him on the stage to Madrid'. The minor matter of his attack on Bahamontes while he was leading the race at Valencia was, strangely enough, never mentioned by Loroño.

Tension levels in the Spanish 'A' team reached the point that after a crucial eighty-one-kilometre time-trial from Zaragoza to Huesca, the Spanish Cycling Federation decided they had to intervene. Their warning that both riders would be excluded from the race unless the insults stopped, coincidentally, arrived by telegram. A truce was officially agreed and toasts were drunk to mutual loyalty for the press's benefit. Loroño and Bahamontes even shook hands publicly, and the media dubbed it 'the Huesca Pact'. Nobody was fooled, though, except perhaps the Federation; behind the scenes the war continued unabated.

Later, the organising newspaper *El Correo Español* ran a story in which it claimed Puig had taken the two riders into his hotel room, showed them the Federation telegram and told them in no uncertain terms to stop fighting otherwise they would both be excluded. He also apparently told Bahamontes, *sotto voce*, that if Loroño did not win the Vuelta, 'there was no way either he or Bahamontes would be allowed inside Bilbao [where the race finished]'. To add to the intrigue, it later emerged that Bahamontes tried to abandon the race the same night, and was only persuaded not to by his 'godfather', the Catalan businessman Evaristo Murtra.

Bahamontes rode flat out in the time-trial the following day, using a twenty-eight-spoke front wheel from a track bike, despite them being prohibited for road-racing. He was given a one-minute penalty which dropped him from second, six seconds behind Loroño to third in the time-trial. But he had the minor satisfaction of ousting Ruiz from second place overall. 'They told me those wheels were banned, but then why were the French team all using them?' Bahamontes complained to me more than fifty years later. Loroño bitterly criticised Bahamontes at the time-trial finish, saying: 'It's really annoyed me that he uses a wheel that he knows is illegal, even telling the race officials about it, because he'll get more benefit from using it than whatever he was going to be penalised. I'd have rather died on the road than lose the yellow jersey to him that way.'

For the last three days, with nothing to lose, Bahamontes attacked as and when he liked. However, given Loroño and Ruiz were now firm allies, he was effectively fighting against two teams not one. Furthermore, Ruiz was happy to tip off Loroño if Bahamontes made a move. 'Bahamontes was officially going for mountains points whenever he attacked, but there was one time when he got a one hundred-metre advantage on a climb,' Ruiz revealed to me. 'I told Loroño, "Don't trust him, he only needs to be twenty metres ahead, not leading by minutes". And so Bahamontes was chased down. They kept on insulting each other all the time, though. It was incredible. Like something out of a film.'

Bahamontes rode brilliantly in the final mountain stages, taking out his rage at losing the overall title by attaining his first Vuelta

King of the Mountains title with ease. Not that Loroño or Ruiz were prepared to let him get too much of an advantage. On the stage to Bayonne Loroño chased down every charge by Bahamontes, 'who attacked and attacked and attacked', according to *El Mundo Deportivo*, 'turning around to see each time what Loroño could do'. The report continued: 'But Loroño went from strength to strength, hammering on the pedals every which way in order to be totally sure he was gaining the maximum distance possible. When he brought back Bahamontes to fifty metres, Bahamontes sat up, looking at him with a mixture of hatred and admiration. Loroño kept on baring his teeth as if to show that even if he ran out of physical strength he'd defend himself by biting.'

Again, Bahamontes' apparent change of mind over the instructions to lose the race so late on raises yet more doubts about the existence of a telegram that nobody, barring Bahamontes, has apparently seen. However, it is difficult to conceive another explanation. Why should a rider who was in total control of a race suddenly allow a rival he loathed to gain such a huge margin and throw it all away, even if then he changed his mind again and tried to get it back? Ultimately, there are four possible explanations for Bahamontes' behaviour on the Valencia-Tortosa stage: extreme carelessness; a sudden attack of indifference; lack of team support; or external orders, perhaps from Elola. Whichever reason is the right one, fifty years on it is pretty clear that Bahamontes' bitterness endures. Furthermore, given he cannot turn the clock back he has no choice but to belittle the entire event. 'The Vuelta?' Bahamontes says. 'In those days it was just a bit of a joke.'

'That telegram?' says Josu Loroño. 'If he's got it, then he should produce it, which he never has. The day he shows somebody that telegram, that's an end to any arguments.' Until he does, Loroño has his own interpretation. 'It's basically sour grapes. He's pissed, too, that he never won the Volta, the Vuelta or the Bicicleta Vasca. He's got a magnificent *palmares*, but in that area he feels sore.' Loroño argues that from a political point of view Bahamontes' claims are illogical. 'Given what my father was, from a Basque

Nationalist family with two brothers in exile and a third doing time in a hard-labour camp in Cadiz because of the Civil War, the ruling regime would have far prefered Bahamontes to have won. Nobody can deny Bahamontes' achievements which are huge. But at the same time, he shouldn't deny what other riders achieved. It's all "me, me, me" and the rest are a heap of shit.'

Chapter Seven
The Dangers of 'Go-Fast'

7 July, 1957, Eastern France: In many ways it is the least significant of acts. In a quiet country lane, a bike rider draws up on a roadside, dismounts, takes off his watch and his shoes, and sits down on the ground. Yet how can it be insignificant? Federico Martín Bahamontes, the race's big favourite, is abandoning the Tour de France. Instantly a huddle of journalists, spectators, race officials and team personnel crowd around him. They offer him water – it was already 36 degrees when the stage started in Besançon a couple of hours back in one of the worst heatwaves of the 1950s – but Bahamontes refuses it. 'It's over, I'm not going on,' he insists.

Not everybody is convinced: a Spanish team mechanic attempts to put his race shoes back on his feet, but Bahamontes grabs them from him and flings them into a ditch. The same mechanic then attempts to pick Bahamontes up and physically put him on the bike. 'Fuck, I said I'm not going on,' Bahamontes yells at him. He leans so heavily on the mechanic that he has to let him fall back down on to the ground.

When his sports director Luis Puig gets out of his car and demands an explanation, Bahamontes says nothing but points at a swelling in his left arm. It has been caused, it will later emerge, by an injection given to him by Puig himself. Bahamontes cannot steer his bike, he claims, though that has not stopped him from taking part in the first break of the day.

Grainy photographs of the scene show a glassy-eyed

Bahamontes drawn up into a semi-fetal position, lying at the centre
of a crowd which is steadily growing in size and variety. Two of
his Spanish team-mates, Carmelo Morales and Antonio Ferraz, see
his bike flung on the ground, stop, and plead with him to get back
on into the race. 'Do it for the sake of your mother, Fede!' Ferraz
shouts at Bahamontes over the heads of the crowd. Back from
somewhere in the middle of the knot of people comes the muffled
but increasingly determined answer: 'No.' 'For Fermina!' 'No!' 'For
Spain!' 'No!' Then Ferraz plays his last card, and theoretically the
best: 'For Franco!' Again Bahamontes spits out the answer: 'No!'
He then picks himself up and gets in the race's 'broom wagon', the
vehicle for riders who have abandoned.

Meanwhile, Puig's initial sympathy has been replaced by anger.
He refuses to believe that the injection is the real cause of the
abandon and he attempts to provoke Bahamontes by claming he is
not 'man enough' to continue. 'Go on then, quit,' Puig sneers. 'But
when you're getting changed out of your clothes and putting on
your trousers, take a look down at your chest and you'll see you've
grown tits!' Bahamontes just ignores him and the broom wagon
heads off: a spectacularly undignified exit for a Tour favourite, and
arguably one of the most melodramatic and farcical in the race's
history.

Long-term, Bahamontes' departure will force Spanish cycling's
top brass to finally face up to the country's chronic lack of unity
and carry out a much-needed overhaul of the Federation. Above
all it will produce a change of national team director, from Luis
Puig to Dalmacio Langarica, from a director with whom
Bahamontes was incapable of collaborating and who oversaw his
most humiliating abandon of any bike race, to one whom he
described as 'the best I ever had'. In fact, one of the most important
seeds of Bahamontes' success in the 1959 Tour, the crowning
moment of his career, is sown on a day when success is probably
the last thing on his mind.

Bahamontes was interviewed a few days later in a hairdresser's shop
in Toledo by the newspaper *Informaciones*. 'With the "closed" sign

on the door and the guy in the chair, where better place to have a chat?' the reporter shrewdly observed in his article. During the conversation Bahamontes claimed that he had no choice but to abandon. '[Race director Jacques] Goddet told me that even if I reached the finish outside the time limit, I'd be allowed to continue,' he said. 'And I wanted to continue but my arm was far too swollen and painful. I had fever, sinusitis and laryngitis as well. I had to ride with my arm on my *musette* [food bag] for the first eighty-five kilometres, the only part of the stage where things were calm. I didn't abandon for good reasons or bad reasons, I abandoned because I had no other choice.'

Not everybody believed him. 'He was playing chicken,' Bernardo Ruiz told the Mayor of Barcelona, Juan Antonio Samaranch, a few days later. 'I've had those injections and they hurt a bit, but not that much. In any case, Fede is stronger with one arm than most of us are with two.'

The injection Puig had administered the night before was variously reported as containing lime, calcium, vitamins B and C or a combination of all four. The problem was not the mixture of medicines themselves, outlandish as it sounds. Rather, according to Bahamontes, Puig messed up the injection, jamming the needle in twice, which caused severe swelling and pain in his entire arm. In consequence, he could not control his bike, so had to stop.

But quite why Puig had given Bahamontes the injection in the first place was harder to establish. According to Puig, Bahamontes' morale was low and he needed a boost. And as he cheerfully, and very unwisely, told journalists: 'It's perfectly natural for me to give the riders injections.' The U.C.I. did not see it quite like especially since in France only doctors were allowed to inject patients. Nor were the Tour de France organisers impressed; even if the police cast a blind eye to some laws being infringed by the Tour, the only doctor allowed to administer injections was the official medic, Pierre Dumas. As a result of Puig's bragging, on the same day that Bahamontes abandoned Goddet told the Spanish Federation to make sure Puig 'did not return to the Tour next year, because he is unwelcome'. Politely worded as Goddet's message was it was still a bombshell: being unable to direct the national team in the biggest race in the sport meant Puig's career as national coach was over, and the French knew it. And Bahamontes? 'Federico Bahamontes has fallen from grace,' Goddet later wrote in his usual poetical vein in *L'Equipe*, 'just at the point when he was the sole favourite of the race, and his departure leaves the way open to new challengers. It's perfectly logical that Federico suffered as a result of the injection his sports director gave him in his left arm. But what's not so comprehensible is that the Spanish champion has not tried harder to overcome his problem and to give it time to pass.' He was not the only person who thought that.

The scandal did not fade into the background immediately. The Spanish Federation banned Bahamontes and, separately, Miguel Poblet from racing abroad for a month, both for abandoning without due reason. The aim was to stop them making money from post-Tour criteriums. In Poblet's case this seems particularly harsh. Sixth in the Giro, and therefore with reasonable hopes of a strong ride in the Tour, the race was going to have a stage finish in his home town of Barcelona and he had been keen to win there. However, he was forced to abandon on stage four because of a boil 'the size of a golf ball in the part that most hurts a cyclist. Whenever I sit down, I see stars'. Bahamontes was also required to re-state his explanations for abandoning before a medical tribunal in Madrid in the autumn and ordered to undergo a health check before he was allowed to race again. 'I had to go to Madrid to prove I hadn't taken anything [illegal],' he said. 'Puig was a doctor and before the Alps, he injected me with Binerva and Redoxon [the brand names for vitamins B and C] in my arm. I was in agony. [Team-mate and future Vuelta winner Antonio] Suárez told me that I shouldn't give up, but I refused to go down a climb steering with only one arm. By then the damage had been done, anyway. It fucked up my Tour completely.'

The word that was never mentioned throughout the controversy was, of course, doping. Though lists of banned substances existed at that time, very rarely was any concerted action taken to fight drugs. However, allusions to the problem are plain: Tour organisers made dark hints in their official report of the affair about 'practices of which we don't approve'. Then there were the unstated aims of the medical commission who investigated Bahamontes on his return. As far as I have been able to establish from a cross-section of professional cyclists and team doctors, calcium has no performance-enhancing benefits whatsoever. Nor does lime. Either Bahamontes did not know that and fell for some of the quackery prevalent in cycling at the time, or he did not know what was in the syringe but assumed that if Puig was administering it, it could only do him good. Either way, Puig had crossed a red line given that officially the only provider of legal medicines for the riders – be it injections or otherwise – was the Tour's doctor, Pierre Dumas. Brian Robinson, the British rider, recalls: 'Dumas would tell us which vitamins to buy. He told me the American products were the best. I'd bring it over with me from England and he'd inject me with it. He used to come by every couple of days. I remember I went to the local chemists in Yorkshire and asked for vitamin B and C in five hundred milligram ampoules, and they said, "What do you want with that?" When I told them, they said, "Bloody hell, it's what we give horses!"'

Unlike Robinson, many riders wanted more than Dumas would give them. Far more. Les Woodland's *Yellow Jersey Guide to the Tour de France* records that in cycling half a century ago: 'There were *soigneurs, fakirs*, who came from the six-day [criterium] races. Their value was in the contents of their case. Riders took anything they were given, even bee stings and toad extract.' This was not a new development. As one of the toughest endurance sports, cycling had been infected with doping as early as the 1890s. It was particularly prevalent at track events where strychnine and arsenic were among the substances used. In 1896, the death of Bordeaux-Paris winner Arthur Linton was suspected, though never proved satisfactorily, to have been the first in sport caused by drug use. And that was only the beginning. As William Fotheringham's *Cyclopedia* notes, in 1924 professionals Henri and Francis Pelissier once gave a graphic description of their doping to leading Tour journalist

Albert Londres. Opening a pillbox, Henri showed Londres 'cocaine for the eyes . . . chloroform for the gums, and do you want to see the pills? We ride on dynamite. When the mud is washed off us, we are white as sheets, we are drained by diarrhoea, we dance jigs in our bedroom instead of sleeping'. Just to add to the grotesque horror of the interview, which was entitled 'Convicts of the Road' when published, Francis claimed that six of his ten toenails had fallen out, the strong implication being that it was due to doping.

By the 1930s drug-taking was so widespread that historian Benjo Maso records that the riders' contracts in the Tour stated that the costs of 'stimulants, tonics and doping' had to be paid for by the competitors. And two decades later Bahamontes' old training partner Ian Brown was to discover that, while it was possible to complete a race without dope, the decision not to take drugs could destroy what had looked a promising career. Brown had been disappointed not to be named as one of the future stars at the end of the Simplex camp. 'As I said to [Charles] Pelissier, I didn't want to go back to England. In fact I was a bit desperate to get out of the normal life of Britain,' he says.

Brown's professional career started almost by chance, though, thanks to Simplex generously putting him up for a week in a hotel outside Brussels' Gare du Nord 'because Pelissier said the only racing on at that time of year, if I wanted to do it, was in Belgium. So I had to go there'. Its only initial drawback was that it was in the middle of the city's red-light district. 'There were all these sexy women in the shop windows, which was a bit of a surprise; we didn't have anything like that in Morecambe,' Brown recalls. 'But there was a race the following Wednesday, and I got third and a load of money when I hadn't even realised where the finish was and that I'd crossed the line. And I thought, "Holy crikey, this is easy!"'

However, while some of his discoveries about life and professional racing abroad were appealing, others were not and led him to retire early. Brown makes it very clear when interviewed why he packed up prematurely: drugs, principally amphetamines, 'though there was other stuff going around. What, I don't know, because I never took it'. Brown has a collective term for all the substances, in any case: 'go-fast'. The evidence of Brown and other British riders indicates that there was little drug-taking in cycling on their side of the Channel. However, in mainland Europe the opposite was true, and Brown decided, with decidedly bleak logic, to opt out. 'I knew a lot of riders who later died by taking too much "go-fast", guys in their twenties or thirties, and I wasn't taking that stuff,' he says. 'Somebody who'd been Belgian pro champion twice, about ten years older than me, once offered me something called *la bombe atomique* to win races. The next spring when I came back to the cafeteria where I was staying, he'd died. I'd see them head off the side of the road in the middle of races to get injections. And in Belgian races, with about two hundred riders, it was hard and fast to start with, so with about fifty kilometres to go they'd all take their pills. They called it "parachute time" because all the pills were in little bits of paper and when the bits of paper came flying back through the bunch they looked like parachutes.' Brown's career fizzled out in 1958, he says, 'because I knew if I'd gone back to try and win races the following season, I'd be asked to take stuff and I wasn't doing that'.

Bahamontes, on the other hand, maintains that it was still possible to win without doping. Not only does he state categorically that he did not use drugs, he claims there was little evidence of it, and that he only once saw 'somebody put something in a flask'. At most, he says, his success was caffeine-induced; in the 1959 Tour he drank two cups of coffee before destroying the field in an uphill time-trial at Puy de Dôme. His comments could sound like a deliberate under-exaggeration given the extent of drug-taking that went on in the 1950s when there were no anti-doping controls in racing. In addition to Brown, it is easy to find people who disagree that the sport was relatively clean. When Josu Loroño, the son of Bahamontes' arch-rival Jesús Loroño, was asked what he had heard about drug-taking in that era, he answered, without batting an eyelid: 'There were a lot of amphetamines going around.'

However, Bahamontes decries the idea that he personally could have taken drugs, saying: 'Your health takes priority over everything. If you don't take care of it, it's like not taking care of your wife or your car. Wherever you go, make sure your car has good tyres and good petrol, and make sure your wife has money so she's got nice clothes and good food. Because if you don't, then – pardon my being so direct – somebody else is going to fuck your wife and somebody else is going to steal your car. I never took anything, never. I saw a *soigneur* put something in a *bidon*, once, and that was it.'

But Bahamontes also refers to many of his former rivals 'being in the grave already'. As he puts it: 'You can be alive and not have much money, or have all the glory and be dead these thirty years past.' Bahamontes does not state it outright, but the implication is there: he got through the major Tours without drugs; others didn't and paid the ultimate price.

Robinson partly supports Bahamontes' claims that it was possible to compete and win major races like the Tour without drugs. 'I could go along with that: that it was due to his athletic ability. I know I got over those hills myself [without drugs],' says Robinson. 'Anquetil . . . said you can't ride the Tour on water, but I proved you can . . . with a little bit of vitamin C, a bit of cola and a bit of this or that. Nothing drastic. On the other hand, I did the job as it was supposed to be done. I didn't bugger about at night. That's why [Tom] Simpson' – Britain's greatest professional who died of a mixture of amphetamine abuse and dehydration on the Mont Ventoux in 1967 – 'and I split. He went to Belgium to further his career in that line, which was sad because he was the one [rider] who didn't need it.'

Robinson's view that it was possible to race at a high level even if you were clean is corroborated by Brown, who says: 'You could ride just as well without [drugs] if you were crafty. I was better at stage races than I was at one-day races, because if you weren't taking "go-fast" then you'd be hanging for grim death in the first two days, but in the third you would be all right.' It should be noted that Brown's experience is based largely on week-long stage races, in which he did very well without being outstanding. However, the demands of week-long races are nothing compared to a three-week

Grand Tour. Brown only did one of those, the Vuelta a España in 1955, from which he abandoned. Bahamontes rode up to three major Tours in one year, and one season finished them all. Furthermore, while Bahamontes had numerous major highpoints in his career, Brown says simply and bleakly: 'It was just make money and eat and sleep well. I never had one [a highpoint], there weren't any at all.'

While officially turning a blind eye, the Tour de France organisers were far from unaware what their riders were up to. Dumas himself spoke of 'medicine from the heart of Africa . . . healers laying on hands or giving out irradiating balms, feet plunged into unbelievable mixtures which could lead to eczema, so-called magnetised diets and everything else you could imagine. In 1953 and 1954 (Tours de France) it was all magic, medicine and sorcery. After that, they started reading *Vidal* [the French medicine directory].' At best, the organisers carried out damage limitation when the doping got too blatant, as was the case in the 1955 Tour after the abandon of Jean Mallejac and Charly Gaul falling ill. Mallejac lost consciousness while ascending the Mont Ventoux and pulled out, almost certainly after using a 'bad batch' of drugs. Gaul was allegedly close to following suit, according to media reports of the time, because of the same batch. However, Gaul's director claimed in *L'Equipe* that the rider had been victim of an attempted poisoning by being 'forced to dope'. Given the scandal surrounding Mallejac's abandon, the Tour issued a *communiqué* urging directors 'to watch how their riders take care of themselves' and advising that they should 'stop them using certain products that have not been prescribed by a doctor'. But that was as far as it went.

Seven years later, as Bahamontes neared the end of his career, very little had changed. In the 1962 Tour, Gastone Nencini, the 1960 winner, and several other riders pulled out after eating what they claimed was rotten fish from the same hotel. The Tour organisers published a *communiqué* apparently proving their excuse was a lie, and warning grimly that 'the physical limits which athletes of various disciplines seek to attain are beyond all medical and psychological control'. However, they then suggested the best solution to a situation which they were incapable of solving was that Dumas should do a doctor's round of the riders' rooms each evening. The implication was that even if they could not stop them taking drugs, they would at least know what they were.

In that context, for Puig to be injecting his riders with calcium and other substances is hardly strange. However, to admit it in public was too blatant for the cycling establishment to swallow. Puig later stated that he 'only gave Bahamontes the injection because we couldn't find the race doctor in the team hotel'. Since there was no reason why Dumas should have been in the hotel, this excuse was ignored by the Tour authorities: they wanted Puig out. It is quite possible, of course, that Puig was only providing a badly-administered placebo to Bahamontes. As Robinson says: 'There was so much talk about what it does. "You got to take this, you've got to take that". A lot of it [the benefits of doping] is purely in your head.'

After what was a bizarre abandon considering that by all accounts Bahamontes' injuries did not justify it, conspiracy theories abounded. One of the more popular was that Bahamontes was faced with a re-run of his Vuelta 1957 duel against Loroño and psychologically could not take it. There were definitely parallels. Again Bahamontes had moved into a dominating position early in the Tour, surviving a wasp-sting, the blazing heat and the dreaded cobbled farm-tracks on the stage to Roubaix, to become sole leader of the Spanish team. No sooner had he done so, though, than Loroño managed to counter-attack, not once but twice in two mountain stages in the Vosges, and move ahead in the overall. This was eerily reminiscent of the Vuelta stage from Valencia to Tortosa. For Bahamontes such a situation must have been impossible to accept, particularly as since his Vuelta defeat he had slowly been regaining a strong position in Spanish cycling. Now he was faced with that all-too-familiar scenario.

The season had started so well. In May Bahamontes had produced a dominating performance in the Tour of Asturias, his talismanic race. He won the first, the most mountainous stage, and led the race from start to finish before scooping the King of the Mountains jersey.

On top of that the pace set by his Mobylette team was so intense that thirty-four of the seventy-five-strong peloton had abandoned by the finish. By then Bahamontes was showering his team-mates with stage wins. The only disagreeable incident for Mobylette during the race was when one of Bahamontes' team-mates, Rene Marigil, attempted to beat up an Italian rival for trying to get in a break by riding in the slipstream of the Italian team's car. Marigil was allowed to continue racing despite the controversy that followed, and even won a mountain stage. As a morale-boost Bahamontes could not have asked for more. Incidentally, his days of riding by bike to races like Asturias had long gone. As Bernard Ruiz says: 'The top riders of the time, like me and Bahamontes, earned more money than football players.' So, as one of Spain's top earning athletes, Bahamontes now travelled almost everywhere by aeroplane, car or train.

Bahamontes, though, was far less successful in his one venture abroad between the Vuelta and Tour, abandoning the GP Midi-Libre, then a one-day race, with cramp after a spectacular early mountain attack. Though he also pulled out after two stages of the Bicicleta Vasca, his last Tour warm-up race, it was suggested that his form was so good there was no point in him 'over-cooking it'. The only downside from Bahamontes' point of view was that the Spanish team's line-up was full of unfriendly faces like Ruiz and Loroño. Bahamontes chose to make Ruiz, rather than Loroño, the subject of his complaints. With hindsight it was an unwise move, though it revealed the depth of the disunity within the squad. Bahamontes said at the time: 'The whole line-up is wrong, but in particular the presence of Bernardo Ruiz, whom as everybody knows has been my public enemy number one for the last seven years. He envies me and I don't know why, but if he comes to France then I know I won't be able to expect anything from him at all. I suppose he might be useful as a *domestique*, just like Loroño. [Actually] if he comes, I refuse to be leader. He can be leader. I'll go as a *domestique*.' What particularly worried Bahamontes was that Ruiz and Puig were close, both being from the Levante area of Spain, and that Ruiz's far stronger character and veteran status would give him greater authority than the team manager. 'Ruiz is

thirty-three years old and at that age should go for lesser objectives,'
Bahamontes said. 'Everybody knows that if he goes to the Tour,
he'll be the team manager because that's what he's always been.
They ask him everything, right down to what the plans are for the
stage and what time they ought to have dinner each night. I don't
think he should be selected just because he won the [Vuelta] stage
from Valencia to Tortosa.' Puig adopted his usual pose of sticking
his head in the sand, claiming: 'Of course there will be unanimity.
The race is so hard, Ruiz and Bahamontes are bound to get on.' In
a sentence which neatly summed up Puig's inability to sort out
internal team conflicts, he added: 'We'll agree on everything
beforehand, just like we did in the Vuelta a España in Bilbao.' Again
it was Bahamontes who paid the price.

The Tour de France itself started brilliantly for Bahamontes. He
was in two breaks on the first three stages and propelled himself
into to fourth place overall. Significantly, at the same time Loroño
was most definitely on the back foot. After losing a little time on
stage one – 'the Belgians wouldn't let me move even a metre ahead'
– Bahamontes bounced back the next day by making it into a move
of nineteen that gained more than three minutes on 1956 winner
Roger Walkowiak, and nearly five on France's rising star Jacques
Anquetil. Twenty-four hours later, a timely shove by team-mate
Suárez propelled Bahamontes into another big break and he shot
back up the overall classification to fourth, the best-placed of the
favourites. The race was affected by a heatwave, which lasted ten
days, and riders all but stampeded to take on water every time the
race went past a drinking fountain. It was so debilitating that Charly
Gaul abandoned on stage two because he could not stand the high
temperatures. More importantly for Bahamontes was the incident
that cost Loroño his status as co-team leader. On the same day as
Gaul's exit Loroño decided to dismount and stand under a garden
hose to cool down. He was enjoying his cold shower so much that
by the time he came to his senses, more than quarter of an hour
had passed, the race was miles ahead and he was fortunate to finish
inside the time limit.

Stage four to Roubaix, however, marked the beginning of a relentless series of setbacks for Bahamontes. In one day alone he was stung by a wasp, hit hard in the eye by a bottle [flung unintentionally by another rider during the struggle to be first at a drinking fountain] and suffered a severe bout of sunstroke. The heat affected everyone. Of the one hundred and sixteen starters, twenty-eight abandoned in the first four days, while reporters' throats dried up so badly while dictating their copy by telephone they were reduced to swigging cough mixture to keep talking. At one point it looked as if Bahamontes was going to join the list of abandons: he began weaving all over the road, dropping back from group to group. As he did so, he gave the Spanish correspondents covering the Tour more and more cause for alarm. '"Sunstroke!" Suárez yelled at us when we drove alongside him and asked him what was wrong with Bahamontes,' recorded *El Mundo Deportivo's* correspondent. The news from Dumas, the Tour doctor, was even more unsettling. 'Bahamontes had a kind of fit because of the heat,' he told the Spanish journalists, 'and he got off his bike, half-fainting. He recovered fairly quickly, though. When I put him back on it he was off like a rocket.' So much so that he regained eight minutes on the pack in three kilometres, albeit with some team support.

Photographs of Bahamontes at Roubaix after the stage show a miserable-looking figure; the swelling above his right eye caused by the wasp-sting was clearly visible. He was criticised by *El Mundo Deportivo*'s man for failing to combat the sunstroke by putting lettuce leaves on his neck and nape 'as most riders do in extreme heat'. However, while Bahamontes had not lost time he was looking in trouble. Stage five, a longish grind from Roubaix to Charleroi in Belgium over some of the region's best-known cobbled climbs including the infamous Mur de Grammont, dealt Bahamontes a severe blow. Lightly-built climbers like Bahamontes are notoriously vulnerable to this kind of terrain because they cannot ride over the hills in low gears like the heavier Classics specialists. So while Bahamontes had survived the *pavés* of Roubaix, the Belgian murs took a punishing toll. The bunch split completely after an attack masterminded by Anquetil and riders reached the finish line in dribs and drabs. Bereft of team support, not even the encouragement provided by a solid wall of Belgian fans along the stage's one hundred and seventy kilometres could help Bahamontes. He slid from fourth to fourteenth overall. Loroño saw his opportunity and took it with both hands. By sneaking into breaks in two stages in the Vosges mountains, Loroño regained twenty-seven minutes on the main favourites, climbing thirty-eight places to seventh overall. Suddenly Bahamontes' role as sole team leader was severely undermined. The parallels between the Tour de France and the Vuelta a España were evident, right down to Bahamontes' bizarrely passive attitude when his arch-rival went up the road. According to the Spanish team mechanic, Bahamontes' usual tactic when racing alongside Loroño was to 'hide at the back of the bunch. Then if there was a break and the bunch split behind chasing, Bahamontes would sneak into the forward half without anybody noticing and he could claim he was protecting Loroño's position as well as his own'. However, one Spanish newspaper correspondent noted a change: 'When I saw Baha halfway through the second Vosges stage with the Loroño break long gone, he was right at the rear of the main bunch, and I yelled, "Always at the back!" His only response was to smile.'

As Bahamontes slid from fourteenth to sixteenth, and Loroño moved into the top ten, it was little wonder that his morale was sinking and that Puig should provide him with medical assistance. However, again with hindsight, it was not a wise move. 'Maybe a little lime spilled out of the syringe, but that's not why he abandoned,' was Puig's later interpretation of events. '[In fact] he wasn't ready to face up to the challenges of the Tourmalet [tackled the day after Bahamontes abandoned]. He was scared of failing in the mountains and he didn't have a strong enough sense of vocation.'

Bahamontes' business advisor, Evaristo Murtra, partly went along with Puig but like others he pointed out that the Federation and manager had failed to live up to their responsibilities by not

Bahamontes after winning his second ever bike race, in 1947, using his black marketeer's bike and wearing a borrowed baseball shirt – complete with sewn-in shoulder pads. *Courtesy of F.M. Bahamontes*

Bahamontes with his future wife Fermina outside his first bike shop – the 'hole in the wall' he opened in Toledo in 1950. *Courtesy of F.M. Bahamontes*

Bahamontes during his military service in the early 1950s. Much of his time was spent trying to 'find what few black beans there were at the bottom of very watery stews'. *Courtesy of F.M. Bahamontes*

Bahamontes *(second left)* and his amateur 'accomplice', Ladislau Soria *(second right)*, at a race in 1949. With no money for shorts, the entire team wore dungarees.
Courtesy of F.M. Bahamontes

Bahamontes with Alejandro Del Caz, President of the Spanish Cycling Federation. Del Caz's decision to nominate Dalmacio Langarica as national coach was crucial for Bahamontes' 1959 Tour win.
El Mundo Deportivo

Two of Spanish cycling's most promising young guns of the era, Bahamontes and Salvador Botella share some reading material during the 1954 Tour.
El Mundo Deportivo

Bernardo Ruiz during the 1951 Tour. One of Bahamontes' most tenacious rivals, Ruiz later directed him in the hugely controversial 1960 *Vuelta*. *Corbis*

Jesús Loroño *(first left)*. His rivalry with Bahamontes divided 1950s Spain and Bahamontes still claims that the regime ordered him to let Loroño win the 1957 *Vuelta*. *El Mundo Deportivo*

Bahamontes savours the taste of victory in the 1959 Tour de France. Winning on 18 July, the anniversary of Franco's rebellion, was a timely coincidence for the General's propaganda machine. *Corbis*

below: The peloton rolls west past Fougères castle in the 1959 Tour's first week. Bahamontes' rivals would later regret failing to ambush him on stages like this. *Corbis*

below right: Bahamontes receives a warm welcome home after his victory in the 1959 Tour – the most important individual sporting success of the Franco era. *Courtesy F.M. Bahamontes*

Bahamontes with Franco and Spanish sports supremo General Elola *(second right)* after the 1959 Tour: 'Franco told me I'd planted the Spanish flag higher than ever before.' *Courtesy F.M. Bahamontes*

The St Raphael team celebrate their Tour win in 1963. According to manager Raphael Geminiani *(far right)* his dexterity with a pair of pliers secured Anquetil *(third from left)* victory. *Getty Images*

Anquetil *(left)*, Bahamontes and Raymond Poulidor *(far right)* at the head of affairs in the mountains in the 1963 Tour – Bahamontes' greatest opportunity to take the race a second time. *Getty Images*

Bahamontes with Jacques Anquetil shortly before the start of stage 16 of the 1963 Tour. By the end of the day, Bahamontes would be in the lead.
Getty Images

12 October 1965: For Bahamontes, riding his last ever race, the *Subida a Montjuic* hillclimb in Barcelona, the city where his professional career began, 'rounded it all off nicely'. *El Mundo Deportivo*

The Eagle of Toledo in his *peña*'s office – complete with statue of eagle – in early 2011. *Jacinto Vidarte*

designating Bahamontes as sole leader from the start of the Tour. 'Bahamontes' morale has suffered after seeing how much freedom Loroño and Ruiz had,' Murtra told the press in a reference to Puig allowing Loroño to get into two breaks in the Vosges without being reprimanded. 'Combined with the heat, the injection and his constantly being watched by the French, it all got too much for him.' Murtra had only turned up because he wanted to see his rider's attacks on the Tourmalet in person. Instead, both he and Bahamontes returned to Spain empty-handed, Murtra by aeroplane, Bahamontes by train, in a third-class compartment, which was all that the Federation were willing to pay for their fallen star.

If Loroño's breakaways had provided a replay of Bahamontes' worst sporting nightmares, the knock-on effects of his abandon within the Federation were considerable. Not all of them were bad, though. The entire medical commission – three different doctors – resigned. This gave the Federation the opportunity to bring in a fresh generation of young medics who were not so inclined to accept at face value the quackery and outlandish cures that were so popular in cycling, as well as post-Civil War Spain. Even more importantly, Puig was gradually phased out and Dalmacio Langarica was brought in as coach for the 1958 Tour.

For Bahamontes, the arrival of Langarica was a huge turning point. He describes Langarica simply as 'the best coach in the Spanish team that I had, because he knew how to take decisions'. That was despite Langarica being a friend, former team-mate and regular room-mate of Loroño's when he was a professional. Crucially, Langarica was far tougher than Puig. From the word go, Langarica told both Bahamontes and Loroño in no uncertain terms that he was not going to take any nonsense from either of them. He also showed, albeit indirectly, which rider he favoured when he politely but firmly condemned Puig for allowing Loroño to attack in the Vosges in 1957 when Bahamontes was already in a commanding position overall. 'Bahamontes is Spain's classiest rider, the greatest the country has ever known. While Loroño did what he had to, it [the overall strategy of letting Loroño attack] was throwing stones against our own roof,' Langarica was quoted as saying in an interview in August 1957. 'In that context, Bahamontes' abandon made perfect sense.'

Bahamontes will have welcomed this support even if it was clear Langarica did not believe a word of his explanation about the injection and attributed his abandon purely to his rivalry with Loroño. Furthermore, unlike Puig, Langarica showed a keen understanding of Bahamontes' personality. 'Fede is like a child,' he used to say. 'If he doesn't like the people in charge of him, he'll lead you a merry dance. But if you know how to handle him, he'll come quietly enough.'

On 9 July, 1958, Bahamontes turned thirty. He could not have asked for a better birthday present: his first stage win in the Tour de France. The build-up to the victory on a short, sharp one hundred and twenty-kilometre stage through the Pyrenees from Pau to Luchon, was surprisingly straightforward. With the Aspin and the Peyresourde cols as the two main challenges of the day, Bahamontes needed no telling that it was a comparatively short distance from the summit of the Peyresourde down to Luchon, and if he gained enough time on the climb he could be in control. 'We got [team-mate Fernando] Manzaneque into a break with three French riders and then in the village of Sainte-Marie-de-Campan [at the foot of the Aspin] I hit the pedals hard twice, more than just at cruising speed, and left them all behind,' Bahamontes remembers. 'I overtook the rest of the guys ahead on the Aspin, and my advantage was one and a half minutes by the summit. The descent to Arrau was thirteen kilometres long and really awful, the hardest in the Pyrenees, but I actually gained thirty seconds, which ended up being fundamental. Then on the Peyresourde the race blew apart because Gaul and Geminiani attacked and I gave it even more on the climb, knowing that somebody had lit the fuse behind. Finally I got two minutes and a bit on Gaul and two and a half minutes on Bobet and Geminiani, and even though there were fifteen kilometres downhill left, I was determined not to get caught. I finished alone with about two minutes on the field. I'd promised my wife to do something dramatic and give Toledo a triumph to remember, and that's what happened.'

How come it looked so easy? There were a number of key differences between Bahamontes in 1957 and Bahamontes in 1958, not least that he was in exceptionally good form and morale. He finished sixth in the Vuelta after another bust-up with Loroño, which cost them both the race. That was the last race where he would be directed by Luis Puig. 'Just as well he'd never direct me in the Tour again,' Bahamontes commented. Bahamontes nonetheless took a significant consolation prize in the King of the Mountains competition. Then he followed up by scoring his first stage win in the Giro. Bahamontes was part of a powerful Faema squad that year and had decided to use the Giro as Tour preparation. On stage four, with a summit finish at Superga, Bahamontes inflicted stinging defeats on Charly Gaul and Loroño, leading them home by twenty-seven and thirty-seven seconds respectively. Not huge, but enough to convince him that his decision to race the Giro had been the right one.

Another major difference was that on the 1958 Tour there was no Jesús Loroño. After racing flat-out in both the Vuelta and Giro, Loroño decided that the Tour would be asking too much of himself. His absence meant Bahamontes was finally the undisputed leader in a major Tour. In addition Bahamontes' relationship with his team-mates was apparently improving, albeit intermittently. The reported group cheating at the 1958 Spanish National Championships, categorically denied by Bahamontes, but given lavish eyewitness coverage in *El Mundo Deportivo*, would seem to hint at this, too. According to *History of the Spanish National Championships* by Javier Bodegas and Juan Dorronsoro, the 100-kilometre time-trial was completely fixed. In theory it was an individual event, but Bahamontes allegedly joined forces with two other Faema riders, first Salvador Botella, who waited for Bahamontes after a timely puncture, then Francisco Moreno, and the three rode as a unit over the second half of the course. To make matters worse, Bodegas and Dorronsoro claim, the police failed to stop traffic in either direction, allowing riders to benefit from assistance provided by motorbikes. Indeed, Bahamontes' illegal pacer crossed the finishing line just ahead of him. As a result of the alleged race-fixing, the favourite Loroño had no chance despite building a fifty-second lead at halfway. He finally finished third behind Bahamontes and Botella.

Yet more significant than Loroño's absence from the Tour was the change in the man behind the steering wheel in the Spanish national team. The replacement of Puig by Langarica meant Bahamontes could count on a degree of team loyalty, not least because it effectively ended Ruiz's role as the power behind the director's throne. However, Bahamontes respected Langarica for more than that: he also liked his team tactics and was willing to use them. 'Langarica dropped the previous director's strategies,' Bahamontes said in an interview at the time. 'He moved with the times. He was practical. Previously, we attacked where we could, but on the day I won we attacked at exactly the right moment to be sure I got my first of seven Tour stages. It was a daring move, but it was efficent, too.'

Crucially, the Spanish took a large leaf out of the French team's book with Langarica drawing on the lessons learnt from Bahamontes' defeat the previous year. In 1957, after his superb start to the Tour, the French had refused to let Bahamontes go up the road under any circumstances, whereas Loroño had been given a considerably longer leash. The tactic was to deliberately favour the less dangerous rider. This time round the boot was on the other foot and the switch in strategy was particularly effective in the Alps where Bahamontes gained a second stage win over the Vars and Izoard passes. Realising the squabbling French were willing to give Bahamontes some room for maneuvre, Langarica encouraged Bahamontes to come up with a specific plan to win the stage. Initially doubtful, 'because plans are one thing and reality another', Bahamontes finally went along with Langarica since he believed the director had already got him his first Tour stage win in the Pyrenees. 'The night before we talked about the stage and Langarica said, "You have to make the most of the war between the French and the way they're dealing with Gaul. They're all going to be watching each other, and you have to take advantage of that",' Bahamontes recalled. Sure enough, after the Vars climb had whittled down the main pack to just a dozen, Bahamontes broke away on the Izoard, crossing the summit with a fifty-seven-second advantage on his closest pursuer, the Italian Nino Catalano. When he reached Briançon to claim his second stage win, his advantage had only dropped to fifty seconds. It indicated that his poor descending was no longer automatically the handicap it had been.

In the past Bahamontes had used the tactics of eating on the descents, so he could attack with a full stomach on the next, and making early breaks to rack up points in the King of the Mountains competitions before easing back after a couple of cols. However, these strategies limited him, almost deliberately so. If the other contenders for the overall prizes did not 're-fuel' on the descents it was at least partly because they knew they risked losing time. In 1958, though, Bahamontes partly changed tack, and it is no coincidence that at the same time his descending radically improved. Bahamontes puts this down to greater experience, but it is clear from the way he won those two stages that his previous unwritten, unspoken agreement with the other favourites that he would stay away to the finish after making an early attack no longer applied. Rather than just focus on the King of the Mountains title, for the first time in the Tour Bahamontes was starting to think bigger. Now he was able to trust his sports director to come up with a plan that did not weaken his status compared with other rivals inside the Spanish camp. The reward was not only two stage wins but the King of the Mountains title as well. *L'Equipe* still criticised him, though: 'In any other rider, what Bahamontes did would have produced admiration and respect. Not many other riders can get two big mountain stage wins, easily get the overall in the King of the Mountains title and finish eighth overall after being forty minutes down on the race leader prior to the Pyrenees. Only an athlete like Bahamontes can pull off an achievement of this calibre. But it loses its edge when we consider what a rider of his class is actually capable of doing. His tactics are extremely simplistic, and worthy of condemnation, consisting of playing dead in the first few days of the race so he loses any importance to the main favourites.'

The judgment is unduly harsh, but it contains some grains of truth. Bahamontes had been ill in the first part of the race, suffering from suspected appendicitis, but even so he had under-exploited his talent, and that needed to change. Not that Langarica could resolve all of Bahamontes' defects: he still had an almost pathological inability to race in cold weather. The day after he won in Grenoble, as the rain teemed down Bahamontes was dropped by Gaul on the Col de Luitel, the second of five Alpine cols. On a stage with nearly one hundred kilometres of climbing Bahamontes ended up losing five seconds short of half an hour on Gaul and dropped to tenth overall. He pulled back a couple of places overall in the race's final seventy-four-kilometre time-trial at Besancon to reach Paris in eighth place. Once again it showed that even if he was nowhere near as good as specialists like Jacques Anquetil or Roger Rivière, at the very least he could hold his own. And the following year in the Tour de France, that ability was to prove crucial.

Chapter Eight
1959 – 'That Man From Toledo'

Luis Otaño has barely opened the door of his fourth floor flat before he comes out with a joke about the rider he helped guide to victory in the Tour de France, back in 1959. And it is not a polite one. 'I bet you anything in the world, Federico's asked you for money to do his biography, hasn't he?' he says. Before I have time to deny it, he yells through to his wife in the kitchen, 'Hey, I told you, Bahamontes asked him for money!' Chuckling to himself, Otaño leads me through to a sunlit living room. We are high above the town centre traffic in Renteria, just outside San Sebastian. Through the windows the green foothills of the Spanish Pyrenees are visible in the distance. Just beyond them, but out of sight, lie the roads and climbs of France where more than fifty years ago Otaño rode as part of the Spanish team who had Bahamontes at its head.

Career-wise, the Pyrenees mark a dividing line for Otaño. On home soil he recorded numerous top-five finishes in the Vuelta, including second overall behind Raymond Poulidor in 1964. However, once on the other side of the mountains it was a different story: Otaño rode in eight Tours de France and each time it was purely as a *domestique*, a behind-the-scenes worker for whoever was Spanish team leader. That included Federico Martín Bahamontes, of course. 'But not Fede's personal *domestique*, eh,' Otaño says with a grin. 'That was [Juan] Campillo. Bahamontes used to have him wash his socks and clean his shoes, he did.' The bald, sturdy man with a piercing stare lets rip a cackle. 'Me, I used to argue with Fede all the time, asking him, "Why are you doing this?" and "Why are you doing that?" even though I was younger than him. And he would mutter, "Anquetil this" or "Anquetil that". If Anquetil hadn't been there or if there had been more summit finishes, I'm sure Fede would have won a lot more.'

Of Bahamontes' eleven team-mates on that 1959 Tour, Otaño is one of three still living. So what was Bahamontes like to work for? 'Odd,' Otaño says. 'On and off the bike. For example, he used to insist on us not eating any tomatoes for dinner because he said they were bad for our health, and we'd ignore him. When Loroño used to drink a bottle of wine a night, that would piss him off even more because even a little wine used to make Baha dizzy. If he didn't like something then he tried to make sure none of us had it.' Not that they paid him much attention. Nor did the top French riders when he addressed them. 'Mostly, they'd laugh at his French. He'd say, "*J'ai . . . gran fusil, j'ai . . . gran fusil* ['I have the top gun']",' says Otaño.

Communication was not at a premium in any case. Unlike today the countdown to racing did not start with anything remotely approaching a meeting to discuss strategy. Instead, Otaño says: 'We'd talk a little bit among ourselves, decide who would help who. But that was as far as it went. There was no real plan, no tactics. At most, "Wait for him if he punctures". We'd mostly all wait for Fede when he did puncture, even Bernardo Ruiz in 1958. It'd always be pretty dramatic, though, lots of people shouting, "Fede's punctured! Fede's punctured!" In fact, everything was a drama with Fede.'

Despite their antipathy, Otaño agrees with Bahamontes on one key point: that incoming team director Dalmacio Langarica played a crucial role in pulling them together, and that he did not beat around the bush when it came to letting the riders know who was boss, either. 'Langarica was very tough, but good. He knew what he was doing,' says Otaño. 'I remember when he came into the Tour de France hotel he brought a big walking stick with him. He put it down the middle of the dining table where we were sitting as if to say, "Don't mess with me". Only [Jesús] Manzaneque and [Antonio] Suárez didn't pay much attention to him. Suárez was always banging on about how he'd won the Vuelta and the Nationals, and they both wanted their own chance to go for the overall.' In the event, Manzaneque finished fourteenth in Paris, and Suárez abandoned.

Despite two 'renegades', support from nine team-mates was not bad compared with what Bahamontes had been used to on previous Grand Tours. However, some of that number are convinced that Bahamontes only succeeded because of them. Speaking in an interview in 2008, José Gomez del Moral said: 'If it wasn't for me, Bahamontes wouldn't have won. There was as much about him that was cack-handed as there was pure talent. He should have won four or five Tours and he only won one. The rest of the Spaniards finished outside the time limit and I was the one who guided him through the Dolomites.' Since the Dolomites did not feature on the 1959 Tour itinerary, or any other for that matter, it is difficult to know how seriously to take Gomez del Moral's comments. That said, his lack of sympathy towards Bahamontes is notably similar to Otaño and his description of how he first fell out with Bahamontes sounds plausible enough. 'I first came across him in a race in Jaén [in Andalusia], a hard one through a lot of hills that was one hundred and fifty kilometres long. It was called the Turkey Race because it took place at Christmas and because apart from a cash prize you got a turkey. My father heard Bahamontes boast he was going to give us a feather each from the turkey. Finally, though, I won.' By 1959, however, it was Bahamontes who ruled the roost.

As a rider twenty kilos heavier than Bahamontes, and no climber, Otaño's main job was to lead the pack on the flat and watch out for breaks. Bahamontes required a lot of 'nannying', particularly when it came to being shepherded through the bunch. Otaño reveals his subversive sense of humour again when he grudgingly admits that Bahamontes was not the worst strategist. 'He wasn't bad. He knew how to calculate, even if he calculated wrongly most of the time. On the stage to Aurillac, for example, he told us, "Work until such-and-such a point, and then I'll go for it". And he did.'

With his severely limited capability in the mountains, Otaño's direct contact with Bahamontes was mainly in the early stages, as well as providing support when the climber was in trouble. He had a particularly inglorious personal mission: pushing his leader along on the rainy stages when Bahamontes was having one of his off-days. One of those came in 1958 on the stage into Aix-les-Bains, won by Charly Gaul, when Bahamontes lost thirty minutes. 'It was nearly dark, thunder and stormy, almost nobody around and Bahamontes was crying, grabbing any food he could get, and Langarica kept on yelling at me, "Help him! Help him!"' The pair finally finished twenty-nine minutes fifty-five seconds down. 'If I hadn't stayed with him, I'd have been second,' Otaño says with no indication of resentment, just what he considers to be an indisputable fact. 'He would say, "I'm the best, I'm the best", but we pushed him just the same, his hand holding on to your leg. And he would fret while we did it, saying, "What if somebody's attacking now?" Us *domestiques* did nothing more than push the big names, you see?'

A solid ride in the Vuelta, when he finished eighth overall, guaranteed Otaño a slot in the 1959 Tour team. However, nothing he says suggests he had any enthusiasm for Bahamontes' quest that year. This is more surprising than it sounds. As Charly Wegelius, Britain's top mountain *domestique* in the last decade, has pointed out: 'Even if you don't like your leader, the fact that you're all riding together with a common objective ends up binding you. You get emotionally involved. It's inevitable.' Not so, it seems, for Otaño. He went through the motions all right, but he seems devoid of any passion for the Tour in general, let alone for Spain's first win in it. Part of this lack of motivation could be because there was no guaranteed money from the Federation for taking part, not even expenses. 'I once got called up to Madrid to go over my taxes, and they said, "You've raced the Tour, so you've earned x". And I said, "No, I've not earned a penny". The same went for the World Championships. The kit the Federation gave you was rubbish, right down to the trousers [for wearing in the evenings]. We got nothing, absolutely nothing, not even a bike. We had to pay for all our equipment, right down to the inner tubes of our wheels. All we got was what we could make in prizes. I often thought somebody must have run off with the money from the travel expenses we were supposed to get.'

As if that was not enough to lower morale, the Spanish also had the most ramshackle equipment of all the top teams. 'In 1958, my bike had a range of gears from fourteen to twenty-two,' says Otaño. 'I didn't have any higher gears. For time-trials, climbs, the lot. Try getting over the Alps with a bike like that. Bahamontes might have had slightly better gearing, maybe a twenty-four, but not much. Still, that bike was an improvement on the equipment Bahamontes used to have. I can remember when he first raced up here in Euskadi, he didn't have enough money to buy any race shorts; he'd wear a pair of those baggy dungarees like mechanics used to have.'

It was not just their clothing and equipment that were dire. With two mechanics, two *soigneurs*, a sports director and two jeeps for twelve riders, the back-up team was stretched to the limits, although any accidents that the consequent fatigue inevitably caused were seen as amusing rather than annoying. Indeed, when a Spanish mechanic fell asleep at the wheel during the 1959 Tour, and fell out of the vehicle, his misfortune was greeted with hoots of laughter. No one seemed to be worried if he was injured.

If Otaño and the other Spanish riders were not one hundred per cent concentrated on the racing, it was hard to blame them considering they were almost economic refugees from a half-starved Spain. Otaño says: 'The best thing about the Tour was the food. In the Vuelta all we'd get was meat so tough it was black. It looked like they'd taken a horse and cart and cut the whole thing to pieces, cart included. To follow would be boiled rice pudding in paper, and the paper would be soaked in the liquid from the rice so you'd eat that, too. In France, you'd get some amazing food, some of it even came wrapped up . . . chicken, all sorts.'

However, despite the better 'fuel' on offer in France, Otaño did not make it to Paris. He had to abandon on stage thirteen. 'It was on the stage to Aurillac,' he says. 'It was baking hot, the tarmac was all twisted in the heat, and I punctured close to a control point. There wasn't anybody there, but I found a bag lying on the ground with an inner tube in it, so I used that. Then I punctured again, and [French rival Jean] Robic gave me another inner tube, and I changed it again. By that point Bahamontes was twenty minutes ahead and there were forty kilometres left to race. I said to myself, "What's the point of killing myself to finish if I'm going to be outside the time limit?", so I quit on the spot. Langarica wasn't too happy. He said they would have let me back into the race if I'd finished the stage. But there were four of us Spaniards outside the limit that day, so I don't know what would have happened.'

Though not there to see it in person Otaño was not surprised Bahamontes won the Tour that year. 'To win in 1959 he needed Langarica, that was for sure. Without Langarica he wouldn't have done it. But we could see it coming. He was in good shape. He's got a great *palmares*. What surprises me, though, is that he didn't win more.' It was not easy for Otaño to discover why. Even though they were team-mates for two years in the trade team Margnat in the early 1960s, Bahamontes tended to keep his own counsel. 'There were stages like one in Briançon in 1962 when we asked him why he hadn't won instead of some Belgian non-climber [Emile Daems], and he muttered something about Anquetil. Very odd, because Baha could have won it.' The professional relationship between the pair ended as soon as Otaño packed his suitcase in the Margnat team hotel one autumn evening in 1963 and headed for another squad. On a personal level, it remains non-existent.

'I read he said that if he'd had the support that Pedro Delgado or Miguel Indurain had, he'd have won several Tours,' Otaño says now. 'All I can say is that some days us *domestiques* would be going well, on others we'd be out the back with our tongues sticking out. We'd hold on for as long as possible; we'd try to be there. But we did what we could, whatever the circumstances. And he never said thank you.' In anybody else that lack of gratitude might be considered rude. But given Bahamontes' constant reference to how he 'moved alone', as well as his tendency to criticise team-mates for being disloyal or useless, it is hardly that surprising. What is strange is that Bahamontes did have some solid, loyal *domestiques*, like Julio San Emeterio and Juan Campillo; indeed, from his days at Margnat, André Darrigade still prides himself on the amount of work he did for Bahamontes. True, nobody in the 1950s would have gone to the extremes of Britain's twenty-first century star Mark Cavendish, whose first words after a victory are almost always to thank his team-mates. But Bahamontes' relationships, even by 1959 when he no longer had to worry about Loroño or Ruiz, never seem to have been fully functional. That did not even change under his greatest manager, Fausto Coppi, whose dealings with his *domestiques* appear to have been extremely good. 'Compared with say Eddy Merckx, Coppi's *domestiques* were more menial,' says William Fotheringham, who wrote the biography *Fallen Angel* about the Italian champion. 'Coppi was more austere and certainly more capricious, even getting them to look after his daughter while he was with his mistress. I certainly can't imagine Coppi playing cards with them and larking about like Merckx did. They also never got to race for themselves in big races, unlike Merckx's. It was more feudal. That said, Coppi clearly appreciated them and they were devoted to him.' That is not something that can be said of Bahamontes.

Perhaps part of the problem was Bahamontes' character. Climbers tend to be reclusive. Charly Gaul certainly was; so was Britain's best climber, Robert Millar. 'I think Millar's default mode was suspicion,' says his biographer, Richard Moore. 'He distrusted people, which made him an awkward leader. Yet at Peugeot he had great support from [team-mates] Allan Peiper and Sean Yates. Ronan Pensec was fond of him as well as Pascal Simon, though Millar felt the French generally resented him. He wasn't really suited to leading a team; he couldn't rally the troops.' However, neither Millar nor Gaul laid into team-mates with as much relentless gusto as Bahamontes did throughout his career.

Another reason *domestiques* often have such poor opinions of their leaders, and vice versa, is connected to the claustrophobic lifestyle they endure during a major Tour. For nearly a month there is no escape from the other members of the team: they eat, sleep, room and ride together. The constant travelling means there is no opportunity to sneak off to the cinema or for a quick coffee as there would be in, say, a major football tournament. The only valid comparison in sport for such lengthy, intimate and unwanted contact with another person of the same sex is probably ocean racing. That, in turn, has parallels to life in prison. Both are intense bonding-experiences while counting the days until you are back on *terra firma*, or on the right side of the walls. In cycling, once the final stage is over and the celebrations start, those harsh memories tend to fade very fast and the benefits of bonding remain. However, during the two hours I talk to Otaño there is no sense whatsoever that he is proud to have been part of the first Spanish team to win the Tour de France. His attitude is partly because of the contradiction that underpins professional cycling: it is the only team sport where an individual wins. So no matter how many kilometres of pushing their leader they do, how often they clean his shoes, how many hours of the day they spend together and how many ricepaper containers they eat, the rest of the squad receives almost no recognition in return. If they had won football's World Cup, they would barely be able to get out of the front door without somebody offering to buy them a drink or do their shopping.

This degree of neglect strikes home even harder when Otaño's wife comes in halfway through the interview, camera in hand and takes a picture of me talking to her husband. There could hardly be a more graphic illustration of how completely forgotten Otaño's contribution to one of a handful of sporting highpoints in an impoverished, war-torn, politically repressed country, has been. So on the day, fifty-two years later, when a stray foreign journalist turns up to talk about the 1959 Tour, Otaño and his wife want a photograph for their album, if only to be sure it really happened. Strange as it sounds, my only regret about interviewing Otaño is that it mattered to him and his wife that much.

The start of Federico Bahamontes' *annus mirabilis* was predictably dogged by the latest in his disputes with Jesús Loroño. To his credit, Bahamontes had spent most of the previous six months avoiding his arch-rival. During the winter he had deliberately chosen not to re-sign for Faema, where the pair would have remained team-mates in name at least, opting instead to race for Fausto Coppi's Tricolfilina squad. Bahamontes had prepared the ground carefully for his move by inviting Coppi to go greyhound hunting with him in Toledo during cycling's closed season. Coppi, partly drawn by curiosity, and partly by his interest in signing Bahamontes, was keen to accept. After a morning's hunting, a midday meal of typical Madrid stew and some joking over how to drink wine out of a wineskin that invariably ends up with wine all over the novice's face, Coppi 'popped the question'. Coppi's logic was simple: as 1959 was to be his last season he would be racing more in spirit than anything else and he needed a star rider. Bahamontes' attempts to bluff and make his future employer nervous by pretending he had not heard the question, failed completely. 'You heard me perfectly,' Coppi told him. But even Bahamontes was not expecting what Coppi told him next: that he could win the Tour.

Bahamontes has since claimed that this was the turning point for which he had been waiting. Not so much for joining the team, who turned out to be far weaker than he would have liked, or the half a million pesetas a year wages [£85,000 in modern money] which he never fully received, but because of the faith an international star (and double Tour winner and a rider considered a pioneer in so many areas) was prepared to show in him.

The deal was agreed there and then and Bahamontes' sadly brief spell as a team-mate of Coppi's began. Given that Coppi would only live for another year, and that 1959 was Bahamontes' most successful, what would have happened if Bahamontes and Coppi had collaborated together for longer? But the little time they had together they used to the full.

There were several reasons why Coppi worked so well with Bahamontes, says Raphael Geminiani. For instance, the older man realised the degree to which the younger rider's real potential had been underexploited. 'Coppi had his team, and his sponsor, though not a lot of money, and he knew that Bahamontes was a climber, and a climber in the Tour always plays a pivotal role,' explains

Geminiani, 'So he told Bahamontes to forget the King of the Mountains and stick with Anquetil and Rivière. He told him to switch strategy and he gained his trust. It's as simple as that. He transformed him.'

But it was not just mind-games that Coppi was so good at. As Geminiani points out, the other techniques for racing which the Italian used as a rider, and briefly as a team director, were way ahead of his times. 'Coppi operated with a level of authority about all sorts of things that nobody else had,' says Geminiani. 'He was really advanced in terms of race strategy, training, equipment, nutrition. He was a pioneer in a lot of things. He knew how to direct a team when director and he inspired me as a manager. To give an example, Coppi's principles in the evening were to let the riders have their bath and massage, talk to them afterwards, but never discuss the next day's racing until after their meal. Then out the strategy would come: this, that, that, this, that . . . like a game of chess. Not before and certainly not five minutes before the start. That way, the message really sinks in.' With an impulsive rider, that was not always straightforward. But as Langarica observed, Bahamontes had a child-like nature, meaning that if treated the right way he would usually come round to your point of view.

However, allying with Coppi would not help on a day-to-day basis in the event itself where riders again raced in national teams. In the last few weeks before the Tour the question of how Loroño and Bahamontes could possibly race under the same flag intensified. Bahamontes, with his usual direct style, had made it quite clear what his position was. 'It's him or me,' he told Langarica in private conversations. On the record he was only slightly more polite. 'We haven't spoken in over a year and I won't eat at the same table as him,' Bahamontes told the Spanish press. 'But if he's leader, I'll play my part. He'll have my help, even though I don't actually rate him as a rider.' Loroño was even more uncompromising. He insisted he would not support any other Spanish rider under any circumstances, and 'particularly not that man from Toledo'. To complicate matters further, another Spaniard, Antonio Suárez, had won the Vuelta a España in April. He also claimed that he could be a good leader of the Spanish squad in France. Langarica finally decided to go for Bahamontes and dropped Loroño, a choice 'that man from Toledo' unsurprisingly thought was the right one. 'I could win the Tour and Loroño couldn't,' Bahamontes reasoned later. 'And Loroño hadn't won a single race in the whole of 1959, either.'

However, the situation got completely out of hand when Langarica called all the riders to an emergency meeting in the Spanish Federation's offices to explain his decision. At the same time a list of the Tour riders was published outside the office building. 'In those days,' Bahamontes recalls, 'the line-up was as important in Spain as whoever got to play in the football World Cup.' Loroño refused point blank to accept his exclusion and the conversation grew more and more heated. Then when he heard Suárez had been admitted to the Tour team, talking gave way to shouting. Loroño stormed out, slamming the door behind him. 'A few minutes later a gentleman whom I had never seen before came in asking for me,' Langarica recalled in an interview with *Informaciones*. 'He said to me, "You can't direct a Spanish team because you are an undesirable Commie separatist".' Provoked by what was arguably one of the most insulting of insults in 1950s Spain, Langarica lashed out at the fan, who responded by thumping him back. 'I must confess,' Langarica said rather laconically later, 'that I lacked enough internal calm and I reacted violently.' The fighting only stopped when one of Langarica's fingers was broken after he swung a particularly enthusiastic punch. Then, as Langarica was making his way downstairs to leave the building, the scuffle broke out again.

The Loroño supporter – rumoured to be a journalist from *La Gaceta del Norte* – was finally ejected, but the press were waiting outside and the news spread fast. An overly frank telephone interview Langarica gave during the row to a 'friendly' journalist turned out to have been taped and the resulting conversation published verbatim. It ensured that the latest Bahamontes-Loroño row remained in the headlines for several days. The revenge of Loroño's fans did not end there, either: a few days later, while on the Tour,

Langarica learnt that his bike shop in Bilbao had been attacked and its front window broken. Throughout the race he received anonymous hate-mail. Loroño made a last-minute unsuccessful appeal to Langarica to ride in France, saying he would accept team orders. But he recognised how badly things had got out of hand and belatedly acknowledged the decision to leave him behind. His supporters' behaviour earned him a fine, though, as well as a two-month suspension from racing.

Bahamontes, meanwhile, told Langarica that he would have no regrets about excluding Loroño. 'I told him I'd show him what I could do and I'd make [1958 winner] Charly Gaul suffer in the process!'

Leaving Loroño at home united the Spanish team. In a Tour which French cycling historians believe their country lost because of internal divisions that was no small matter. Bahamontes, though, was still as insecure as ever. No sooner had he seen off Loroño than he began to worry about Suárez's loyalty instead. But even he acknowledged the significance of Loroño's absence. 'The atmosphere in the team will be better because of the absence of one of our team-mates,' Bahamontes rather smugly told *L'Equipe*. 'Our team is more cohesive than last year.'

Bahamontes had few other pre-Tour requests apart from asking for all the Spanish newspapers to be delivered to him twice a week. 'I want to be sure which of the journalists are my friends,' he said to the correspondent of Spanish sports daily *MARCA*. It was a warning he clearly intended to go around the press room. However, Bahamontes knew that he could count on one loyal supporter all the way around France. Jacques Daudé was a French restaurant owner who became a fan after the ice-cream incident on the Romeyere in 1954. Daudé followed Bahamontes throughout the 1959 Tour, paying his own way and organising sweepstakes on a Bahamontes' victory among the journalists. Bahamontes would always stop immediately after each stage to talk to Daudé. In return Daudé would invariably produce a bottle of Perrier, a comb and some eau-de-cologne for Bahamontes to perform his post-race *toilette* while he held on to the Spaniard's bike frame.

With Loroño gone and Ruiz missing, Bahamontes was the only member of the Spanish squad with real Tour experience. Of his eleven team-mates who boarded a flight to France for the race start at Mulhouse, Suárez was now the only possible threat to his authority. How much of a challenge Suaréz posed is hard to estimate. He was four years younger than Bahamontes and had his Vuelta win to reinforce his credibility, whereas Bahamontes had made another controversial abandon in his home race. Following a blistering start, including a spectacular stage win in Granada, Bahamontes had missed some crucial moves in the second week. After falling out with Fausto Coppi, Bahamontes competed in the Vuelta 'on loan' for the K.A.S. team. Coppi was particularly unhappy when he finally made it into a break only for Bahamontes to promptly chase it down. Bahamontes eventually pulled out on stage eleven, allegedly in protest after five of his key rivals from Faema were re-admitted despite failing to make the cut-off time. However, according to *Viva La Vuelta*, the history of the race by Lucy Fallon and Adrian Bell, when asked for an explanation Bahamontes spat out: 'Because it's easier to go by car.' Bahamontes later alleged another reason: that he abandoned as the result of an anthrax infection, a disease usually affecting those working with animals. Yet more reports from the time suggest he had appendicitis.

Furthermore, in June Bahamontes lost the Spanish national championships, a time-trial round Madrid, to Suárez. Conversely, he came within a whisker of winning the Tour de Suisse that month despite a painfully poor start. Indeed, he commented later: 'I remember some woman in a bikini pushing me up a climb. I was creeping.' But he then picked up his form so fast that he took two stages, the King of the Mountains and had received 'an offer to buy the race off me'. This he refused, perhaps unwisely given he did not win. Yet despite those results Bahamontes still felt the need to assert his leadership once and for all. As usual with Bahamontes, there was only one way he knew to do that: attack. But this time he did things slightly differently: rather than wait for the mountains, Bahamontes went for it on the flat.

*

The Tour's first stage from Mulhouse to Metz was held in a downpour. It was the kind of weather that would normally have had Bahamontes grumbling at the back of the peloton. Instead he went on the rampage. Forty kilometres from the finish he suddenly lunged out of the pack. Two more riders, Rolf Graf of Switzerland and Frenchman Michel Vermeulin went with him. Fourteen others finally bridged across, and in a breakneck finish on a circuit through Metz they opened a gap of more than a minute. It was a sign of how fast they were going that the average speed for the stage was above forty-two kilometres an hour, which was very high for the era. André Darrigade took the stage, but the rest of Bahamontes' main rivals for the yellow jersey were nowhere. Best of all for 'that man from Toledo', nor was Suárez. It was an audacious move and one which meant any attempt by Suárez to claim the Spanish leadership had, at least partly, been stomped on. 'Suárez had tried to break away earlier on several occasions, but it did not work out,' MARCA's correspondent wrote that evening. 'His problem is he doesn't like the rain.' Neither did Bahamontes, or so his rivals thought, but he had stolen a march on them of one minute twenty-nine seconds. 'It's very important I've done this because it shows my team-mates I'm not just here to win the King of the Mountains prize,' Bahamontes told reporters afterwards. 'This time I'm after the overall as well.'

The extent of Bahamontes' fear of Suárez was shown later by his actions on stage eleven from Bagneres de Bigorre to St. Gaudens when Bahamontes attacked early on with Charly Gaul. The stage was structured so that the two big climbs of the day, the Aspin and Peyresourde, were crossed a long way from the finish, yet Bahamontes could not resist the opportunity. Bahamontes knew he and Gaul had no real chance of staying away, but he persuaded his unwilling accomplice to continue their near-suicidal attack. Bahamontes recalled: 'I had to shout at him all the way through a village to convince him.' The reason for Bahamontes' enthusiasm was that he had learnt Suárez had been dropped from the bunch.

But if stage one had given Bahamontes the upper hand in his battle to ensure he was sole Spanish leader of the 1959 Tour de

France, then stage two from Metz to Namur showed Suárez was not willing to lie down and take his punishment so easily. Close to the finish he launched several attacks. His multiple moves failed to work out, though, and Bahamontes made a counter-charge at the finish on the steep uphill climb to the fortress of Namur. Only Gaul could follow Bahamontes. Just when it seemed they would be fighting for the yellow jersey, a policeman stationed at the entrance to one of the fortress's numerous tunnels misdirected the pair. By the time Bahamontes and Gaul had found their way out of the tunnel and on to the proper route again they had been caught by the peloton and they all reached the finish together. Suárez complained bitterly afterwards that Bahamontes had failed to let him 'ride my own race, one that does no one any harm, particularly as all the favourites were asleep'. Bahamontes responded: 'Even if it had worked out, all we'd have got would have been a stage win.' He was clearly sticking to his line that the idea of Suárez fighting for the overall classification was inconceivable.

If the Spanish were merely bickering, the French were riven by serious in-fighting. Sprinter Darrigade, the race leader, and the French squad's co-leader Jacques Anquetil were now refusing to talk to each other. Anquetil had apparently not taken kindly to Darrigade working in the first day's break which had directly helped Bahamontes. It looked like a minor tiff, but in fact it was just the beginning of the French team's troubles. The underlying problem was that all of their top contenders were in the same squad. It contained Anquetil, three-times Tour winner Louison Bobet, 1958 runner-up Raphael Geminiani and the up-and-coming Roger Rivière. Team trainer Marcel Bidot had tried to avoid conflicts before the start with the so-called 'Poigny pact' between all four under which they agreed to work for the common goal of a French win. 'It was risky having so many big names in the same team,' Bahamontes recognises. 'But there was more to it than that. Anquetil and Rivière were both time-triallists and that intensified their rivalry. They disliked each other off the bike, too. As for Bobet and Geminiani, they were at the end of their careers and this Tour represented their last chance to go out on top. Finally, when you're only in the same team for one race like the Tour, money becomes a lot more important, too.'

Things had gone awry between the 'Big Four' in the previous year's Tour. Geminiani partly lost the race in the Alps because Rivière and Anquetil had been unwilling to help him. When Geminiani reached the finish line he realised his best chance of winning the Tour had gone up in smoke and he accused Anquetil and Rivière of being 'more treacherous than Judas'. That hardly augured well for the 1959 race. However, in addition to such a strong senior squad, there were three other French teams, the so-called 'regionals', who might lend a hand. Indeed, forty per cent of the riders in the Tour that year were French. For Bahamontes, his best hope was that there were too many big names in one single squad for power to be shared successfully. As Bahamontes put it with his usual directness: 'Which director was going to be brave enough to argue with any or all of them, and even more so when the Tour was the one race that they all rode for the same team?'

The Spanish team was almost unrecognisable at the end of stage three. Just like the rest of the peloton, they were covered in mud from head to foot, having ridden more than half the course through an interminable series of treacherous, waterlogged country lanes in northern France. By the time they reached the finish at the Roubaix velodrome, their nerves were shattered and their bodies jangled by the huge cobblestones that pockmark that part of the country. *MARCA* rather predictably dubbed the stage 'Hell'. The Spaniards suffered twelve punctures between them and Rene Marigil damaged his bike so badly he had to change it three times. Suárez had to change his twice. Remarkably, Bahamontes neither punctured nor crashed. Others were not so fortunate. While most of the Spaniards, including Bahamontes, had avoided the one big pile-up of the day, 1947 winner Jean Robic fractured one of his fingers. He struggled on but never fully recovered and was finally eliminated for falling too far behind on the stage to Chalone-sur-Saône, just two days before the finish.

While the Spaniards were never experts in racing over cobbles and had enough trouble staying upright, the battle for the overall continued and the classification had changed considerably. Fortunately for Bahamontes, though, they were not important in the long-term. The biggest change had come after an opportunist ten-man move, not containing any top favourites, had broken away early on the Grammont 'Wall' in Belgium, which had caused Bahamontes such grief in 1957. Since none of the riders was considered to be any real threat, the break was allowed to gain more than eleven minutes on the main peloton. The French were particularly happy to see it go, gambling that their one representative in it, Robert Cazala, would be fastest on home soil in the velodrome. The gamble paid off. Cazala, who was only in his second year as a professional, not only won the stage but found himself leading the biggest bike race in the world. He would stay in the yellow jersey for a further six days, the highpoint of his career.

For the next week the race wound its way first westwards to the Atlantic, then southwards to the foot of the Pyrenees at Bayonne. Bahamontes concentrated on staying out of trouble. 'There is a midweek time-trial, which though it's short, is where I would like to make my presence known,' Bahamontes told reporters early on in the Tour. 'But essentially I'm riding with the same kind of strategy that Gaul did in 1958: lay low and wait for the mountains.' Cunningly, he even opted to shadow Gaul, who had a much stronger team to back him up. Though not particularly great mountain riders, they were experts at sheltering their climber against attacks by the French and Belgian squads. Where one climber could shelter, Bahamontes reasoned, so could two.

If Bahamontes' spirits were rising 'the further away we get from those *pavés* and the horrible weather in the north', the race itself suffered a major tragedy en route when a five-year-old child was hit and killed by a vehicle from the Tour's publicity caravan on the stage to Rennes.

The time-trial on stage six was won by Roger Rivière, though it had little long-term significance. However, during the race against the clock Bahamontes felt he had been the victim of yet another French 'conspiracy', and he made sure the world knew it, too. This time Bahamontes' opportunity to accuse his rivals revolved around the starting order for the riders, something usually decided by their position in the overall classification. Bahamontes, being twelve places better placed than Jacques Anquetil, should have started the time-trial later than the Frenchman. Instead he found at the start-line that Anquetil was starting immediately after him, not before. The disadvantage for Bahamontes was that Anquetil would be able to use him as a 'moving target' and adjust his pace accordingly. On top of that, given Anquetil's position as one of the world's top time-triallists, Bahamontes was sure to be overtaken. Being 'caught' is always a huge blow to any rider's morale and even more so for a rider with a fragile ego like Bahamontes. His vigorous protests were ignored and he had to make the best of a bad job. When he was caught by Anquetil, Bahamontes simply fell in behind and adapted his pace to the Frenchman's, limiting the time deficit to two minutes. He even sprinted for the line, beating Anquetil by a wheel's breadth. The gesture was not received well by the race organisers, who promptly fined him one thousand francs. Apart from the financial penalty Bahamontes had no other reason to complain. He had finished tenth on the stage, the best-place Spaniard, which helped reinforce his position over Suárez. In addition, while Rivière had gained three minutes on Bahamontes, none of the other favourites had taken more than two. For someone who rode only reasonably well in time-trials, as a damage-limitation exercise it was a significant triumph. Even better, the Tour now headed southwards towards the hotter weather. 'I function on solar energy,' Bahamontes liked to say, 'and with any luck my rivals will melt on the roads of the Pyrenees.'

As it turned out, he did not have to wait that long for two opponents to fall by the wayside. On stage nine from Bordeaux to Bayonne temperatures soared into the high thirties. After one hundred and fifty kilometres of racing through the airless pine forests of south-west France, the peloton was ready to crumble under the slightest pressure. The honour of wrecking the peloton fell to the Belgian team, who had been given a roasting by their director at Bordeaux for failing to ride aggressively enough. So it was predictable that it should be one of their number, Marcel Janssens, who led the attack. Janssens's move quickly split the bunch and twenty-two riders forged ahead, including most of the favourites. However, both Raphael Geminiani and Suárez missed it, as did Cazala, the race leader since Roubaix. Suárez finally lost six minutes, while Geminiani finished twelve minutes down, thereby relinquishing all hope of victory in Paris. France's 'Big Four' had become the 'Big Three'. Eddy Pauwels, a young, inexperienced Belgian rider, took over in the yellow jersey, but with the Pyrenees looming he had little hope of remaining there for long. Bahamontes, meanwhile, was poised to strike.

Seventeen kilometres long, the Tourmalet is the highest and most formidable mountain pass of the Pyrenees. Its nickname in French is *l'incontournable,* the unavoidable one. 'We gave it that name because it's the only way through that part of the Pyrenees,' Phillippe Bouvet, *L'Equipe*'s head journalist, told the British magazine *Cycle Sport* a few years back, 'and because it's been a part of the Tour for so long all of its riders must face it at one point or another.' In 1949, the Tourmalet was the starting point of what remains arguably the most spectacular comeback in Tour history. Fausto Coppi was thirty minutes behind the leaders when the race reached the climb, but his attack there was so stunning he went on to win the race by an incredible ten minutes. Now, ten years later, the riders would take on the biggest single challenge of the Tour on the race's first day in the mountains when they often had problems adapting physically from multiple stages on the flat.

Strange, then, that when eleven riders moved ahead in the 1959 race just before the Tourmalet, the French team failed to react. Surely they would want to control one of the most important stages of the race and win it? Instead, the breakaway group opened a gap of eleven minutes by the foot of the mountain. Behind, the phony war of the Tour's first ten days continued. Finally, after an hour of waiting for the French to increase the pace and start reeling in the break, Bahamontes could contain himself no longer. Eleven kilometres from the summit, on a series of broad hairpins just before the village of Barèges, he charged up the road. It was the first big mountain attack of the Tour and it looked very good indeed. Gaul, Rivière and Anquetil followed at first, but with another blast on the pedals, Bahamontes and Gaul were clear. This could have been a race-winning move, the sort that has earned riders countless victories in the Tour. But then, to the bewilderment of the crowds of Spanish fans lining the route, Bahamontes eased back, inviting Gaul to move ahead and keep the pace high. Gaul did so, but noticing Bahamontes' reticence he did not go flat out either. By the summit their advantage over the first chasing group of Rivière and Fernando Manzaneque was two minutes eight seconds: a good margin but by no means decisive. From the summit of the Tourmalet there was another twenty-eight kilometres to the finish at Bagnères-de-Bigorre. But rather than widen the gap Bahamontes and Gaul crossed the line with an advantage of just one minute twenty-two seconds over Anquetil, Rivière and Bobet.

The big question after the stage was why Bahamontes and Gaul had failed to put more daylight between themselves and the French when they had the chance. Even the traditionally loyal *MARCA* ran a headline the next day: 'Disappointing Performance By Top Climbers on the Tourmalet', which was a none-too-veiled criticism of the Spaniard's failure to drive home his advantage. Bahamontes' explanation was that he had wanted to prove to the French who was the strongest man in the mountains, but with Gaul on his wheel he had not wanted to risk an all-out attack. 'I'm biding my time,' was all he would say. 'I'll go for it when it suits me.' With the benefit of hindsight, Bahamontes' strategy was probably the right one, even if it inevitably provoked a sense of anti-climax. If he and Gaul had opened up a bigger margin on the rest of the field with two weeks' racing still to go they would have had an uphill task defending their lead all the way to the Alps and beyond. The French would almost certainly have become more united against the two clear enemies, and for Bahamontes with an inexperienced

Tour team to back him that was too great a risk. At least short-term, then, Bahamontes needed Gaul as an ally, not as a rival for yellow.

Bahamontes certainly seemed fairly relaxed. In his daily column for the local Toledo newspaper *El Alcázar*, he barely discussed the race during the Pyrenees. Instead he thanked the 'Frutos Ramos' wholesalers of Toledo for sending a box of fresh Spanish fruit every day for the team. He also claimed, in his latest conspiracy theory, that the Italians were getting preferential treatment because 'they've posted a supporter on every corner of the Pyrenean climbs with bottles of water. I hope the race officials do something about this so we're racing on a level playing field'. But there was no comment on why after being so gung-ho in the flatter stages, he was suddenly no longer as aggressive as he could have been in the mountains.

However, there were good reasons for Bahamontes' patient policy. The French squad still dominated the race after one day's racing in the Pyrenees, but their ferocious discussions about who was the leader continued apace. The longer Bahamontes sat back, it seemed, the worse the disagreements grew. 'Our boat is still sailing, but it's leaking from all sides,' was French trainer Marcel Bidot's graphic description of their disunity. 'We have to work harder together and control the breaks, because that's exactly what we didn't do today.' Bidot had formulated the famous 'Poigny pact' between France's top four riders. But rather than work in their favour, the pact became an excuse for the quartet to watch each other like hawks for the slightest sign of weakness as well as failing to agree basic tactics like chasing down breaks.

With Bahamontes not willing to declare open war, and the French too divided to do so this lack of aggression led to some bizarre consequences. The second stage through the Pyrenees was won by Darrigade, a sprinter, not a climber. Even stranger, the Tour left the mountains with the overall classification led by Michel Vermeulin, a rider for the lowly Paris-Nord'Est team whose full-time job was as a telegraph operator in Paris. Vermeulin was part of the eleven-man break over the Tourmalet, but he could have had little idea of what effect the move would have or that he would end up wearing the yellow jersey. Anquetil and Rivière could only look on enviously from the sidelines. 'The Tour is being taken over by greenhorns,' was Bahamontes' acerbic analysis. 'Something's going to have to happen.'

Bahamontes' words proved prophetic. On stage thirteen's trek through the hills of central France the race was finally blown apart. The French were mainly responsible, but it was a day in which the cracks in their team became chasms. For two hundred and nineteen kilometres, on a day of blazing heat and rugged terrain, the Poigny agreement disintegrated as the French relentlessly chased down each another's attacks. Anquetil remained nominally in contention, but France's chances of winning the Tour had suffered a serious setback. Meanwhile, in the muddle of the mutual self-destruction, eight riders failed to finish within the official time limit and were eliminated from the race. The two riders who gained most were Bahamontes and Henry Anglade, the French national champion who bizarrely rode for the regional Centre-Midi team rather than the country's top squad. The rider who suffered most was the winner of the previous year's Tour, Charly Gaul. He had been forced to stop at one point on the Col de Monsalvy climb to beg a farmer for some water and eventually crossed the line more than twenty minutes down on Bahamontes. As he put it: 'I was so exhausted I thought I would end up crawling all the way there in my underpants. I could hardly see, there was so much sweat pouring down my face.' The heat was so extreme that even at 10.30 in the morning, before the stage started, Tour officials distributed free sunglasses and sun cream to the riders. 'We Spanish didn't wear them, but we put them in our pockets,' Bahamontes recalled later, 'just in case.' Gaul, though, was in need of far greater help.

Given how badly the stage ended for the French, it was ironic that it was their decision to attack which caused them to suffer such a stinging defeat. After fifty kilometres, the French 'A' squad had a team worker, Rene Privat, and Darrigade up the road in a seven-man break. By the first feeding station at Rodez, when the leading group had only a two-minute advantage, Bahamontes attacked.

The move had been planned well in advance. Bahamontes had even ordered the Spanish team's car driver to wait with his food bag on the opposite side of the road and wear a red jersey so he would be sure to see him. Nonetheless, with one hundred and forty kilometres left, it looked an insanely bold move. Despite the riders already suffering badly in the heat, Anquetil responded immediately by jumping on Bahamontes' wheel. Rivière and Bobet, happy to see one of their internal rivals take part in such a suicidal long-distance attack, opted to stay in the bunch. Four other riders, among them Anglade, reigning world champion Ercole Baldini and his team-mate Roberto Falaschi of Italy, also followed Bahamontes and Anquetil up the road.

For thirty kilometres, the six-man chasing group hovered somewhere in no-man's land between the early break of seven and the bunch. Finally, on a small third category climb, after Falaschi had driven so hard he cracked completely, the two front moves merged. When Radio Tour reported that the two leading breaks had become a twelve-man group, panic overtook the peloton. After sitting so smugly behind, Bobet and Rivière quickly realised that rather than overplaying their hand, Anquetil and Anglade now held the trump cards. Bobet lost his nerve and broke away from the bunch in an attempt to bridge the gap alone. But Anquetil, on hearing the news that Bobet was chasing, decided to increase his pace at the front of the leading group as well. The situation, then, was that one French rider from the 'A' team was chasing while his team-mate was riding as hard as possible ahead. The much-vaunted French *entente cordiale* had suddenly come apart at the seams. Quickly realising that this was too good an opportunity to miss, Bahamontes started to collaborate with Anquetil. Behind yet more French riders came to Rivière's assistance, while ahead Anglade, Bahamontes and Anquetil had formed what proved to be a highly effective working alliance.

In the blazing heat the leading break shrank to nine. Privat was so exhausted he later collapsed on the line and needed to be taken to hospital. However, Bahamontes, Anquetil and Anglade were in no mood to throw in the towel despite the depleting numbers. On the second category climb of Montsalvy, sixty-five kilometres from the finish, Bobet's lone chase between bunch and break came to an end when he cracked completely. He was overtaken by the Rivière-led group and ended up twenty minutes down, all hope of adding another victory to his three previous Tour wins totally destroyed. He was not the only rider to suffer so badly. Gaul reeled off the road on the Montsalvy and dismounted in a desperate search for water. He, too, lost all chance of victory. The bunch began to crumble as Rivière tried to raise the pace even more. But he had run out of *domestiques* to support his counter-attack and only the Belgian Jos Hoevenaers offered some feeble collaboration. The rest were exhausted. Whatever orders Bidot had given to Rivière behind or Anquetil in front, they were ignored. The speed in the break ahead was so great that press cars and officials had serious problems overtaking them on the Midi's narrow, winding roads. When they finally did, close to the finish at Aurillac Velodrome, it was to find the leading break had now shrunk to just four: Britain's Brian Robinson, Anglade, Anquetil and Bahamontes. 'Robinson went for it [in the closing metres] for the stage win, and I followed him, but I was too impetuous,' Bahamontes recalls. 'We reached the velodrome together, but then Anglade went high up the side of the track and he used his speed from descending again to overtake me to win. Then I saw Anquetil pass me, too.' Bahamontes took third, Robinson fourth.

Behind the four stage leaders, it was carnage. Hoevenaers, who took over the yellow jersey, led in a group containing Rivière at nearly four minutes, while Gaul and Bobet crossed the line a massive twenty minutes forty seconds down. To add insult to injury Gaul had another thirty seconds tagged on to his time for accepting pushes from spectators. Bahamontes, meanwhile, had shot up the overall classification from ninth to fifth and was just over seven minutes behind the leader; twenty-four hours earlier he had been more than fourteen minutes behind.

'We've wiped out Gaul and Bobet, and Rivière is almost out of the running, too. It has been an excellent day,' Bahamontes reflected. It was made even sweeter by news that Suárez had been forced to abandon. As the Tour reached its crucial phase Bahamontes found himself in an ideal position overall. Barring the inexperienced Anglade, he had become the best-placed climber, and still to come was a mountain time-trial followed by three major stages in the Alps. Suddenly Bahamontes had moved from being just another potential contender to the rider most likely to win the Tour.

Since a Spaniard had never won the race before, the country was understandably abuzz with the news of Bahamontes' success. For the first time in his career, Bahamontes felt certain he could live up to their expectations. 'The war has started and it is the most ferocious combat on two wheels of recent times,' reported the newspaper *Informaciones*. 'Bahamontes is the favourite of this year's Tour.' *El Alcázar* even put a photograph of Bahamontes on its front page for the first time during the 1959 Tour with the headline underneath: 'Congratulations, Fede . . . Fede could become the real star of Spanish cycling.' The Toledo publication added: 'Even Jacques Goddet came up to our newspaper's correspondent at Aurillac, pointed at Bahamontes and said, "There you have the winner of this year's race".' Bahamontes would later recall: 'At Aurillac, the time and the day had finally arrived that I was sure that I could win.' However, at the time he did not let the opportunity pass to criticise his team-mates and the rest of the break, saying yet again: 'Nobody would help me.' In his later years he claimed he was fully focused on his future Tour de France win. 'The prince was about to become a king and the eyes of an entire country were waiting for my coronation.' It would not be a long wait, either.

Almost every account of the 1959 Tour, at least outside Spain, has perpetuated the widespread belief that the race that year was all but decided between the agents for the criteriums, the closest that some top riders of the era, including Bahamontes, had to a manager. The theory is straightforward: Rivière, Anquetil and Bahamontes had the same agent, Daniel Dousset, while Anglade was with Roger Piel. Therefore, it was in Anquetil and Rivière's interests that if they could not win, then another Dousset 'client' should, namely Bahamontes. 'The 1959 Tour was the war between the managers,' says Raymond Poulidor. 'Dousset was the well-established figure – I used to call him Al Capone – and Piel the breakaway competition. There wasn't any difference in what they charged: both got ten per cent. But Dousset was only interested in big riders, and Piel was happy to go with the smaller ones while they were still on the way up. In 1959, [that was] Anglade. By the time Dousset got to me, though, I was with Piel; it was too late.' Not everybody agrees that Piel and Dousset made such a big difference to the race. Raphael Geminiani, himself a wheeler-dealer of considerable skill, and unlike Poulidor, part of the 1959 Tour peloton, is convinced Dousset's role was minor to the outcome. But the myth has persisted. Three years later, in 1962, when a satirical 'A–Z of cycling' pamphlet did the rounds of the Tour de France press room, 'A' was for [Rudy] Altig – described as 'a treacherous German in a Spanish comedy' in reference to his 'robbing' team-mate Anquetil of the 1962 Vuelta victory – 'D' for Dousset: 'When he arrives, the Tour is over and everybody can go home.'

While the theory that Dousset helped shape the outcome of the Tour probably contains some grains of truth, it is impossible to prove. Either way it is certainly far too simplistic to say: 'Bahamontes won the Tour thanks to Anquetil and Rivière.' As Robert Millar once said about the Vuelta a España he lost to Pedro Delgado because of a Spanish combine in 1985: 'Other riders can't make you win, but they can make sure you lose.' That is almost certainly what happened to Anglade in 1959. His compatriots' tactics wrecked his race. Not that he would definitely have won, but what they wrecked was his *chance* to win. And there is a big difference between the two. A more pertinent question is whether Anquetil and Rivière combining against Anglade, with perhaps Dousset as 'puppet-master', devalues Bahamontes greatest win? The answer has to be no, not least because if that is the case then numerous other victories in major Tours during the 1950s would also have to be discredited.

Even if we rewind just one year to 1958, the French national team's refusal to help Geminiani, who, like Anglade, was in a regional team, arguably cost their fellow Frenchman the Tour, too. But does anybody claim Charly Gaul's victory was a gift, even if he benefited from these divisions? 'Bahamontes was strong enough to be there in the breaks and there on the attack,' points out *L'Equipe*'s veteran cycling journalist Philippe Bouvet. 'Whatever the French got up to, nobody can take that away.' Anglade himself has refused to condemn the combine that lost him his chance of winning the Tour; half a century ago such skulduggery was far more part and parcel of racing than it is today. Besides, for Bahamontes to win he had to be in the right place at the right time. As Raphael Geminiani pointed out to me: 'It's not like Anquetil and Rivière were called up on the phone by Dousset during the stage. They decided to do what they did, not Dousset. He wasn't in the French national team car giving orders.'

Two days after Bahamontes' knock-out performance in Aurillac, the Tour's next big challenge was a 12.5-kilometre uphill time-trial at the Puy de Dôme, an extinct volcano near Clermont Ferrand. The road up the Puy is well-surfaced and not particularly narrow, and appears deceptively easy at first; it is the second part that causes the damage to riders. Like a helterskelter at a fairground its steepest section winds remorselessly round and round the edge of the Puy to the summit. On the right, painted on the cliffside, are the names of former winners: on the left, a low stone wall, and then a precipice. Though not as long and demanding as the single hardest climb in France, Mont Ventoux, the Puy's gradients are far more challenging. And, like Ventoux, there are no breaks, either, no false flats to catch your breath; it is just one long exercise in pain. The climb had only been used on one previous occasion, during the 1952 Tour, and its appearance then had an encouraging historical precedent for Bahamontes. Seven years before, his trade team boss Fausto Coppi had blasted off to victory there, dropping Dutchman Jan Nolten in the last three hundred metres. However, there was one crucial difference: by the time the Tour reached the Puy de Dôme stage in 1952, Coppi already had the race sewn up; in 1959, Bahamontes still had to prove he could win it.

*

One of Bahamontes' weapons on his most important Tour de France stage win was an artificial stimulant, albeit a legal one. 'I didn't use to drink coffee in those days, but as I was heading towards the start of the stage I was feeling nervous. I knew it was going to be a very important day,' Bahamontes recalls. 'So when I saw a publicity vehicle from the Tour I stopped and grabbed a coffee. An expresso. Then, because it didn't look like much in the cup, I thought, "Hey, have another one, at least that way you'll notice you swallowed something".'

Apart from the caffeine coursing through his veins, Bahamontes had other advantages on his side as the Puy de Dôme loomed, the most important being that standing-start mountain time-trials were his speciality. Indeed, he had won the early-spring hill-climb to Arrate on several occasions. This was only the second time a mountain time-trial had been held during the Tour and Bahamontes had finished second to Gaul in the first one on Mont Ventoux the previous year. He was, therefore determined to make the most of it. In his favour, for the rider who 'functioned on solar energy', was the heatwave France was still enduring. Bahamontes says Langarica told him it was the hottest summer in France for a century. By way of a morale boost the team director cunningly pointed out that Gaul would be suffering more than most in the searing heat as a result. Additionally, for once the Spanish were not to be outdone technically, either. A special combination of gears was put on Bahamontes bike – rear cogs of fourteen, sixteen, nineteen, twenty-one, twenty-two and twenty-three with a forty-four and fifty-one double chainring on the front – were designed to cope with the opening section on the flat. He also had special lightweight silk 'tub' tyres, which were sometimes risky in wet weather but not in the baking heat. Not huge advances by any means, but given the usual ramshackle nature of the team they made a difference.

There were other, smaller issues that were tilting things towards Bahamontes. Rather than driving the Spanish team car, Langarica opted to open the car's sun-roof and lean out of the window to give his star rider orders and encouragement. For Bahamontes, with his love of dramatic gestures, having his director so close was an important plus. Then, though Bahamontes did not know it, Gaul was not his only key rival in trouble. Clermont-Ferrand is an important railway junction and Rivière, who would be starting two minutes before, had been kept up all night by the noise from trains in the marshalling yard close to his hotel.

Most importantly of all, perhaps, the mountain time-trial was a section where Bahamontes needed no external assistance or team-mates. On the Puy de Dôme he was able to do what he always said he did best and 'move alone': and moving alone, he soared.

Even before Bahamontes reached the steepest uphill section it was clear he was going to have an exceptionally good day. After four and a half kilometres of rolling terrain he was clocking the fastest time and was already fourteen seconds ahead of Gaul, fifty-one seconds up on Anquetil, and more than a minute in front of Rivière. With his shorts rolled up extra high so he felt more comfortable, and sitting in his classic climbing position, hands slumped slightly over the handlebars, Bahamontes said before the start he was 'super-nervous and ready to eat the road'. Clearly the coffee had already had quite an effect. Before halfway he had Rivière in his sights and two-thirds of the way up he overtook the Frenchman. Needless to say Bahamontes was the fastest through every checkpoint. By the time he reached the summit the damage he had inflicted on the field was colossal: Gaul had beaten him by thirty-one seconds on the more difficult Ventoux climb in 1958, but over such a short distance he was the closest at one minute twenty-six seconds. Anglade was at three minutes and the two great French time-trial specialists, Rivière and Anquetil, were even further back. This was not a defeat, it was a rout. While Jos Hoevenaers clung on to the yellow jersey, Bahamontes was just four seconds behind, and with the Alps to come his path to overall victory looked increasingly free of obstacles.

Now only Anglade, thirty-nine seconds behind Bahamontes, could be considered a viable threat. Anquetil, the strongest of France's 'Big Four', was now more than five minutes back, and Rivière more than seven. Bahamontes revealed that Rivière's relatively strong performance in the middle section had been the spur to do even more damage, exactly at the point where the climb was steepest and hurt his rivals the most. 'I'd decided not to go too hard,' Bahamontes said, 'because I didn't think the gaps would be that big in such a short a distance. I thought I'd catch Rivière quite quickly, though, and I was surprised that I didn't so I started going flat out to try and get past him. It was only afterwards that I realised he had got fourth and I discovered I'd done a far better time than I'd thought possible.' Bahamontes' time was so good, in fact, that he was the only rider to average more than 20 k.p.h.

The French took their defeat in radically different ways. Anquetil made the most of Rivière being overtaken by Bahamontes to take a sideswipe at his rival and tell reporters: 'That'll teach Rivière to boast.' As for Jean Robic, who finished fifty-second, nearly ten minutes back, he gave the most laconic of answers when asked about his experiences. 'It went brilliantly,' he said, 'I actually had to brake quite often to try and slow down a bit.'

Amazingly for such a short distance nine riders finished outside the time limit. However, the race officials applied a rule that allowed them arbitrarily to increase the percentage of the winner's time within which riders had to finish. As a result, only four were eliminated. One, though, was Bahamontes' team-mate Aniceto Utset, the 1956 Volta winner. 'That was our only worry after the Puy de Dôme,' Bahamontes said. 'I was running out of team-mates. By that point, I only had six left with three big Alpine stages to come.' However, two of the other three were powerful French *domestiques* and that could only strengthen his hand.

The loss of Utset had reduced the Spanish team from twelve starters to just seven. Under the circumstances it was important to look for allies. Bahamontes did not have to look far. Charly Gaul had been performing so badly there were rumours that he had actually left the race, and the 1958 winner was keen to show his face at the front.

Stage seventeen to Grenoble, where Gaul and Bahamontes launched their joint attacks, did not look overly promising. Of its two second category climbs, la Romeyere, where Bahamontes had eaten his ice cream back in 1954, was more than sixty kilometres from the finish. Assuming their rivals were organised then in theory they would make mincemeat of the two climbers on the long, flat run-in to Grenoble. However, that was the point: Bahamontes' main rivals, the French, *weren't* organised. They had shown that again the day before. Rivière and Anquetil had planned a joint ambush of Bahamontes on the lumpy run through the Massif Central from Clermont-Ferrand to Grenoble. Rivière was so convinced of his chances he had even requested a special gear, a thirteen-cog sprocket, so he could blast away that much quicker. However, when Rivière was revving up for the move on a descent where they knew Bahamontes would be most vulnerable, Jean Grazyck, a French *domestique*, came rushing through the peloton with a message. He said: 'Jacques says to tell you he's not coming. His legs hurt.' And so the attack was aborted. Even more telling was that Anquetil did not bother to talk in person to Rivière: with internal communication so limited it hardly suggested they were really prepared to collaborate against Bahamontes.

Then again, perhaps they did not need to worry, given that Bahamontes' first attack on the stage from Saint Etienne to Grenoble the next day bordered on the suicidal. Desperate to take the yellow jersey, and ignoring Langarica's orders for once, Bahamontes rocketed off the front on the Col de Gran Bois with more than one hundred and ninety kilometres left to go. He was joined by Gaul and a Frenchman from Anglade's Centre-Midi squad, Francois Huot, but their lead was only thirty-five seconds at the summit. This was too small and too soon in the day. The trio eased back and were absorbed by the bunch. On the Romeyere, though longer and with some brief, steeper sections, Bahamontes went for it again. Taking advantage of a crash that split the bunch, he attacked 'and this time I wasn't going to stop for any ruddy ice cream at the top'.

Initially alone, Bahamontes blasted up the steady but largely shallow climb with such speed that by the summit he had a sixty-seven-second advantage on Gaul, and was nearly three minutes clear of the bunch. While there was no stop for a cornet, food was still on Bahamontes' mind, an indication that he recognised that the sixty kilometres to Grenoble would be no easy task. 'He crossed the line at the summit of the Romeyere yelling, "Bananas! Bananas!" at us,' MARCA reported. 'We weren't sure what was happening, but if he had the strength to shout for food, we knew he had the strength to pedal too.' In what is surely one of the more surreal moments in Tour de France history, MARCA's correspondent and his colleagues then embarked on a 'banana hunt' to find Bahamontes the food he had requested. The sight of a bunch of sweaty, middle-aged foreign journalists, dressed primarily in singlets and shorts, bursting into local houses and asking for bananas is worthy of French farce at its best. But their mission proved unsuccessful. 'We couldn't find any bananas, not one, all the way to Grenoble,' MARCA reported mournfully, 'and we checked in a lot of houses.'

Crucially, rather than plough on alone, Bahamontes soon realised that Gaul was 'the best company I could have. He needed the stage win, I needed the lead. He was miles back overall and no threat to me. It all made sense'. Equally importantly, Gaul was able to guide Bahamontes on the descent. By the foot of the Romeyere the duo's advantage had stretched to four minutes. Then, even on the flat valley floor that stretches for nearly fifty kilometres through Voreppe and Saint-Egreve en route to Grenoble the two climbers managed to hold off an entire pack. While the conspiracy theorists point to this failure to reel them in as another sign of French indifference to Bahamontes winning the Tour, media reports at the time suggest that on this occasion the French were united in trying to close down the breakaways. It was Rivière who had co-led the chase early in the stage and Rivière again who worked hardest to keep Bahamontes and Gaul at bay towards Grenoble. On neither occasion did the chase work. But rather than their failure to catch the two escapees, there is a more important question: why did Rivière, and to a lesser extent Anquetil, try to keep Bahamontes out of the yellow jersey and maintain Anglade's chances on one day, yet once Bahamontes had the lead why did they then collaborate to keep him there and wreck Anglade's Tour the next? Assuming that this was a sophisticated anti-Anglade conspiracy, the answer could be that on the road to Grenoble Rivière and Anquetil's plan was to make a symbolic contribution to Anglade's chances rather than a real one. That they only pulled back twenty-seven seconds of the four-minute deficit over forty-five kilometres lends strength to this theory. From the French team's point of view, the advantage of keeping Anglade in contention was that the roles of Rivière and Anquetil as 'king-makers' would remain intact, roles which if Bahamontes became a clear Tour winner at this juncture, would be irrelevant. They needed to maintain the illusion of an Anglade-Bahamontes duel for as long as possible before their cards were turned up on the table.

In any case, the results still stand and they cannot fail to impress. Whatever the reasons for the failure to chase down Gaul and Bahamontes, they cannot detract from stage seventeen of the Tour de France 1959 being one of the few occasions when two light-weight climbers managed to break and stay away from the pack over a forty-five-kilometre stretch of flat terrain. It was a monumental achievement. On top of that, while Bahamontes showed strategic sense in waiting for Gaul and striking the bargain with him, he would have needed to ride to the limits of his physical strength to maintain that deal in the two-hour battle against the peloton.

When they reached the Grenoble velodrome Bahamontes had to respect the unspoken deal with Gaul and let him win the sprint. In practical terms he had no choice: he had a punctured front wheel. 'The crowd whistled and booed when I let Charly get the stage,' he recalls. 'It was only when the race commentator held up the front wheel between his finger and thumb and showed them I had punctured that they started to applaud me, too. Letting him win was the right thing to do. I had got the yellow jersey and increased my lead in the King of the Mountains competition. That was enough.' Bahamontes was not the first Spaniard to lead the Tour (Miguel Poblet had worn the yellow jersey for a day in 1955 in Dieppe), but with a four-minute fifty-one-second advantage over Anglade, he was certainly the first from Spain with a real chance of winning it. 'We just thought he was going for the mountain points,' Anquetil told *Informaciones* at the finish. 'If he isn't just interested in the King of the Mountains, then the Tour is his.'

As usual, Bahamontes opted for a melodramatic description to sum up his achievements. 'Grenoble was the city where three hundred years before Bayard the "Knight With No Fear" had died, I showed I had no fear, either,' he wrote in his privately published account of the 1959 Tour. It was not strictly true as Bayard was born close to Grenoble, but died in Italy, though Bahamontes' point was clear. 'The Alps were still to come,' he went on, 'but for me the race was done and dusted because I was clearly superior in all areas. The only possible problem was the lack of a strong team.'

In his daily column in *El Alcázar*, Bahamontes said: 'Getting the yellow jersey was not as hard as I expected. In my terrain, the mountains, nobody bothers me. Anquetil is my closest enemy and he is at nine minutes, Rivière and Baldini at over eleven, and Gaul at over twenty.' Pointedly, he did not mention Anglade. However, as he rode around the velodrome on a lap of honour, clad in yellow and soaking up the applause, Bahamontes could be forgiven for not wanting to think about the next day's racing. Just getting this far was impressive enough.

The eighteenth stage from the Lautaret valley in France to Val de Aosta in Italy started and finished with the same rider in yellow. And Bahamontes managed to maintain an almost identical advantage overall. However, what happened during those two hundred and forty-three kilometres caused one of the biggest scandals in French sport as an unholy, though unspoken alliance between Bahamontes, Anquetil and Rivière all but ensured the Spaniard, not Anglade, won the Tour.

The mammoth Alpine stage across the Galibier, Iseran and Petit St. Bernard passes, which included sixty-nine kilometres of climbing, should have suited Bahamontes. Instead, he twice came within a whisker of losing the lead. The French, logically enough, attacked Bahamontes on his two weakest points, the descents and in wet weather, and on both occasions their strategy worked perfectly. But the scandal arose because they then failed to follow through with their initial success: it seemed to be enough for them to have Bahamontes in trouble, not out for the count. The first attack came on the descent of the Iseran, where Geminiani took off on what Bahamontes later called a 'suicide mission', and took with him Anglade, Anquetil and eight of the top eleven overall. Neither Gaul nor Bahamontes were present, and Anglade upped the pace as best he could to haul back some of his five-minute deficit. However, neither Anquetil nor Rivière offered their help. After five kilometres of climbing on the Petit St. Bernard Bahamontes and Gaul had managed to rejoin the main group, thus resolving what Langarica later called 'one of the most dangerous moments of the entire race'.

'They could have had me up against the ropes,' Bahamontes recalled, 'but the fact that Anglade was in a regional team was impossible for them to handle psychologically.' However, if Anquetil and Rivière deserve at least part of the blame, the bulk of the responsibility has to rest on the shoulders of Marcel Bidot, the French team trainer. Bidot had no money to make from criteriums and no deals with Daniel Dousset, just his duty to ensure a French victory. 'Rather than organise the break with Anglade, for some reason Bidot stayed driving alongside me,' Bahamontes recalls, 'to be sure, so he said later, there were no "dodgy tactics". Under what were very critical circumstances, given he gave up on what were his real duties, Bidot was a real ally for me.'

The second crunch moment came forty-five kilometres from home on the descent of Petit St. Bernard. Bahamontes had no problems keeping up with the rest of the pack on the climb, but when the heavens opened on the descent he was in trouble when he punctured. The only good news was that he was not the only favourite to suffer: so, too, did Anquetil, Rivière and Geminiani; one Italian, Michele Gismondi, punctured six times. Indeed, just six riders in the front group, among them Bahamontes and Anglade, did not have to dismount at one point or another in the freezing rain. One by one, the field slowly picked their way down the treacherously wet single-track dirt road. If racing was the last thing on their mind it would have been hard to blame them. That, though, was not the case.

Anglade took advantage of the drop in pace to go clear and steadily increased his lead on the pack. When Gaul and several others joined him, Bahamontes was again in trouble. With only Gomez del Moral to help him, Bahamontes' fear that lack of team support could be his undoing looked more than justified. But again Anquetil and Rivière were willing to give him their support, this time directly as they hammered away at the front of the group to chase down Anglade. In the end, the gap between Anglade's group and Bahamontes was halved to forty-seven seconds. But that was nothing compared to the damage done to French morale. 'At the finish, all that anybody could talk about was the way Anquetil and Rivière had betrayed their country,' Bahamontes said. 'On France's national holiday [14 July] as well. What a great way to commemorate it.' To increase the host nation's humiliation, Louison Bobet abandoned the Tour in the most melodramatic of fashions on the summit of the Iseran. He never returned.

'I had to make a great effort on this stage,' Bahamontes said in *El Alcázar*, 'but I'm sure my enemies have worked even harder. Some people were thinking I would attack, but when you're in yellow you can't take any risks. The shame is that it's not sunny otherwise I would annihilate all my rivals.'

While the Spanish press chose to ignore how Anglade had been stabbed in his back – 'an uneventful day' was *MARCA*'s anodyne description of the stage – the French were forced to admit that beating Bahamontes was now almost impossible. 'It's not complicated,' claimed Rivière. 'Bahamontes has won the Tour.' Langarica, the Spanish team director, did not agree, claiming that Bahamontes' advantage was insufficient for him to be sure of victory. 'If Bahamontes doesn't attack on the last mountain stage, he could lose the lead in the final time-trial,' Langarica warned. But he then explained, presumably tongue in cheek, that Bahamontes had only lost time on the final descent of the Aosta stage 'because he had more to lose than the rest, so had to be more cautious'. Had it not been for the French disunity, though, Bahamontes might have lost the race completely.

Across Spain, and particularly in Toledo, the news that Bahamontes was just days away from winning the Tour de France left few people unaffected. 'When the news broke that Fede had taken the yellow jersey, you could hear the cheers right the way across Toledo,' reported *MARCA*. 'Shop windows across the city were filled with posters congratulating Fede on his victory in the Tour. And the demand for yellow ribbons to pin to lapels was so great that the haberdashers ran out of yellow cloth. One photographer's shop displayed an enormous photo of Fede with a yellow ribbon pinned to his chest. And in Bahamontes' bike shop it was as packed as Charmartin [one of Madrid's two main railway stations] on a cup final day.'

Congratulatory telegrams galore were sent to the team hotels, though Fermina reported that in her one telephone conversation with her husband, the connection had been so poor they were unable to hear each other. However, the couple would soon be reunited as she was heading for Paris in a relative's Seat car, along with the president of the Spanish Cycling Federation, Alejandro del Caz. All that was needed now, of course, was for Bahamontes to win.

If the first Alpine stage of the 1959 Tour was dominated by thunderstorms and French self-destruction, the race's final day in the mountains, from Aosta to Annecy, was a damp squib. Once again, the weather was the main reason. The Col du Gran St. Bernard, the first climb of the day and the most difficult, was shrouded in fog and the riders refused point-blank to attack if it meant risking their necks on the descent. The only excitement came when Gaul started yelling at Bahamontes after a Spaniard, Carmelo Morales, attacked close to the summit. 'His only objective was to stop my rivals gaining any points in the King of the Mountains competition,' Bahamontes primly explained a little later. On the descent, with cars crawling at ten kilometres an hour through the thick fog, the whole peloton regrouped. 'The descent was lethal,' said Bahamontes. 'I had some broken spokes, but I didn't stop for fear of being attacked. Everybody was waiting for a chance to attack me.'

The Forclaz, far shorter, much steeper, but fog-free, did a lot more damage. An attack by Switzerland's Rolf Graf and regional French rider Gerard Saint shredded the bunch to twenty-two with Bahamontes' support reduced to just Morales. It was at this point that Bahamontes, having played it conservatively all day, took the one option still open to him and attacked. Yet again Bahamontes showed that even if the civil war between the French had all but guaranteed him the Tour, nobody deserved the win more. Anglade attempted to follow, but was dropped, thereby proving that for all the French rivalry, in their first and only full-on mountain duel as the two top challengers, Bahamontes beat Anglade hands down. By the summit, with Gaul by his side again, Bahamontes had a two-minute five-second advantage on the field. For once the French rallied round the common cause of helping Anglade, but they only seemed to do so when it was clear he was going to lose. On the descent Anglade's bad luck continued with a puncture. By Annecy, though Graf won the stage Bahamontes had added another sixty-three seconds to his overall advantage. With his recently-arrived trade team boss Fausto Coppi nodding sagely by his side at the finish, Bahamontes pointed out that: 'The French tried it on the first day in the Alps, but in the second they had to admit they were beaten.'

The sixty-nine-kilometre time-trial round Dijon remained, but even if it all went disastrously wrong at least Bahamontes now had an unassailable lead in the King of the Mountains classification. Whatever the final result, he would go down in cycling history as the first rider to take the mountains' title three times. 'I had one bottle of champagne ready to celebrate that particular achievement,' Bahamontes said, 'but I had the feeling I might need a few more.' Anglade, now five minutes forty seconds adrift, was more forthright about his chances. 'What will it take to beat Bahamontes now?' he said to reporters. 'Somewhere between here and Paris I'd need to cut his legs off. That might do it.'

The time-trial was more confirmation of what had been clear since Annecy: that Bahamontes was going to win the Tour de France. The citizens of Toledo continued to dream up more exotic ways of celebrating Bahamontes' victory with the unofficial prize going to the shopkeeper who put a bike in his window with a live eagle perched on top. Bahamontes, meanwhile, prepared for the most important time-trial of his career with a rather more mundane twenty-kilometre training ride through the Bourgogne vineyards. And then he was off. As Bahamontes preferred, Langarica avoided any vocal encouragement from the following car, simply providing him with advice and updates on the number of kilometres covered. At the time, with no radio communication between riders and the team cars, there was no way for Bahamontes could know how his rivals were doing except from the timekeepers' boards at fixed points on the side of the road. There was a brief moment of panic when Bahamontes suddenly slipped to three minutes behind Anglade after fifty kilometres, more than sixty per cent of his overall advantage. However, that was as bad as it got: Bahamontes opened up the throttle and finished ninety-nine seconds down on Anglade, the Tour safely in the bag.

Bahamontes explained later that he preferred only to go all-out at the end of the time-trial 'because if you go hard earlier and start thinking you might be about to crack, that could make you feel even more nervous'. Langarica said: 'He's lost more or less what he should have, but we didn't want to go too hard because the race isn't finished yet.'

As still tends to happen in cycling whenever there is an exceptional performance, certain elements of the press, in this case the Italians, tried to breathe life into some insinuations, albeit minor ones, that Bahamontes was guilty of doping. Even after the time-trial, amid all the euphoria, Langarica felt obliged to respond to these accusations. However, given how clumsy his comments were, he might have been better off saying nothing at all. 'For the record Bahamontes didn't "take" anything,' Langarica said, 'although I'm sure there were other riders who did today.' Now, though, barring one final, marathon stage to Paris in which the leader was traditionally not attacked, the Tour was effectively over.

While Anglade remained in second place overall, the battle for third was far tighter. Finally, despite Rivière taking a second time-trial victory, Anquetil moved on to the podium, displacing Francois Mahe, whose one moment of Tour glory remained leading the race way back in 1953.

The media attention was now all on Bahamontes. Yet while the camera flashes popped, the journalists scribbled away in their notebooks and the praise poured in, there were no tears or emotional tributes to those who had helped him along the way. Instead Bahamontes, despite having sealed the biggest prize cycling could offer, kept his eyes firmly on the financial benefits. One of the first questions he was asked was what he would do when he completed the Tour. Bahamontes' disarmingly frank response was: 'Talk to Dousset to see what kind of criterium money I can get. Anquetil, Rivière, Bobet and Baldini race for a quarter of a million francs each, and I don't want any less.'

His first message to the good folk of Toledo was equally pragmatic: 'Tell the Mayor if he's willing to give me that land he promised me for my house [if I won] then that would be wonderful.'

Chapter Nine
'The Bullfighter on Two Wheels'

From the Nationalist Government's point of view, Federico Martín Bahamontes could not have chosen a better day to win Spain's first Tour de France. The final chapter of the country's greatest individual sporting achievement of the Franco era was written on 18 July, the day the Generalísimo had begun the so-called 'glorious uprising' back in 1936. Fast forward twenty-three years: the newspapers' front pages across Spain carried the usual anniversary photograph of General Franco, complete with thanks to the man who had apparently singlehandedly made it possible for generations of Spaniards to be brought up in an atmosphere of, and to use his words quoted in *MARCA*, 'peacefulness, hard work and renewal'. However, in 1959, in addition to the images of Franco there were huge photographs of Bahamontes pedalling away during the last three hundred and thirty-one kilometres towards Paris and victory.

The treatment of the two subjects by a conservative, traditional newspaper like *ABC* was typical: on its cover it carried a full-size picture of Franco, and inside a lengthy editorial insisting that the Spanish remain 'on guard and alert' against the 'Soviet virus' of socialism and anarchism. 'It has been twenty-three years since the uprising and we can still find new and legitimate reasons to justify it,' *ABC* trumpeted. 'Look how there is barely the slightest difference between the last will and testament of [Russian emperor] Peter the Great and the Communist International Congress' plans

for expansion. But we remain alert and [maintain] the same spirit
. . . of 1936, [fighting] against those who attempted to subjugate
our country to the rule of the hammer and sickle.'

The editorial's aim was clearly to remind Spaniards why Franco
was so good for them politically. But after a series of strategically-
placed advertisements came some of the best evidence about why
Franco had been so good for Spanish sport, too: a picture of a
triumphant Bahamontes in Paris. The subliminal message was
depressingly simple: just as Franco was writing a glorious page in
Spanish political history, now Bahamontes was in the process of
doing the same in sport, approved and overseen by the ruling
regime, of course. No doubt about it: this was a victory signed,
stamped, sealed and sent out from the Nationalist headquarters in
Madrid in triplicate on the tissue-like multi-coloured folios so
beloved of twentieth-century bureaucratic Spain. What else could
be possible, given that the Spaniard had managed to win on such a
hallowed date as 18 July?

The telegram sent by the governor of Vizcaya province to
Bahamontes and Dalmacio Langarica, care of the Spanish embassy
in Paris, shows just how neatly Nationalist and sporting pride
blended together thanks to the '18 July factor'. It read: 'Your
triumph embodies our Spanish pride and our admiration, enthusiasm and praise goes to the hero of the Vuelta [sic] in a victory for
our fatherland that is, above all, [placed] in the indelible context of
such a glorious date.' The tone of the telegram suggests that the
sender might be congratulating one of Franco's generals on
winning a battle against the Communists, rather than the winner
of a bike race. Celebrations for Bahamontes' win became so
absorbed by the anniversary of the Civil War that it effectively
became a political hijacking. Bahamontes quickly discovered this
for himself. When he arrived at the Spanish embassy in Paris during
the evening of 18 July for the *de rigueur* round of congratulations,
it was to find that they were already in the midst of a party to
commemorate Franco's uprising. Bahamontes' success simply
became an excuse for an even bigger and more patriotic fiesta.

'Bahamontes' win made an already beautiful date even more

beautiful,' exclaimed the editorial in *MARCA*, the most important sports daily in Spain outside Catalonia. It then went on to outline how victory in such a non-elitist sport like cycling could transform all areas of Franco's supposedly ideal society. 'Bahamontes' triumph pushes the pedals of the priest as he goes to say mass in a village, of the worker as he goes to his building site, of the road-mender as he goes to work on his stretch of road, of the message boy as he rushes through the streets of Madrid at midnight to the newspaper printer's with this article. Football is too specialised in comparison with cycling. From today onwards, all the bicycles in Spain will be lighter, happier, as if the wind of Bahamontes' triumph were pushing them onwards.'

Looked at with fifty years of hindsight, such claims seem corny at best, sinister at worst: a crass line of Fascist propaganda, idealising the working class and reinforcing the illusion of a harmonious pyramid of a society topped off by a benevolent, beloved dictator. Yet it was difficult to find anything else in the Spanish press. The Madrid daily *Informaciones*, for example, not known for its hard-line pro-Franco stance, had an almost identical presentation of Bahamontes' victory. It started with a speech by Franco and an editorial celebrating the anniversary of Franco's uprising and Spain's successful onward march to economic stability. At the bottom of the front page were photographs of Bahamontes. 'Spain is not rich but it is on the way towards becoming so . . . in twenty years we have done more than in the last hundred,' the editorial claimed. 'With Franco we advance and conquer new international credibility in a world in which Red Imperialism barely had any problems until we, the Spanish, took up arms against them. And now we work in the common task of fighting Communism, whose only real defeat has been at the hands of Franco.' Given Bahamontes' defeat of the French was just underneath these claims it would have been difficult not to associate such political 'victories' with his success. This association continued inside the newspaper. The first report in *Informaciones* was dedicated to Franco's inauguration of the Ministry of Housing headquarters in Madrid and the handing over of 20,931 low-rent, state-owned houses to needy families. Then came a double-page special describing in lurid detail the 'Communist Plot' of July 1936, which Franco's rebellion foiled. And after that it was straight on to the Tour de France, and another feather in Franco's cap.

Curiously enough, Toledo's 'local' newspaper, *El Alcázar*, was one of the rare cases where Bahamontes' victory was afforded a low degree of prominence. But that was down to its early press deadline which meant it could not include pictures from Paris. Instead *El Alcázar* opened with details of a study showing that Spaniards were on average two centimetres taller than a decade before, and continued with a report of military manoeuvres in Castille, complete with photographs of Franco peering at a model landscape and a spectacular fake nuclear explosion, giant mushroom cloud included. A feature on page four reported on the 'crisis in British pubs'. The article claimed in shocked tones: 'The ones in London date from Queen Victoria's time and nowadays have stacks of greasy sandwiches in display cabinets on the bars.' Only now did *El Alcázar* describe the opening section of the final stage into Paris. However, it made up for lost time in the edition of 20 July (no newspapers were published on 19 July) when the front page consisted of a large portrait of Bahamontes. Inside there was a special pull-out that included a first-person piece, 'Fede – how I won the Tour', plus all the details of the celebrations in Toledo, and the first segment of a week-long mini-biography entitled 'This is the Eagle of Toledo'.

Bahamontes' Tour victory was the only sport shown on Spanish television on 18 July, 1959. Not surprisingly, since the footage would have been flown in from France, the fifteen-minute programme of race coverage was shown late at night on the country's one channel. However, the number of people who had access to a television set in 1950s Spain was extremely small, and radio together with the cinema newsreels were a far more important means of communication. Typically, villagers in rural Spain would gather around the *pueblo*'s one radio to listen to major events. Indeed, it acted as a social 'glue'. But the broadcasts were no freer of the shackles of Franco's censorship than any other type of media and his regime was able to exploit shamelessly the success of Bahamontes and other leading sporting stars, most notably the football team Real Madrid. By way of example, in 1955 when Real Madrid won the shortlived Latin Cup tournament, Franco gave the entire team the Imperial Medal of Yoke and Arrows, the symbols of the Fascist Party, as part of his 18 July celebrations.

However, the most significant method by which Bahamontes could be pushed forward as the poster boy of Franco's regime was through the *noticias-documentales*, widely known in Spain as *no-dos*. These were eleven-minute newsreels, produced from 1943 onwards, which were shown before feature films in Spanish cinemas. They were the only newsreels permitted and were an obligatory part of all schedules across the country. 'They were the main access to any kind of information on current affairs for a large percentage of Spain's population,' says Margarita Lobo, an expert in *no-dos* at Spain's Ministry of Culture. 'Given the level of illiteracy in Spain at the time, more than the press, they were the most important form of internal propaganda. People would go to the cinema which, appealingly for an impoverished population, was cheap and warm, for up to seven hours at a stretch, from three to ten, and watch the double bill of films twice over. This meant watching the *no-dos* twice over, too. The *no-dos* were very anodyne and always had the same structure. They would start off with a news item, some kind of inauguration of a building by Franco, say, then be followed by a catastrophe – a bridge collapsing, maybe, or a flood. But this catastrophe would always be in a foreign country, to remind the public that in Spain nothing so awful happened. Then there would be the Spanish news section, more often than not featuring Franco, and finally the "miscellaneous" section, which would include sport.'

Lobo says that Bahamontes would have been obvious, prime-time, *no-do* material in 1959. 'Up until 1950, internationally Spain didn't "exist" because of the boycotts. From the 1950s onwards Spain slowly started to create links with the outside world again, particularly with the United States. As a result, any event [such as winning the Tour] that could be used to bring us closer together was given huge importance. If the *no-dos* exploited any kind of success so intensely, it was because they had very few other options. In Bahamontes' time there were barely any other top-level athletes – perhaps a horse rider or two as well as the gymnast Joaquin Blume [winner at the European Championships in 1957, but whose career was cut short in its prime when he was killed in a plane crash in 1959]. On top of that, if a person did not have a high level of sympathy for the regime then they wouldn't be given as much importance.' That is why Jesús Loroño, for example, rarely appeared in the *no-dos:* nor was Loroño's King of the Mountains title in the 1953 Tour covered, yet Bahamontes crossing the Tourmalet in first place in 1954 was given its own special report.

On 27 July 1959, Bahamontes' victory opened the sports section with paeans of patriotic praise ringing out. 'The most famous race in the world sees a brilliant performance by our Spanish hero, taking our first ever triumph,' the commentator crowed. He then listed Bahamontes achievements (King of the Mountains, a stage win, fourth in the points prize and so on) before finally describing him as a 'bullfighter on two wheels'. A month later, on his return to Spain after the criterium *tournée* ('Triple the number of engagements we expected,' according to his agent, Daniel Dousset), a homage in the comparatively minor city of Mataró, just outside Barcelona, was given headline billing. The film showed Bahamontes receiving rapturous applause in a rather dark outdoor velodrome, Bahamontes receiving a gold watch in recognition of his success, Bahamontes wobbling rather nervously round the track into the gloom. 'He has done twenty-eight criteriums in thirty days,' says the commentator in awed tones, 'and travelled twelve thousand kilometres.' Its position on the *no-dos* news agenda is designed to give the public the impression that in Franco's Spain such successes can almost be taken for granted. But only successes: after the disastrous 1960 tour for the Spanish, the only sports the July *no-dos* covered were a horse race in Hamburg, car racing in Reims and a regatta in Kiel. It was as if the Tour had been cancelled.

However, the bottom line of the authorities' desire to appropriate Bahamontes' triumph and make it a universal success was down to the fact they had absolutely nothing to lose by doing so.

Coming from Castille, Bahamontes was the perfect rider on whom to base the regime's unspoken aspirations. Unlike Loroño or Catalan Miguel Poblet, there was no chance of a region with separatist goals appropriating the victory. Even so, thanks to Langarica's role in Bahamontes' success, fans in the largely anti-Franco Basque Country could join in the fun and enjoy a rare excuse for pro-Spain celebrations. That was equally true in Asturias, one of the staunchest Republican areas in the Civil War but also a cycling heartland. Bahamontes' regular success in their local Tour, with two overall victories and two wins in the King of the Mountains competition, had brought him huge popularity. In the final days before he reached Paris local newspapers had recalled repeatedly that Bahamontes' first major triumph had been in the Tour of Asturias in 1953. Six years later fans poured into the newspaper offices in Oviedo, seeking news from France. As a result, the offices had to be barricaded and loudspeakers installed to broadcast news of the race to those outside.

Bahamontes implicitly recognises that his victory was appropriated by Franco's regime, recalling that when he met Franco, 'the Caudillo [Franco] told me I had planted the Spanish flag at a height it had never reached before.' However he also insists that 'it was a great moment for all the Spanish Communists in France who'd been there since the [Civil] War. They could all come out of hiding and say, "We're proud to be Spanish again"'. As Bahamontes sees it, his victory briefly managed to close the old Spanish Civil War wounds – but politically at least, Franco's propaganda machine, always interested in keeping those wounds open, saw his Tour win very differently, and the winner's personal opinion would barely have counted.

Unsurprisingly, though, Toledo could not be matched for 'Baha-mania'. From the moment he took the lead in Grenoble the streets and shop windows had been plastered in yellow ribbons and the local council put up a giant neon sign over the town hall saying 'Bahamontes King of Toledo'. When Radio Toledo confirmed at 4.40 on the afternoon of 18 July that he had won the Tour outright, the city went Bahamontes crazy. For more than a week the daily post was delivered in vans adorned with yellow ribbons, the market where Bahamontes had worked was similarly decked out and the city's bars re-dubbed the standard 'caña' measure of beer a 'leader' or a 'yellow jersey'. Some doctors' prescription forms even had the words 'Bahamontes will win the Tour' stamped across the bottom. 'All the rockets in Toledo's one pyrotechnics shop have sold out and to judge from the noise here it often sounds like they were all used to celebrate Bahamontes' win at the same time,' said *Informaciones*. 'Every car I see with a Toledo number plate still has yellow ribbons on it,' wrote *El Alcázar*'s columnist German López a few days later, 'and the streets of Madrid are still full of people with Bahamontes flags.' A newsagent in Toledo added: 'All my newspapers are sold, two hours before their usual time. I don't think anybody, as an individual, has ever managed to sell so many newspapers as Bahamontes just because of what he's managed to do.'

Just like the most famous Spanish bullfighters, it was only a question of time before Bahamontes had a '*pasodoble*' (the traditional folksong and dance) dedicated to him. Entitled with predictable unoriginality, 'Bahamontes King of the Tour', and like many *pasodobles* eminently forgettable, the song starts by claiming that 'on his steel steed, he rides towards Paris, what honour and glory will await him there . . .' Dire though it may have been, it was an indication of how deeply Bahamontes' success had struck home in Spain.

The unofficial prize for the most diehard Bahamontes fan, though, must go to Señor Talavera, president of his fan-club in Toledo. Talavera purchased a live eagle and planned to fly with it to Paris so he could release the bird in the Parc des Princes when Bahamontes climbed on to the podium. However, last-minute visa problems meant both he and the eagle remained in Spain.

Even if an eagle from Toledo failed to make it to the Parc de Princes velodrome in time for the finish of the Tour, the Eagle of Toledo himself, resplendent in his yellow jersey, was most definitely present. Yet even as he received the final bouquets of flowers, and Fermina broke down in tears on the stadium steps, Bahamontes insists that the scale of his had not sunk in. 'I don't think it will do, to be honest, until I cross the Spanish frontier,' he said. 'I do know that I won this race more with my head than with my legs.' For all Bahamontes' climbing skills his greatest win did not come just because of his ability to get up mountains faster than anybody else, it was also down to the tactics worked out with Langarica. As Tour director Jacques Goddet pointed out: '[Strategically] he has changed considerably. He is not the rider I used to know. The reputation he has of being a dreamer is no longer valid. I'm sure he's had to keep a handle on his temper and impetuosity at times, too.' Goddet also recognised that Bahamontes had outwitted his rivals by anticipating them, claiming the lead before they expected. 'He moved into yellow a day early, and for that reason on the last day in the Alps he barely had to push himself. If there had been any real battles in the Alps, in any case, he was so strong he would have been at a real advantage. If he had done what he did this year in previous Tours, I'm sure he would have won the race before.'

Bahamontes acknowledged the huge differences Langarica had made in planning his strategies. 'I could never have won with Puig,' he said after the time-trial in Puy de Dôme. 'Langarica was much more intelligent and Puig had never ridden a bike.' Langarica was also more practical. Every evening, without fail, Langarica would go to Bahamontes' room with a copy of the overall classification and the stage route for the next day. It might take hours, but only after they had hammered out an agreement on the strategy to be employed would Langarica get up and leave.

'The French team was tied up in knots by their friendships,' argued *Informaciones*. 'Bidot went for compromise, even if he knew this fantastic "cocktail" of riders would not yield any particular result. Langarica, on the other hand, dispensed with Loroño. And it would be useful to ask all those critics [of that decision] what they think of a result when a Spaniard tops the Tour de France for the first time. The years of [directing the Spanish team by] Luis Puig, incapable of taking the same kind of responsibility that Langarica did, make it clear what the consequences would have been.' Langarica told *Informaciones*: 'I never managed to convince Federico he could win until this year. I could not accept the war that went on inside the Spanish team in 1958. Then, after one man from Vizcaya [Loroño], advised by another man from Vizcaya, said he would not take part . . . a real Spaniard arose, Bahamontes, labelled as being mad and with all that past history of failures, abandons and betrayals. He called me to tell me he would come with me to the Tour, and that's where it all started.' Team-mate Carmelo Morales said simply: 'He would have won more often had he been directed better, sooner, in his career.'

The influence of Fausto Coppi on Bahamontes, for many the most crucial factor in his victory, was only highlighted in the Italian press. The man who Bahamontes said had inspired him to win during the course of a long conversation over the meal in Talavera the previous winter, had been convinced his star rider would take the Tour as soon as the day after the Puy de Dôme. 'My only fear,' Coppi told Italian journalists, 'was that Bahamontes would do something stupid, because of the strange ideas that sometimes run through his mind.'

Bahamontes told *El Alcázar:* 'I had a huge sense of responsibility before the race started. Hadn't I been forced to abandon the Vuelta a España? I knew that everybody would expect more of me, and I expected more of myself. That said, I was a bit hurt by the way the French newspapers only put me as sixth favourite before the start rather than making me an indisputable top favourite. But, in fact, not racing the Giro and being forced to abandon the Vuelta made all the difference. I was a lot stronger and in the mood for a fight. By the time I had won the Puy de Dôme time-trial, the race was practically won. Gaul even came up and congratulated me then, saying, "This year it's yours. Don't let it slip out of your hands".'

The French, predictably, were hammered mercilessly by their national press and fans, who whistled and booed Jacques Anquetil as he stood on the podium in Paris in third place. Apart from pointing out that Bahamontes had defeated four former Tour winners in Jean Robic, Louison Bobet, Charly Gaul and Anquetil, *L'Equipe* added that he had defeated 'French egotism'. The disputes rumbled on, with the blame being placed on the overly conservative approach of Bobet, who was conveniently absent in Paris after his abandon.

Roger Rivière, meanwhile, directed his ire at another of his other team-mates. 'If I had known Jacques Anquetil a bit better I'd have won the Tour,' he said. 'And without Bobet in our line-up, either Jacques or I would have beaten Bahamontes.' He said the French had expected the winner to self-destruct, and that they had under-rated Anglade, even though he was the French national champion. 'We watched everybody we were supposed to – Gaul, Ercole Baldini – but we forgot about Anglade and Bahamontes. The only times we thought about Bahamontes we remembered his eccentricities, which generally end up wrecking his chances. So we let Bahamontes seem to lord it over the rest of us and then we expected Charly Gaul to wipe him out. But instead of that Gaul did nothing and Bahamontes, whom nobody rated, ended up taking the yellow all the way to Paris.'

The French were not the only ones to underestimate Bahamontes. 'We all thought that Bahamontes was just going for the mountain points, and look what happened,' said Baldini, the reigning world champion, and 1958 Giro winner. *Informaciones* summed it up: 'In sporting terms, the Tour has been mediocre. Some of the stars were not up to scratch and others feared to lose what they had. Only Bahamontes has really given it any life.'

André Darrigade shakes his head as he tells me: 'That year it was a disaster.' The Frenchman's green jersey in the race, plus his stunning victory in the World Championships, effectively saved his country's season. He was one of the few riders who willingly sacrificed his chances for his team-mates. 'He was the perfect *domestique* and our default winner,' Bidot said. 'If he had raced more for himself and he hadn't been so unlucky, he'd have won ten more stages.' Darrigade is unfailingly polite and does not make a single disparaging comment about Bahamontes. He seems curiously innocent, too, and fifty years on he still finds it difficult to believe that two of his country's greatest stars could destroy the chances of a third (Anglade) simply because their egos would not let him triumph.

Darrigade watched the greatest team France had fielded in a decade disintegrate in front of him; the only words to describe what he seems to feel are barely disguised despair. 'It was really, really bad. Bobet and Anquetil: that [their relationship] was terrible, and Rivière and Anquetil, that was even worse. Anglade could have won the Tour when he broke away, but Anquetil and Rivière agreed to bring Federico back up to Anglade because they preferred Federico to win. On top of that, Geminiani and Coppi were close friends and don't forget that Coppi was Bahamontes' manager. The rivalry was a problem. Each one preferred Bahamontes to win rather than the rest.'

For Spanish cyclists, Bahamontes' success ended their role in the Tour as a sideshow confined to the mountains. 'Climbers of the calibre of Vicente Trueba and [Julián] Berrendero were known here as the Fleas of the Pyrenees,' recalled leading French journalist Rene Dunan of the winners of the King of the Mountains titles in 1933 and 1936 respectively. 'They only appeared when the Tour approached the mountains near their country, and their victories were applauded all the more warmly because they were clearly without any long-term significance. The Spanish were like marionettes who did their "number" on the stage and then left. They created the legend of the Spanish climber, but they've always been considered eccentrics.' Bahamontes might initially have appeared to be similar to Trueba and Berrendero, but his win brought Spanish cycling up to a completely different level.

On a wider plain, the Tour de France was just one of many examples of progress being made by Spain in 1959. That winter United States President Eisenhower paid his first visit, thereby symbolising the end of the country's political isolation. Severo Ochoa's Nobel Prize for Medicine confirmed that scientifically Spain was no longer a backwater. Economically, too, Spain broke out of the recession that had gripped the country since the Civil War. In the future, 1958 was to become the last of the so-called 'Años de Hambre' [Years of Hunger], and 1959 the first of the 'Años del Milagro', the years of Spain's economic miracle. And this was not just Nationalist propaganda: in 1959 a 'Stablisation Plan' was implemented, backed by the International Monetary Fund, and the peseta devalued; Spain's economic revival began with a radical increase in foreign investment. On the day of Bahamontes' victory, there was also a high-level political meeting in Brussels to decide whether Spain had advanced enough to join the Organisation for European Economic Cooperation, the O.E.C.E. or O.E.C.D. as it was later known. A week later Spain was in.

The biggest development, though, was in tourism. The ending of the requirement for Western Europeans to obtain entry visas that year might not seem an earth-shattering change, but it was to have a huge effect on the travel industry. It opened up the country to package holidays in which Spain would do a roaring trade during the 1960s and 1970s. At the same time Spain began its transition to a far more urban society; the number of agricultural workers fell by half between 1960 and 1976 as they sought better living standards in the towns and cities.

Bahamontes appeared in his last *no-do* as an athlete in 1964 when they recorded an homage to him in Madrid. The newsreel amply reflected the developments and giant strides the country had made in just five years. The film opened with news of a trade centre in Bilbao, then introduced a new long-distance bus 'complete with a bar, a hostess and headphones, just like the best aeroplanes'. A longer feature showed university students going to help out in the country, pitchforking hay and teaching classes of grimy-nailed farmers' wives, 'wiping out the last traces of illiteracy from the country', according to the documentary. If such activities, vehicles or buildings were unthinkable even ten years before, so too was the location of Bahamontes's homage: Madrid's Sports Palace. As he and several other top riders wheeled around a specially-built artificial track on special track bikes, waving to the fans, behind them were advertisements galore: for rum, cigarettes, a festival and even *El Cortefiel*, Spain's first major chain of department stores. Compared to a decade earlier, the opulence and comfort on offer in Spanish society was manifest.

In 1959, though, the fruits of change lay ahead. From the regime's point of view Bahamontes' Tour de France victory was just the sort of image-changing international success the country needed. Apart from an indisputable display of modernity, it was also proof positive that even for the poorest, least developed sectors of Spanish society there was some light at the end of the tunnel after decades of misery and civil conflict. 'Bahamontes represents the transition of a person from the "Spain of hunger" to the "Spain of develop-ment",' historian Manuel Espin said in an interview published on 21 June, 2009, in the newspaper *El Mundo*. 'He took the path from that hard, battered Spain to a nation that started to open up to the world.'

However, no matter what a trailblazer Bahamontes was for cycling in his country, the fact remained that when the Eagle of Toledo finally got his claws into the Tour he was not the young, fresh-faced Anquetil of 1957, or Eddy Merckx in 1969, set to dominate for nearly a decade. Bahamontes was thirty-one. As such, Bahamontes was therefore no pioneer: rather, after years of trying to get the pieces of the jigsaw the right way round, in 1959 the puzzle had finally fallen into place.

And in 1960, while Spain made giant leaps forward in social and economic areas, for Bahamontes it was back to square one.

Chapter Ten
Goodbye to the Vuelta

Federico Martín Bahamontes basked in the glory of the greatest triumph of his career for the rest of the year. However, within months of the start of 1960 it all went sour. He was about to become embroiled in the greatest sporting scandal of his life.

Bahamontes' season had gone askew almost from the start of 1960. Initially it looked as though he was en route to making a fortune by building on his success in the Tour de France. The first setback came when Fausto Coppi's team collapsed when the Italian died in January from malaria. Bahamontes bounced back quickly by signing for Faema, his former enemies, allegedly for the astronomical sum of eight hundred thousand pesetas [£450,000 in modern money] a year. He was not deterred by the presence of Bernardo Ruiz, his old rival, as sports director or having Antonio Suárez, who had attempted to usurp him as top Spanish contender in the Tour the previous year, as a team-mate.

It was just as much of a rollercoaster once he was on the bike. Following a crash on 13 March in the Tour of Levante, Bahamontes spent thirty-six days with his fractured femur in plaster. He returned, after just twenty-five days' training, to win the Arrate hill-climb. Then came the Vuelta a España. It was a race Bahamontes was on the point of not starting because he was ill and had fallen out with his team. Later, on 17 May, he would tell *MARCA* that he had not been able to 'move his guts' since before the start of the race, hence his unwillingness to take part.

But that was only the beginning of his problems. As Chico Pérez writes in *The Vuelta 1935–85:* 'The great Federico was constantly polemical and in only ten days went from the "genius" of Spanish cycling to its *"enfant terrible".*' The Vuelta had barely begun in Gijon when Suárez crashed in the opening team time-trial and suffered major bruising and huge scrapes all over his body (the dreaded road-rash as cyclists call it). Bahamontes also went down in the crash, ripping off half his right thumb-nail. Without Bahamontes wishing it, Suárez's accident had conveniently sidelined his main opposition from inside the team. Then, on stage five from Orense to Zamora, Bahamontes underlined his suddenly improving form and position in the squad by embarking on a long-distance attack. To call it long-distance is actually an under-exaggeration: he was off the front alone for two hundred and forty-three kilometres, the longest single breakaway of his career, and the longest in the history of the Vuelta at that time. But since he was the reigning Tour winner his move was impetuous in the extreme: the peloton were never going to let a figure of his stature establish such a commanding lead so early in the race. Bahamontes was caught thirty-two kilometres from the finish, first by Frenchman Antoine Abaté and then by the bunch. *El Mundo Deportivo*'s headline the next day, 'A genius or a madman?' summed up the general consensus. Likening his 'stupid, useless effort' to the adventures of Don Quixote, the writer's only explanation was 'that like every big star, he has ended up having a psychological dependence on getting into the newspapers'.

Bahamontes' strange attack contributed to a widespread feeling that something was not quite right in the Vuelta. The underlying unease continued even as Bahamontes attempted another dramatic breakaway the next day on the stage from Zamora to Madrid in which he was accompanied by Faema team-mate Fernando Manzaneque. This time the gamble paid off: the move gained almost four minutes on the peloton, and even if the stage win went to an earlier breakaway, the leader's jersey still ended up on the shoulders of Manzaneque. Bahamontes, though, was still twelve minutes down despite those two gung-ho performances. Conscious that he could not lose any more time he fought back hard when

Charly Gaul made his one and only major attack of the race on stage seven, a mountainous trek through the sierras of Madrid. Gaul jumped twenty-one places to fourth overall and ahead of Bahamontes by seventy-four seconds. Despite complaining of an upset stomach, Bahamontes ended the stage with a tenuous lead in the King of the Mountains competition.

The narrow gap between Gaul and Bahamontes briefly raised expectations of a duel between the two mountain kings: however, that particular battle was overshadowed by a more significant turn of events the following day when the entire race started to go off the rails. The stage from Madrid to Zaragoza was an extremely long run, one of five exceeding two hundred and fifty kilometres and seven in a row that were more than two hundred kilometres in length. The riders requested another feeding station mid-stage, and when the organisers refused they went on the first of five major go-slows which turned the Vuelta into a farce. As a result of the first protest the race reached Zaragoza at nearly half past nine at night, two and a half hours later than scheduled. The thirty thousand spectators whistled and booed as the riders inched their way around the finishing circuit. But worse was to come. The near-unanimous apathy continued for another four days. There were isolated incidents of picket-breaking: an eleven-rider break of non-favourites gained a forty-minute advantage over the bunch on the stage into Barcelona; a ten-man break claimed a nineteen-minute advantage on the next stage into Barbastro and, after a rest-day, a four-man break finished twenty-four minutes ahead into Logroño. Just a handful of young Belgian riders seemed interested in racing, and they dominated the overall. The rest of the reduced peloton of forty-seven was effectively on strike, and the race had become, as Chico Pérez put it, 'a total disaster'. Race organiser Luis Bergareche begged the directors to get their riders to do more than pedal mechanically at ridiculously low speeds, but nobody paid him any heed.

Bahamontes and Gaul were now more than fifty-one minutes down on Belgian leader Armand Desmet. 'No "Bahamontes miracle" today', *El Mundo Deportivo* sardonically reported. However, the next stage from Logroño broke the pattern of the previous five days. A breakaway by Bahamontes, all but from the gun, managed to stick this time. Two hundred kilometres later at the finish in San Sebastian he was still ahead of the field with a three-minute twenty-two-second advantage over his closest pursuer. Such a spectacular move could have saved the race's image. However, after four days of trundling across Spain the general mood of disillusion among the press and fans was so great that day-long breakaways like Bahamontes' had a decidedly hollow ring to them. If the rest of the field were so apathetic, what did it matter what one rider achieved? Had Bahamontes opened up a bigger gap on the stage – ten minutes, say, or even twenty – it might have resurrected a sporting corpse. But the organisation shot themselves in the foot. For some reason nobody had bothered to give Bahamontes details of the time difference he had over his rivals as they should have done. Instead, Bahamontes pedalled away for two hundred kilometres with no idea of the effect he was having until he punctured close to the finish. By then, though, it was too late. His stage win strengthened his lead in the King of the Mountains competition and in the race's 'most combative rider' classification. However, since he only moved from twenty-eighth to twenty-first overall this was barely noticed. Bahamontes' answers to the press at the finish – even if they were serious – did little to alter the view that the race had become meaningless. When asked what his objectives had been with such a long attack, without batting an eyelid, he replied: 'To get over the mountains first and finish half an hour ahead of the field. Why not? That's what has happened every day up until now.' When Suárez staged an eight-hour breakaway to win the 'Queen Stage' to Vitoria the following day it gained the same lukewarm reaction from observers. There were even rumours that the race was so discredited there might not be a Vuelta in 1961.

Then, in the early hours of the morning after the Vitoria stage, the news began to circulate that Bahamontes was threatening to stage a 'go-slow' because the organisers were refusing to readmit Julio San Emeterio, Bahamontes' prized *domestique* after he had failed to finish inside the time limit. If carried out, Bahamontes' departure would be a major blow to the race, especially as it came just hours after Gaul had quit stage fourteen for no clear reason other than he could not be bothered to continue. The organisers could ill afford to lose another star. Yet they were faced with a dilemma: if Bahamontes' demands were met, and San Emeterio reinstated, then two other teams, Licor 43 and K.A.S., said they would abandon en masse. With the race already reduced to thirty-four riders the organisers risked either losing Bahamontes or another twelve riders, five of whom were in the top ten. According to Bernardo Ruiz, now Faema director, the reason the teams decided to put the Vuelta organisers in such a position was because they had learnt of Bahamontes' strategy to save his Vuelta and knew that San Emeterio was crucial to it. Bahamontes had deliberately told San Emeterio to take it easy, even if he finished outside the time limit, because the next day they would make a joint attack. Unfortunately for Bahamontes, San Emeterio blabbed about this cunning plan when he finished the stage: small wonder the rival teams did not want to see him start, particularly when they discovered the organisers had initially acceded to Bahamontes' demands.

'I directed Bahamontes that year and he was a man out of control,' Ruiz told me. 'Julio San Emeterio finished outside the time limit in Vitoria and said afterwards that he had taken it easy because he wanted to win the stage to Santander. At first the organisers readmitted him without anyone knowing, but then the other teams got wind of it, protested and they kicked him out again. I went to talk to the director of the Vuelta and I said, "Look, does it really matter to you [if San Emeterio is readmitted or not]? I've got Fede sitting outside your office and he's a shade annoyed about all this. And Bergareche said to me, "Don't get me annoyed about this either. I can't do it because of what San Emeterio has said about winning in Santander".' Ruiz went back to Bahamontes and told him that San Emeterio was out of the race. 'So I said to Federico, "It's not going to happen", and his response was, "Right then, I'm going to finish outside the time limit to see if they exclude me, too". And that's what he did. On the next stage he went deliberately slowly and of course they threw him out. I said to him, "Who the hell do you think you are?"'

Even half a century afterwards Ruiz's anger towards Bahamontes is still palpable to the extent that he talks in the present, as if the controversy had happened yesterday and not in 1960. 'What do you want me to do, [should I] kill him? [During the stage of the go-slow] I give him a couple of riders to bring him up to the front of the bunch and he stops, he tells them to go on, because "I'm going to finish outside the time limit".' And then Ruiz repeats: 'What do you want me to do, kill him?'

The confrontation with Bahamontes, and the general mood of discontent among the riders, was not all the Vuelta had to face that grim morning in Vitoria. On the same day one newspaper ran a story in which Lucor 43 rider Miguel Pacheco claimed he had been 'exiled' from Faema, the team with whom he had initially signed that year, because of his good relationship with Bahamontes. 'I could not imagine my friendship would end up with me being barely considered for races [by Faema],' he said. 'I have been declared an outlaw.' Pacheco claimed that as Bahamontes' decision to join Faema 'was not seen favourably, they took it out on me because I was his friend'. He even said that attempts had been made to bribe Licor 43 so that he would not take part in the Vuelta, and that Faema had formed an alliance with the Belgians to try and squeeze him out of third place overall. Quite apart from highlighting Bahamontes' difficult position in the team, Pacheco's allegations were effectively confirmed on the final stage to San Sebastian when he punctured and the Faema-Belgian alliance tried to eliminate him. Pacheco's claims were the latest bombshell for a Vuelta already cowering under the table, and they did not go down well with the fans lining the roadside and reading their morning newspapers as they waited for the race. After Gaul's abandon Bahamontes remained the main target for the public's dissatis-faction. And given his duel with Jesús Loroño, Bahamontes' popularity was precarious anyway with fans from the Basque Country where the race was due to pass. While news of the

Pacheco story circulated at the start in Vitoria, Bahamontes was in the middle of a blazing row with Bergareche about San Emeterio. As Bahamontes pointed out, in the 1959 Vuelta a similar situation had occurred when Roger Rivière and five members of the Faema team had been allowed back in despite finishing outside the time limit. At the time Bahamontes' protests had gone unheard and he had pulled out of the race. A year later his protests on the start-line were just as fruitless. San Emeterio was also present, ready to start, but Bergareche refused to succumb to what he described as 'blackmail' and threatened to take the case to the Federation. Bahamontes took his appeal to the international *commissaire* for the race, but it did no good: San Emeterio was out and he stayed out.

The stage kicked off with spectators shouting insults at Bahamontes and these increased when they realised that he was about to stage what looked like a deliberate go-slow. The newspaper reports about Pacheco only added to the tension. Around the eighty-kilometre mark, just outside Bilbao near the town of Sollube, Bahamontes could no longer handle the constant jeering and insults and dismounted, bicycle pump in hand.

'He assaulted a group of fans both verbally and physically,' the official report into the incident said later. At that point a pro-Bahamontes supporter intervened in an attempt to calm everybody down. It did not succeed. According to newspaper reports, as well as Antonio Jiménez Quiles's account of events, Bahamontes' team-mate Herrero Berrendero dismounted as well. In the midst of the argy-bargy and shouting he apparently accidently struck the Bahamontes supporter, thinking he was about to attack his leader with a bottle. 'I didn't hit anyone,' Bahamontes told me. 'There's a photograph of me with my arm raised and a pump *about* to strike someone, but I didn't manage to do it. It was Herrero Berrendero and he got the wrong person.' At this point Luis Bergareche intervened and told Bahamontes that he had to go on riding, and reportedly adding: 'If you don't, I will take you to the U.C.I. and I assure you that you will remember me for the rest of your days.' Finally everybody calmed down and the race continued.

If Bahamontes had intended to cause chaos and delays he

certainly succeeded. The fact that thirteen other riders joined him, albeit protesting about something else, was another indication that the Vuelta was coming apart at the seams. 'Half the time we were starving because they wouldn't let us take on extra food,' Jiménez Quiles, who joined the protest, recalls. 'It got to the point where we'd end up stopping, get off our bikes and break into people's houses to rob bread. So that's why I was in that group with Bahamontes that day.'

Keen to see the outcome of the fourteen-rider 'strike', around one hundred and fifty vehicles containing journalists and race followers formed a massive convoy grinding along at snails' pace behind the mini-peloton. But if they could not see much of the race they had no need to worry about getting bored. As the press cars rolled through one village Bergareche and Faema representative Miguel Torelló could be seen standing on the pavement arguing at the tops of their voices. Then, at the entrance to the town of Castro Urdiales the fans' ill-feeling towards Faema and its director Bernardo Ruiz was clearly expressed in a huge poster reading: 'Bernardo: this is a country of *hidalgos*: no traitors here'. Bergareche also ran the gauntlet of spectator protests, which had developed into death threats. After the controversial abandon of another Vuelta rider, Pérez Frances, a poster greeted the race director at the entrance to one town in northern Spain: 'Bergareche: Pérez Frances was born here'. That might have been inoffensive in itself except that the message appeared to be written in blood. Another sign went up in San Emeterio's village, which the Vuelta passed through the day after Bahamontes' exit: 'Bergareche, San Emeterio will be your cemetery'. If anything was designed to make Bergareche feel less favourably towards Bahamontes and the riders in general it was messages like these.

Fifty kilometres from the finish in Santander four of the fourteen realised that they were almost certainly facing expulsion and darted away from the Bahamontes group. They finished between thirty-five and forty-five minutes down on the winner, the Belgian Arthur DeCabooter, twenty minutes or more behind the rest of the field, but more importantly just inside the cut. There was no reprieve for the rest. Like Bahamontes, they were summarily thrown off the race. According to the official inquiry into the stage, as well as some well-publicised accusations from Faema sports director Miguel Torrello, Bahamontes was the ringleader of the rebellion: he had allegedly urged the others to remain with him and even refused any support from his team-mates who had briefly dropped back to try and guide him back to the main peloton. Instead, the report concluded, Bahamontes had continued his two-wheeled protest. Combined with the incident involving the bicycle pump and the fan, there were a multitude of reasons why Bahamontes could not be allowed to continue. Quite apart from anything else the organisers had race regulations of the most mundane kind to back them up: by the finish the Bahamontes group was more than fifty minutes slower than DeCabooter and they were outside the time limit. End of story.

Bergareche told the newspaper *El Diario Montañés:* 'With people like this it is impossible to organise a Vuelta. My only regret is that I tried to do so.' Bahamontes responded in kind: 'With these people [organising it], I'm not racing the Vuelta again.' His defence to the press, which was contradicted by everybody from the organisers to eye-witnesses, was not that he was annoyed about San Emeterio, but that he 'did not feel well and could not go any faster. Do you want me to die on the roadside just because the race is going to Bilbao?'

The organisers were not the only ones upset by the scandal. Antonio Anglade, Faema's chief executive, said he was 'obliged to consider' withdrawing sponsorship of the team, as well as expressing 'displeasure at what has happened'. He added: 'These events are far beneath the category of this race and the dignity of this sport.' *El Mundo Deportivo* summed up the prevailing mood: 'Bahamontes has not known how to digest the huge number of homages and tributes he gained after his phenomenal win last year and he believes he can wreck the essence of this sport. There is a path to take for every rider who does not consider himself a demi-god: either withdraw from the race or withdraw from his profession.'

The Vuelta itself was in major trouble. Quite apart from the fact that only around a quarter of the starters made it to the finish, the winner Frans De Mulder was a Belgian of very little standing whatsoever. His winning margin of fifteen minutes from another team-mate, Armand Desmet, confirmed the abysmally low level of competition in the race.

If Bahamontes' reputation was damaged, the long-term financial consequences were minimal. Though the Vuelta's official communiqué confirmed he had been excluded from the race, the Federation's investigative committee fined him the risible sum of twenty thousand pesetas and declared the case closed. If Herrero Berrendero was involved in the fracas with spectators, as Jiménez Quiles claims, that was not even mentioned. There have been suggestions that Bahamontes was too important a figure, after his Tour de France win, for the Federation to mete out the level of suspension he probably deserved. But the Tour was less than a month away and for the defending champion not to go to France was unthinkable.

Yet there was a price to pay for letting him walk away from the Vuelta of 1960 all but unscathed: Bahamontes had been allowed to put one over on his country's cycling authorities. Giving one rider that much unspoken power was not the wisest strategy, particularly in view of the way he had already behaved in the Vuelta. 'Everything that happens here is a consequence of his personal interpretation [of events] or a consequence of his absence,' *El Mundo Deportivo* complained the day after his expulsion. In a lengthy interview with *Alcázar*, Bahamontes denied that he had even got off his bike and that, contrary to what the photograph published in *ABC* suggested, he had not planned to hit a spectator on the roadside. Somehow Bahamontes managed to draw his old enemy Jesús Loroño into the conflict, claiming that the person he was gunning for was 'an individual in Loroño's team car who had been laying into me for three or four days'. Bahamontes also claimed that Faema director Torrello had only warned two of the riders in the go-slow protest that if they did not reach the finish within time the jury would show no mercy and they would not be allowed to start the next day, and he was not one of them. 'I am ill,' he said, 'and that's why I was unable to race properly. I should be able to cure myself. If they ask me to do the Tour, I'll go, but that doesn't depend on me.'

Whoever was right or wrong, the failure of those in authority to punish Bahamontes more stringently was an admission of their dependency on him for results. However, if the short-term consequences were minimal or even beneficial to Bahamontes, in the longer-term they had a considerable knock-on effect: the events of May 1960 saw a definitive rupture between the rider and Spanish cycling. Except for a final, low-key appearance in the 1965 Vuelta, Bahamontes never returned to his country's biggest race; from 1961 he spent the last four and a half years of his career in foreign squads.

The clearest indication of what the Bahamontes affair meant in the wider political arena came from the reaction of Franco's regime: they simply blanked him of their *no-dos*. He only made fleeting appearances in the big-screen documentaries during 1963 and 1964; as Margarita Lobo, the *no-do* expert, pointed out, anyone who failed to deliver the goods disappeared from view. In the newspapers, never again would Bahamontes be hailed as the social and sporting example to follow in the unqualified way he was in 1959. Instead the old labels of the 'unpredictable genius' were revived to describe him, and they stuck for the rest of his career. 'Physically Bahamontes is gifted for racing, but mentally he is not at the same level,' claimed *MARCA* in 1963. Later that summer, after an equally controversial Tour, *ABC* described him as having 'justified fame as a champion, but at the same time [also] for being over the top and abnormal'. The authorities were no more sympathetic. 'Any problem can affect his nervous system,' Federation president Alejandro Del Caz said. 'He is like a child and has to be treated as such.'

As for the Vuelta, it never reached such a low point again, not even in 1978 when protests by Basque separatists forced the last stage to be cancelled. As *MARCA's* special correspondent wrote: 'The 1960 Vuelta is over: may God forgive it.'

★

If Bahamontes turned around both his season and his career after a disastrous Vuelta in 1959 by his performance in the Tour, there was to be no repeat in 1960. Quite the opposite, in fact. 'The Eagle of Toledo has become a corn-fed chicken and corn is all he has in his head,' Tour director Jacques Goddet said after Bahamontes pulled out on the second stage in France. 'He has lost his honour as a cyclist and has shown himself to be unworthy of the attention he received last year from his compatriots who were so proud to have a Tour winner in their midst. [The Eagle] has let himself be stripped of his plumage without any desire to put up a fight.'

Indeed, Bahamontes was a shadow of the 1959 champion. After losing time early on during the second stage across northern Belgium to Malo les Bains in Dunkirk due to a mechanical problem, Bahamontes began drifting out of the back again in the final hour of racing the same day. 'I couldn't respond when the peloton accelerated,' he recalled later. 'My guts hurt too much.' The constant bashing along the cobbled roads of north-west Flanders that day probably made any pain even worse. Eight riders from the fourteen-man Spanish team stayed with him for support, but it was no good. Forty-five kilometres from the finish Bahamontes slowed to a standstill, wrapped himself in a blanket and sat down by the side of the road. Then, for the second time in four years, the last his team-mates saw of him was a gaunt, dejected figure, slumped in the back of the race's 'broom wagon'. His compatriot's noisy attempts to persuade him to continue had failed, though this time there were no appeals to his patriotic duty or loyalty to his wife. Those minor details apart, history really was repeating itself.

It is not difficult to understand why Goddet was so furious: Bahamontes' abandon so early left the Tour director without the leading favourite for no clear reason other than a lack of motivation; for a former Tour winner to act like that was nothing short of treachery. Physically, for all he claimed his stomach hurt, Bahamontes did not seem to be in bad shape. Unlike 1957 there were no wasp stings, no reports of sunstroke or suspect injections. Nor did anybody see this one coming: Bahamontes had finished with the main bunch in the first section of the opening stage, between Lille and Brussels. Though he lost nearly three minutes to Anglade and Britain's Tom Simpson, so too had Rivière, for example. And while he lost nearly four and a half minutes to Rivière in a twenty-seven-kilometre time-trial on the race's second section in the afternoon, that was only slightly more than he had lost to the Frenchman in the final time-trial at Dijon during the 1959 Tour.

Again, with the benefit of hindsight there was perhaps one indication of what was to come: Bahamontes' anger at team-mate Fernando Manzaneque because he had misunderstood a race official's instructions and as a result the Spanish team leader had to start the time-trial earlier than he wanted. Instead, Bahamontes had to roll only a few minutes after eating his lunch, the time when his digestive system apparently hurt the most and he found it harder to pedal. But the team, it seemed, had no real idea that anything was wrong right up until he decided to pull out. 'If the doctors don't know what's wrong with him, how am I expected to know?' Team trainer Julián Berrendero fumed over the phone to a journalist that night. 'He's sitting in his [hotel] room refusing to eat anything but pills.' Team-mate Rene Marigil added: 'It's incomprehensible that he abandons like this. If he was so ill he shouldn't have asked the rest of us to lose time as well. All of us, barring three Spanish riders, stayed back with him.'

If everyone was at a loss for an explanation it was hardly unfamiliar territory. This was Bahamontes' fourth controversial Grand Tour abandon in just over three years and his enemies were quick to take advantage. 'It is just like 1957 all over again,' his old director Luis Puig said, 'except there is less of a show than there was back then. But the substance of the matter is the same.'

On one point at least Puig was wrong. The scandal in Spain surrounding Bahamontes' latest premature exit was far larger than three years before: Bahamontes was the country's first Tour winner after all. His victory then was supposed to be representative of the new, dynamic, prosperous Spain. Instead, the grainy agency photographs which appeared in the next day's newspapers showed an ill-looking rider in Spanish team kit, clearly ignoring the cameras and jammed into the back seat of what looked like an Army jeep. It gave Bahamontes the appearance of a war refugee trying to clutch on to the last shreds of personal dignity as his world collapses around him; certainly not that of a top athlete or the poster-boy for Spain's international success.

Neither did Bahamontes' behaviour in France on the way home do anything to deflate the sense of national disquiet. After catching a train in Dunkirk to Paris he stopped off at his friend Jacques Daudé's restaurant. There an immaculately suited Bahamontes was photographed drinking some light soup. It was the only thing, he claimed, that his stomach could handle at the time. However, he looks perfectly healthy in the picture which was exactly what he did not need if he wanted the Spanish authorities to feel better disposed towards him. The photograph is odd for another reason: the presence of Swiss rider Willy Trepp, the only other occupant of the broom wagon when Bahamontes abandoned. For some bizarre reason he stayed with the Spaniard the next day, too, all the way to Daudé's restaurant. It contributed to the sense that something was out of place, but nobody knew quite what. This time, though, the Federation was not going to let Bahamontes off the hook so lightly.

No sooner had Bahamontes set foot in Spain than he was summoned to the Federation by its president, Alejandro Del Caz. Bahamontes turned up for the appointment half an hour late, but even he was not able to avoid the formal, full-scale inquiry into why he had abandoned. As usual with Bahamontes, the reasons for pulling out never quite added up. One of the more surreal stories behind his Tour-start-and-instant-abandon was the case of the poor translation service. Del Caz had apparently tried to get in touch with Bahamontes in France five days before the race began. Bahamontes had arrived early to see a doctor to try and sort himself out, though he later claimed he was taking part in criteriums. Del Caz called to tell him he had to return to Madrid for the obligatory pre-Tour medical check-up. However, Bahamontes was unreachable, and Del Caz was sidetracked into talking to a

Tour de France official who apparently assured him that Bahamontes was well enough to start the Tour. It emerged later that Del Caz had little idea what the official was telling him. The conversation had been in French and by the time the official translator was roped in, Del Caz had already got it into his head that he was being told Bahamontes was in good shape. By the time the opposite was discovered to be true Bahamontes was out of the Tour and on his way home. This could have reflected badly on Del Caz, of course, except Bahamontes was equally insistent that things had been going fine. How could he possibly have wanted to start a race, Bahamontes said, if he knew he was going to have to abandon so soon? Bahamontes pointed out he had even paid twenty thousand francs (around £10,000 today) to the French doctor who saw him before the Tour to ensure all was in order. (There are unconfirmed reports this was Dumas, the Tour's own medic.) Even after the opening time-trial, Bahamontes was still telling journalists that his stomach pains had disappeared.

However, there were wheels within wheels: much later Bahamontes claimed that he had been under massive pressure from the Federation to start the Tour, which he had not wanted to do. Others, he argued, should have read the signs correctly and noticed, for example, that he had finished nine minutes down on the leaders in the Tour des Pyrenees, a warm-up race immediately before the Tour. 'I shouldn't have started,' Bahamontes said. 'I felt really bad, as bad as in the Vuelta. But I wanted to please everybody.' Neither the last-minute trip to Paris to try and cure a stomach upset that had plagued him since the Vuelta, nor the few days' rest in Melun at Jacques Daudé's country house, did much to solve the problem. The key point, though, was that there was too much at stake for Bahamontes *not* to start. The Spanish authorities were so keen to have Bahamontes in the Tour line-up that they were prepared to bend their own rules over the obligatory check-up and assume a French official was telling them what they wanted to hear about his condition. While Bahamontes knew he was ill he felt obliged to start. Berrendero, who had the least to lose over the whole affair, thought it was nothing to do with illness or cramps, 'just that our *vedette* [diva] had a real attack of nerves. It was completely out of the ordinary.'

Meanwhile, as the Spanish newspapers ran full-page photographs of Bahamontes' abandon, it seemed that everybody had an opinion, which they were invited to express. One magazine, *Información*, even placed advertisements in the daily newspapers asking readers 'from Madrid, Toledo and Spain', to send in their reactions for a special edition about the issue.

Over the years another possible contributory element to his untimely exit has emerged. Following disagreements a year earlier, it seems the night before the start in Lille an unwilling Bahamontes was forced to sign a deal with his team-mates over how prize money would be shared out. Could the answer to the Bahamontes question have been financial? Bahamontes has denied that he had been paid a prime by the Tour organisers to start that year, so there was no initial slice of the cake for the others to have. Luis Otaño, for one, said that he received his correct share from the 1959 race. However, if disputes over money did affect Bahamontes, it would not be the last time financial disagreements tipped the balance when it came to him pulling out of races of whatever size. It is perhaps worth noting, too, that when Del Caz gave Bahamontes a public roasting in the Federation's offices, one of the things he berated Bahamontes for was putting financial interests above representing Spain.

What is most striking about how the Federation dealt with Bahamontes is their total lack of faith in what he told them. From the word go they insisted on seeing the reports from the French medic who had examined Bahamontes before the race to compare them with their own doctors' analyses. At one point this was not going to be just a physical check-up, either: Del Caz wanted Bahamontes to see a psychiatrist. Initially the Federation president had defended Bahamontes, but he ended up roundly criticising him for failing to communicate with the Federation in the run-up to the Tour. As the scandal grew, any sympathy for Bahamontes evaporated completely.

However, unlike 1957 when it was relatively straightforward for the Federation to give Bahamontes the green light again, this time their investigation was exhaustive. He was poked and prodded by nine different doctors, from specialists in the heart and lungs, ear, nose and throat, the digestive tracts, the stomach, as well as an ophthalmologist, the Federation's head of medical services, a family surgeon and another medic with unspecified skills. They found four specific physical problems: breathing, chronic throat and sinus infections and dyspepsia, which produced large quantities of wind. None of these were exactly life-threatening even if combined, as Bahamontes claimed, with a major dental trouble. Bahamontes later revealed that he was suffering from caries in four canine teeth and had to have them removed in the aftermath of the Tour. Strangely, given how thoroughly he was investigated, this operation was not mentioned anywhere in the official report. However, when the problems were combined they were enough for the Federation to 'declare him useless', as *ABC* rather cruelly put it, and take away his racing licence. That effectively barred him from racing in any of the profitable post-Tour criteriums had there been any invitations in any case. Typically, Bahamontes was so annoyed his licence being withdrawn that he initially refused to apply to renew it. It was thanks to his wife that his career did not finish there and then. 'Finally it was Fermina who did it,' Bahamontes recalls. 'She and [Bahamontes business associate] Evaristo Murtra, went and got the licence sorted out again behind my back. Evaristo told me later he knew that was the only way it would get resolved – if Fermina did it.'

The Federation turned a blind eye when he made his return to racing on 31 August, four weeks earlier than he was supposed to. However, his performance in the two-day GP Priego de Cordoba was a minor triumph. Though it was hardly a major race, Bahamontes took both stages, the King of the Mountains classification and the overall. Suddenly it looked as though a strong end to the season was in prospect. The looks were deceptive. In the Spanish regional championships, his final race of the year, Bahamontes made another abandon described in the press as 'incomprehensible and unjustified'. Bahamontes' three-man

Castille squad were the reigning champions in the team time-trial event held in front of a huge home crowd in Madrid's Casa del Campo park. However, after the first four of eight laps the Castillians were losing time and were ninety seconds down on the time set by the Catalans. They were still just about on course for a respectable result until first Fernando Manzaneque and then Bahamontes lost contact with team-mate Suárez for reasons none of them were prepared to explain. In Manzaneque's case, the local media claimed it was a lack of general fitness. Indeed, he collapsed on the side of the road and needed medical assistance. Suárez and Bahamontes raced on without Manzaneque, and with a minimum of two riders required to finish could still have defended their title. But rather than work together the two longstanding rivals began racing on opposite sides of the road. Suárez finally dropped Bahamontes and continued alone. Bahamontes then abandoned and cunningly left Suárez and Manzaneque to face the outraged fans at the finish by flinging his bike into the back of a car and driving off. His high-speed getaway probably neatly summed up his feelings about 1960: he could not get away from it quickly enough.

Why Bahamontes should have cracked so badly in the two most important events of the year was probably down to a lack of external guidance. The two biggest factors missing from his life in 1960 were his directors: Fausto Coppi died and Dalmacio Langarica was unavailable to manage the national squad in the Tour. He had resigned on 21 May, 1960, telling the press it was because of expanding business in the bike shop he owned. That did not stop him returning to directing later on, though, with the legendary K.A.S. squad. Bahamontes has always maintained that these two individuals were the keys to his racing success, albeit in different ways: Coppi had inspired him to win the Tour; Langarica had shown him how to do it. Crucially, Bahamontes respected them both in a way he never did Luis Puig or Bernardo Ruiz.

In the 1960 Vuelta with Faema, it is arguable that Bahamontes' volatile personality, combined with his increased sense of self-importance after the Tour win, was a fatal combination. His ego would not let him accept that one of his main support riders could be eliminated from the race. Having Ruiz, his old enemy, as director can only have heightened the tension inside the team. As far as the Tour was concerned, it seems Bahamontes underestimated his own problems.

However, with his worst season following hard on the heels of his most outstanding one, not even Bahamontes could avoid the key question: how on earth was he going to put his career back on track?

Chapter Eleven

Exile

André Darrigade is a gentle, softly-spoken man who is keen to please. As he talks he springs around the room, dragging out boxes and bulging envelopes containing mountains of photographs from the time when he was a friend and team-mate of Federico Martín Bahamontes. His office in the well-appointed bungalow in one of the more chic areas of Biarritz is crammed from floor to ceiling with trophies, medals and pictures of his victories. And they are not from the smallest of races. The winner of a staggering twenty-two stages from fourteen starts in the Tour de France, as well as being the 1958 world champion, Darrigade was one of France's greatest cyclists. A sprinter by profession, he won the opening stage of the Tour five times out of a possible six: not even Mark Cavendish, the 2011 World Champion and unquestionably the fastest rider of modern times, has matched that yet.

Even half a century on, and with limited contact between the two, Darrigade still feels a great deal of affection for Bahamontes, who was a respected colleague in the French Margnat squad for four years from 1962 to 1965. Darrigade's presence was a key reason why Bahamontes stayed so long with the team and did not keep switching at the end of each season as he had done before. For the first time in his professional career he felt sufficiently appreciated to want to stay. With a team-mate like Darrigade that is hardly surprising. Bahamontes once told me that Darrigade was his 'only friend among the foreigners in the peloton'. Darrigade recalls: 'We liked him, we really did. He wouldn't shut up, but he talked to everybody. He was a good rider. He could be cunning strategically and he wasn't the type who'd go out and party on stage races. In fact, I can remember him once ordering the entire team to get to bed.'

The universally popular Darrigade was a top sprinter who could climb well. But he was also a superb *domestique* to the extent that he was sometimes criticised by directors for sacrificing his own chances to help the team's overall contenders. It was rare to find that degree of selflessness in the cut-throat world of cycling in the 1950s and 1960s. 'There was never a problem with Fede as a leader,' Darrigade told me. 'I'd do my work for the team and then I'd sprint, too. I did that for Anquetil, for Bobet and I did it for Federico. If he was ahead in the mountains, I'd try to slow down the rest [by chasing down counter-attacks], including Anquetil.'

As a heftily-built, tall sprinter, Darrigade's principle role within the team was to take care of Bahamontes ahead of the mountains, guiding him through the pack. By positioning himself just ahead of Bahamontes he could ensure that his leader had plenty of elbow room and would not get blocked in. 'It was difficult for Federico,' Darrigade says. 'Without me he'd have had to try to find enough space by himself. That's why he lost so often with the Spanish because they wouldn't pay him much attention. He was particularly vulnerable in side-winds and in echelons and he'd invariably lose time there in the north, in Belgium. So when he got to the mountain stages he'd be out of touch. I could warn him when problems were coming up. I would look at the maps and warn him what was going on, right down to looking at the width of the road. It was the kind of stuff I'd done with Anquetil countless times.'

Like Miguel Poblet, Darrigade says that Bahamontes post-1962 was a different rider than in his younger days. 'Federico was willing to learn new tactics, like when he went training for an hour in 1964 before the start of a big mountain stage in Andorra, and he did the same again in Luchon the next day. Even before the stage started, he'd ridden over the Peyresourde pass to warm up. And as I knew

Anquetil and Poulidor really well, I could tell how they were feeling and pass that information on to Federico, too.' Both Darrigade and Bahamontes point out that their new director at Margnat, former French professional Raoul Remy, was another catalyst in Bahamontes' renewal. Unlike Fausto Coppi, Remy was not a pioneer in terms of technology. But he did not have to be. Some of the changes Remy introduced were very straightforward, and quickly integrated, but they produced major results. For instance, in 1963, he suggested changing the gearing on Bahamontes' time-trial bike, so that he used a fifty-three-inch chain-ring rather than a fifty-two; it enabled Bahamontes to improve significantly when riding against the clock. Astute signings, such as bringing Darrigade and Jean Grazyck into the team, took longer to engineer but were equally beneficial.

Darrigade repeatedly expresses his incomprehension that Bahamontes had received such poor support from the Spanish in the past. He partly blames Bahamontes, though, saying: 'It was in his character.' Things changed at Margnat after the Tour returned to trade teams rather than national squads in 1962. 'He was our leader,' says Darrigade. 'We knew he could win the Tour, so he got a team that worked with him. *C'est normal, non?*' However, as Darrigade emphasises, by now Bahamontes was thirty-four and within sight of retirement age for a professional. 'The tragedy was that it all happened too late.'

Bahamontes' career can be characterised as a series of brilliant flashes interspersed with sudden, dramatic falls from grace. However, after the turmoil of 1960 he went through a comparatively calm patch for two years which led to some of his most consistent and impressive results. The most significant development during 1961 and 1962 was that Bahamontes discovered that even at his age, and after a two-year absence from the race, he still had it in him to go for the overall classification in the Tour. Equally importantly, he also found that he was far better off in a French trade team than in any Spanish squad at the time. Neither discovery was straightforward: Bahamontes missed the 1961 Tour because his trade team, the Italians V.O.V., did not have the money to enter. In his one Grand Tour that year, the Giro d'Italia, he abandoned, citing injuries, though it later transpired the team had been unable to pay its riders for the entire season. If leaving a team because of money problems was not new to Bahamontes – he had run up against similar problems when he raced for Tricolfilina and would again, he claimed, in his final year with Margnat – he did not simply turn his back on the foreign option, as he might have done before. Rather than return home to ride for, say, Faema, Bahamontes decided to stay abroad in 1962 and join the French team. 'I was respected more outside Spain than in it,' he explains. He was also able to stipulate some basic conditions in this contract: he would not ride in the Classics as he had been forced to do with V.O.V; a definite ride in the Tour de France; plus the signing of a loyal *domestique*, Juan Campillo.

In a sense the decision to stay abroad was the culmination of an ongoing process that began with Dalmacio Langarica and the Tour in 1958. Bahamontes had realised then that with the right tactics, and the right man in the driving seat as sports director, he could do more than just win the King of the Mountains prize. But after changing his attitude towards the Tour even more after Coppi's insistence that he could win it, 1960 proved Bahamontes was as good at forgetting advice as he was at taking it on board. However, in 1961 he lurched back towards taking a more objective, less impulsive approach to racing. After the 1960 debacle it seemed he might be changing for good on a personal level. 'Federico was very different in his later years, very different,' recalled Miguel Poblet. 'When he started racing, and we were sharing rooms, he was a right tearaway. You couldn't teach him anything. I remember at some point, in some race, we started being given these clear plastic cards, and I'd rip out the page of the route book and put it inside them. Bahamontes was lying on his bed, and he says, "What's that? Can you do me one please?" So I did. And when the race was over I ask him how using the card had gone. And he said, "What card? It's still in my jersey. I don't understand it at all!" That was Bahamontes in his early years. Later on, the more he raced, he got more sophisticated. He was willing to learn. There was a transformation over three or four years. It made sense because either you changed or you'd have to be a numbskull and Bahamontes was never a numbskull. He just liked to say what he thought.' One thing did not change, though, according to Poblet: 'He was very disorganised in the hotel room. His suitcase was so chaotic you'd have to walk round it on tiptoe and get the *soigneur* to come and clear it up. But he was growing up all the same. With age he got a whole lot sharper.'

Bahamontes' various analyses of the advantages of being with Margnat vary wildly: while he admits in his account of the 1959 Tour that he had a better structured season with the French team, and that Remy was a great director, on other occasions when asked if he ever had a good team, he responds categorically: 'Never.' He elucidates: 'In the companies [teams] I joined, if there were [good riders], they didn't pay them, so they weren't there long. In a sporting sense it was always a disaster. If I'd ridden with [the legendary Spanish team of the 1960s] K.A.S., I'd have won more than one [Tour].' It is certainly true that in 1962 Margnat did not have a strong squad, underlined by the fact that they had only three finishers in the Tour, one of them Bahamontes. To their credit Margnat brought in some top reinforcements in 1963 as Bahamontes had requested.

At the same time Bahamontes recognises that going to Margnat solved a dilemma: it meant he did not risk offending either of the two top Spanish teams, K.A.S. and Ferrys. 'Margnat was the team who paid the best,' he says. 'They all turned up in Toledo – K.A.S., Ferrys and Margnat – with offers of half a kilo [five hundred thousand pesetas – £210,000 in today's money] each. I had a letter and a verbal offer from Raoul Remy [at Margnat] and I said to myself, "If I race with Ferrys, then K.A.S. will race against me all season; if I race with K.A.S., then Ferrys will be against me". So it was neither K.A.S. nor Ferrys; I was off to France. I took Juan Campillo with me [in 1964] and Antonio Blanco [in 1964]. I went for 475,000 pesetas a year, [£200,000] which was less than I'd get in a Spanish team. But the difference was they even paid my social security.' On top of that, he points out, as a 'foreigner', he could charge start money for races in Spain, which was apparently impossible if he was racing with a local squad.

One race Bahamontes did not ride again was the Vuelta. After the events of 1960 that probably suited both sides perfectly. Since his Tour win he had a lot to lose in smaller races he would be expected to win, and little to gain. In France, though, he could concentrate on the Tour with a squad who would support him. After a comparatively lacklustre 1961, Bahamontes' return to the Tour in 1962 followed an impressive first half of the season. Just as in 1961, Bahamontes hit the ground running. Whereas twelve months earlier his successes petered out after he abandoned the Giro when his old femur injury played up, in 1962, the good results stretched into July and beyond.

Bahamontes' return to form started with memorable victories in the Mont Faron time-trial and road race. 'I told my team-mates that when we got to Toulon [at the foot of the climb] they could go to the hotel and I'd handle the last part myself.' It was no idle boast. Just as the year before he won two hill-climbs back-to-back near Nice. But this time he followed them up with wins in May and June, on the Arrate hill-climb for a fifth time, then in a stage in the Tour of Romandie, widely used as the warm-up race for the Giro d'Italia. Even more encouragingly he was fourth and King of the Mountains in the week-long Dauphiné Libéré, France's third biggest stage race after the Tour and Paris-Nice.

'He was in great shape in the Dauphiné Libéré,' confirmed fellow Spaniard José Bernárdez. 'If he was brave enough to descend fast then he'd be unbeatable. But I don't think he's a match for Anquetil and Van Looy's strong teams.' *MARCA* was wary about Bahamontes' Tour chances, saying that he was 'in great shape, but we'll have to give it a couple of stages to see what his real condition is like'.

MARCA's caution proved to be wise. On the opening stage from Nancy to Spa, a front group of twenty-three containing all the race favourites barring Bahamontes and Gaul, gained a massive margin.

While Gaul lost two minutes, Bahamontes finished seven minutes forty-two seconds down with just Campillo supporting him. It was not quite game over but it was definitely not the return to the Tour for which Bahamontes had been looking.

Most of the media attention centred on the post-stage bust-up between Belgium's sprint legend Rik Van Looy and stage winner Rudy Altig, the Vuelta champion. But the Spanish journalists were waiting for Bahamontes, who informed them he had been caught out. 'We rode well but the bunch split. It was hot and we were unlucky,' was Bahamontes' facile explanation. This time, though, Bahamontes did not just abandon and go home. He simply continued to lose chunks of time here, there and everywhere: ninety seconds to Jacques Anquetil on stage two's time-trial; six minutes on the first section of stage seven to Henry Anglade and Tom Simpson; and three minutes to Anquetil in the afternoon time-trial the same day. The totals were adding up and Bahamontes had little to say to the press apart from bland clichés: 'The important thing is to stay close to the front,' he said after one stage; 'The Spanish are doing well, I'll try to do something in the mountains,' after another. Perhaps more notably, he recognised that Luis Otaño and Antonio Suárez 'are the ones defending our country the best'.

There were parallels to his disastrous performance in the first part of the 1956 race when he found himself even further behind the frontrunners. But unlike six years before this Tour was following a standard pattern rather than being what Brian Robinson called 'a blank sheet every day where you never knew what was going to happen'; it was going to be harder for Bahamontes to regain time. There were occasional attacks which raised hopes and when he chased down a break at the finish of the stage into San Malo it earned him his first mention of the race in L'Equipe. There were also brief flashes of the old self-confidence. As Raymond Poulidor recalls, Bahamontes would be telling riders when and where on the course he would eliminate them. In 1962 it was not just the more impressionable Tour rookies like Poulidor who could receive their marching orders from the Eagle of Toledo, it was big names like Rik Van Looy, too. 'Van Looy was attacking every single stage with his famous Red Guard. We got to the foot of the Pyrenees racing at 45 k.p.h. all the way from the start,' Poulidor told me. 'Then on the morning of the first Pyrenean stage we're all there at the signing-on, me, Van Looy and Bahamontes . . . and Bahamontes goes up to Van Looy and says, "You, this evening, you're on the train out of here. It's me that's got the keys to the race now". And, sure enough, that day Bahamontes was on the attack in the Pyrenees and that evening Van Looy was on the train, just like Bahamontes had told him.' And that was Bahamontes' level of confidence on an average Tour.

More than half the Tour had passed when the race finally headed into the Pyrenees and Bahamontes duly took off. He went over the Tourmalet, Aspin and Peyresourde in first place. It was as spectacular a performance as any of his earlier mountain rides and earned him the front cover of *MARCA* with the headline: 'The Eagle Takes Flight Again.' However, while it racked him up a healthy twenty-three-point lead in the King of the Mountains competition, in terms of the overall it was all but meaningless. Caught by Rolf Wolfshohl on the Tourmalet's descent, and again on the Aspin, Bahamontes was duly reined in sixty kilometres from the top of the Peyresourde. Game over. 'When you see that [Robert] Cazala, a sprinter who got over middling-size hills in reasonable shape, won the stage, that just about sums it all up,' Bahamontes fumed. 'I couldn't have won. To go on would have been crazy.' Next up, though, was an 18.5-kilometre mountain time-trial from Luchon to Superbagnères, one of Bahamontes specialities and he duly delivered. But though he won the stage by eighty-five seconds over race leader Josef Planckaert, and gained seven minutes on the Belgian overall, he was still nearly twelve minutes behind the yellow jersey and remained pessimistic. 'I can't win, it's impossible,' he said. 'I've taken ninety seconds on Anquetil, but he'll regain six minutes on me in the time-trials.' As was so often the case in Bahamontes' mind, others were responsible for the situation. 'My team isn't sufficently strong for me to pull this off,' he claimed, 'though I'm ready to say that I prefer it to the one that was with me in 1959.' Bahamontes may have been critical of the Margnat team but they were not as weak as he made out: Otaño, for example, was lying fifth overall after Superbagnères.

Unhappily, the Alps lost their relevance for Bahamontes in terms of the overall before he even reached them. Like Otaño, he lost a huge amount of time the day after his stage win and trailed into Carcassonne more than thirteen minutes down on all the other favourites. Having praised him for his classy performance during the two days in the Pyrenees, *MARCA* now highlighted his erratic nature, saying: 'He is a formidable rider – he gets formidable wins, then formidable defeats.' This tongue-in-cheek attitude was reinforced when they dragged up an old anecdote in which Bahamontes had apparently said he had suffered from a non-existent illness called *limaquitis*. 'Remember when he caught *limaquitis*? Nobody knew what it was because it was only an illness for him, and only he knew what that illness was.' For once Bahamontes blamed himself for a momentary lack of attention: he was at the back of the bunch when a sudden acceleration wrenched it into two. It left him with only the King of the Mountains jersey and another stage win as possible goals over the eight remaining days before Paris.

Bahamontes succeeded with the former, but not the latter. He blasted away alone in the Alps on the Tour's first assault of the Restefond Bonnette, Europe's highest pass at 2,802 metres above sea level. On the Izoard he was twenty seconds ahead of the main favourites. However, he was easily caught on the drop into Briançon and had to settle for sealing his fourth King of the Mountains jersey. Once again that competition had been a one-man show: Bahamontes had a colossal sixty-point advantage over Italy's Imerio Massignan, who had won the title in his absence in 1961. At the finish in the Parc des Princes the French press dubbed the only three Margnat riders to complete the course (Otaño, Campillo and Bahamontes) 'The Three Musketeers'. They had all finished inside the top thirty which led journalists to wonder what would have happened had the race been ridden with national teams.

Bahamontes' popularity remained high in Spain as one journalist from *El Mundo Deportivo* testified when he came down into the lobby of the team hotel after Superbagnères to find it overflowing with telegrams congratulating Bahamontes on his win. His old French friend, Jacques Daudé, was equally delighted by Bahamontes' return to winning ways. Just as in 1959, Daudé funded his own trip around the Tour so he could be there at each finish with a bottle of water for his favourite rider. He had also become Bahamontes' minder, forcing journalists, and particularly Spanish ones, to ask him permission to talk to Bahamontes. 'It's easier if you're a foreigner,' one huffy Spanish journalist wrote.

The Tour route in 1962 did not particularly favour Bahamontes as he constantly pointed out. It contained four time-trials, albeit one of them uphill and one of them a team time-trial, making one hundred and eleven kilometres of racing against the clock. Made to measure, in other words, for Anquetil. Many of the finishes were also placed a long way from the top of the last mountain pass: it occurred after both the Tourmalet and the Izoard. Bahamontes was undoubtedly not helped by a lack of team support, not least because the last of the seven Frenchmen who started had abandoned in the Alps. But that would have been more significant if Bahamontes had been in contention, and that, as he admits, was at least partly his own fault.

So the 1962 Tour was a classic case of whether the glass was half-full or half-empty. Bahamontes felt the pros outweighed the cons. 'The important thing about 1962 was that it put me back on the map, even for those people who had claimed that I was on the way down,' he says. That in itself, given he was now thirty-three, was no mean achievement. So, too, was Bahamontes finally finding a trade team that suited him – and vice versa.

Chapter Twelve
A Pirate With a Pair of Pliers

My ears hurt. Raphael Geminiani has just yelled, 'Who? Where? Who says Anquetil tried to buy Bahamontes?' at the top of his voice. For good measure he has slammed his fist on the kitchen table. Even at eighty-six, '*Le Grand Fusil*' – Mr Top Gun is probably the closest translation – remains a force to be reckoned with. Interviewing Geminiani is not for the fainthearted. At six feet tall, he is a mountainous man with huge hands and tree-trunk thighs to match his girth. His laugh is like a long, dry drain and he has a leery, shark-like grin. If Geminiani had a previous life, it probably had something to do with bottles of rum, high seas and buried treasure. Instead he played the role of pirate on dry land. He had a near-legendary ability for wheeler-dealing and was one of the great managers, directing everybody from Louison Bobet to Anquetil, Lucien Aimar to Stephen Roche, and even briefly Eddy Merckx. Geminiani was and remains cycling's ultimate buccaneer, a champion of the sport's non-conformists. He was expelled from France's 'A' squad to a regional team in 1958 for being a firebrand. But only a raging storm in the mountains of Chartreuse, and a climber of the talent of Charly Gaul, prevented 'Gem' from embarrassing France's top team by winning the yellow jersey outright.

Geminiani was equally fearless when it came to taking on race organisers and cycling's governing body, the U.C.I. Indeed, he staged a near one-man battle to have the names of trade sponsors included on team jerseys, something that is now taken for granted. In fact, in one race as a team director he instructed his riders to take off their jackets to reveal their logo-encrusted jerseys only seconds before a stage was due to begin to beat the ban on sponsorship. Just as fascinating is Geminiani's penchant for ridiculing the authorities. Typical is the story of the pet donkey he received from a fan at the 1958 Tour start and named after the French national trainer, Marcel Bidot, in revenge for his non-selection to France's 'A' team for that year's race. Parading it around the streets of Brussels where the race began, Geminiani then presented it as a gift to Bidot before as many photographers as he could assemble at the World's Fair, held in the Belgian capital that year. It was the kind of publicity stunt he took a positive delight in.

That, though, was more than half a century ago. These days, as Geminiani potters around his village near Clermont-Ferrand in central France, his giant frame squeezed into a tiny car, cigarette jammed into one corner of his mouth, he looks almost inoffensive. But this is the man who had one of cycling's stormiest and most intensely-lived careers.

Right now, he is furious that anyone could suggest Anquetil wanted to pay off Federico Martín Bahamontes. He yells again at the top of his voice: 'Where? Who?' In that mythical former life Geminiani would probably have been jabbing a sword in my chest. A neighbour has dropped in with a home-grown lettuce the size of a large cannonball for Geminiani's lunch; he watches this verbal dust-up across the kitchen table with all the impassivity of a countryman who has seen these kind of fireworks many times before. At this point I cop out. I do not have the nerve to tell Geminiani that the allegation comes from Bahamontes himself, who describes how Geminiani rang him one night during the Tour and offered to buy the race from him on Anquetil's behalf.

In any case, I have given Geminiani the right of reply. When he finally calms down he insists: 'I only ever had one rider in my team, a Belgian, who once sold a Paris-Roubaix, and when I threw him out and Anquetil said I'd been tough on him, you know what I said? "My sponsor doesn't pay riders to make their rivals win". But that's typical, they [the press] never say it's the strongest who wins, it's always a cheat, a doper or someone who's been bought. You say that Bahamontes helped Anquetil? I've got two sons and four daughters, and my honour, and I'm telling you [on all of them]: no. Never did anybody help Anquetil win anything. Whatever.' I leave it at that. After all, this is a man who allegedly swung a bicycle pump so hard during a Giro d'Italia he knocked five teeth out of a fan's mouth. His biography is titled *400 Fits of Bad Temper and Rifle Shots*. I have no desire to become the victim of the four hundred and first. As he reaches for his fifth cigarette in about an hour, and pours another black coffee, we continue.

Geminiani was one of the first French riders to get to know Bahamontes well, and that as far back as 1956. So he was able to witness first hand the growth in the Spaniard's popularity in France. He also knew his weak points. 'We did the whole of the *tournee* [post-race series of criteriums] of the Tour de France in 1956 in my car. It was me who drew up the route, me who chose the hotels and me who – he-he-he – chose the restaurants,' claims Geminiani between loud sucks on his cigarette. 'Daniel [Dousset] had told me to look after Bahamontes because he had no idea about France.' In the criteriums, Geminiani recalls, Bahamontes proved to be just the sort of ally he wanted. 'I remember we went to a crit in Chateaulin, the best paid in France. We got to the start and there was the Bobet mafia and the Anquetil mafia. And I said to Gerard Saint, "Gerard, you do the first five laps and get all the primes". Then, "Federico, it's you [to another five laps] and afterwards it's me". It worked. The mafia only got to win the fifty-franc primes and we got all the hundred thousand primes. And that evening in the distribution of the primes at Chateaulin town hall, I remember saying to the two mafias, "All right, lads? Those fifty-franc primes feel good?"' He hoots with laughter at the memory.

'With time, we grew to trust each other. I taught him some French. He didn't speak much, but when he did people liked it.' Just as André Darrigade had suggested, Geminiani says that Bahamontes was enormously popular, 'even more so here than in

Spain. They liked him here, he was *spectaculaire*. Everybody knew
about that ice cream incident and they loved him for it. Maybe he
only ate it because he'd needed a wheel change, but it caught their
attention. But he wasn't so big in Spain because he'd never won the
Vuelta. Whatever.'

The massive round of applause Bahamontes received in 1962 at
the Tour presentation in Nancy goes some way to indicating how
much he was appreciated in France as the leader of a French team.
And there is some more intriguing confirmation of his fame in the
most unlikely of places: the film *Amelie*. The heroine finds a box
of toys left behind in a flat and upon returning them to their owner,
a middle-aged man, he is reminded of watching Bahamontes win
the 1959 Tour. Bahamontes concurs with the verdicts of Geminiani
and Darrigade about how he is perceived in France. He once told
me: 'Go anywhere there and ask a Frenchman who the best climber
in the world has ever been? Bahamontes.' Geminiani, being
Geminiani, could see Bahamontes' popularity in France was
something he could exploit. When he sought alliances to defeat
Bahamontes, he went to the Spanish riders. 'Given the situation it
was easy to work with them against Bahamontes,' he says. 'It
wasn't just that he was the man to beat. The aim of the game for
the Spanish was to beat the man who was popular in France. But I
can't say anything bad about him, he was somebody I liked.'

For all that Bahamontes was popular in France, it was no longer
something he could take for granted on the other side of the
Pyrenees. By early 1962 Bahamontes was no longer the number
one sports star, let alone cycling star, in Spain. Two years of failing
to make an impact in Grand Tours, and the rise of new stars like
Angelino Soler and José Pérez Francés, contributed to a drop in
interest in the man from Toledo. Furthermore, Bahamontes raced
for a foreign team and never took part in the Vuelta. By the time his
old rival Jesús Loroño retired at the end of 1962 the two rarely
raced against each other any more: Bahamontes competed mainly
abroad and Loroño seldom ventured out of Spain. Besides, the
external factors of an inward-looking, isolated and economically-

backward Spain that had helped drive their conflict had begun to fade. Not that Bahamontes was complaining. Racing for a French team automatically made the Tour the number one target of his season, something which in the Italian squad V.O.V., with its huge interest in the Giro and the home market, had by no means been guaranteed. Bahamontes was happy to be where he was, too: in 1963, for the first time in his career, he opted to stay with the same team for more than one season. Margnat were delighted with his success in the King of the Mountains in 1962, but their signing of two double winners of the Tour's points jersey, Jean Grazyck and Darrigade, showed they had bigger ambitions for Bahamontes than the previous summer. Indeed, ensuring he did not lose time on the flat could only mean one thing: Margnat wanted their star rider to have a crack at the overall title.

If news of Bahamontes' switch of strategy towards regaining the Tour overall had filtered out of Margnat's team before the race start, most French fans would not have been displeased. However, among French riders his new-found ambition drew a mixed reaction. 'We used to detest Bahamontes, but only because he was so good,' Raymond Poulidor says. 'Whatever the stage he would always be positioned a long way forwards on his bike, pedalling furiously. He'd attack at the foot of the first col and we wouldn't see him until the evening of the same stage. We didn't want to let him get out of our sight, but we didn't have any choice. He used the "coffee-grinder" style of pedalling: he would use a big gear to get away for his first attack, but then he'd spin a small gear really fast and keep up the same speed to create the really big time gap. If you tried to go with him, it was like committing suicide.'

Even in 1963, when he turned thirty-five, Bahamontes made a great start to the season, gaining resentment and respect in equal measure from those who were less prepared. Poulidor recalls: 'It was always the same. Every year. I remember the Mont Agel hill-climb race early in my first year as a pro in 1960. Nobody had done any training – I'd maybe ridden three or four hundred kilometres before it – and we just had a pump on our bikes to carry as little weight as possible. Bahamontes, though, had a pump, a bottle and spare wheels on his. But who was the first at the top? Bahamontes.'

In 1963, then, Bahamontes came to the Tour de France with far more ambitious plans than 'just' another King of the Mountains jersey. 'Raoul Remy [Margnat's director] told me that there was no point in going for it again, people would take that for granted,' Bahamontes recalls. 'On top of that, the route was far more mountainous than usual. We had to go for the overall.' Anquetil won the Tour despite the organisers doing their best to level the playing field by cutting more than thirty kilometres from his strongest suit of time-trialling, reducing it from one hundred and eleven kilometres in 1962 to seventy-seven in 1963. However, what nobody expected was, as Tour director Jacques Goddet put it: 'The one rival who would be at his level was our old acquaintance, Federico Bahamontes.'

Bahamontes' crowning moment of glory came in the ski resort of Isere. A day after taking an Alpine stage win in a lone break, for the first time in four years he captured his first yellow jersey since 1959. True, his overall advantage over Anquetil was almost risibly small: just three seconds. Yet given he celebrated his thirty-fifth birthday the day he took the lead in the Tour for the second time in his career, it was a landmark achievement.

Everything had fallen into place in 1963 starting with morale-boosting King of the Mountains wins in both the Midi Libre and Dauphiné Libéré warm-up races in June. Significantly for his team, on the first stage of the Tour Bahamontes had managed to get into the earliest possible break alongside Britain's Alan Ramsbottom and Belgian Eddy Pauwels and gained an eighty-eight-second advantage over Anquetil. For a squad like Margnat's this was crucial: just as today, much store was set in a team by a contender's ride in the Tour's prologue. Bahamontes gaining time *outside* the mountains so early in 1963 showed his troops that their often erratic leader was on form and keen to do battle. Small wonder Margnat rallied around him, and he had some powerful team-mates to back him up. 'Bahamontes had a great team for the flat in 1963,' Poulidor recalls. 'Darrigade and Grazyck were two key players. His only weakness, curiously enough, was in the mountains: not many riders to support him there.' *MARCA* waxed lyrical about this early success: 'He has turned up with the same kind of strength he used to have as a junior. Bahamontes is "Baha" again, flying over the Tour.' However, they added a sting in the tail, noting that in previous years, 'Anquetil has shown he is the best'.

Bahamontes' early break meant that even after an unremarkable seventh place for Margnat in the team time-trial on stage two he still remained fourth overall. He continued to go from strength to strength, staying out of trouble on the *pavés* to Roubaix. Then he lost just ninety-eight seconds to Anquetil in the first individual time-trial on a technically difficult course which contained sixty dangerous curves in 24.5 kilometres. 'I'm in great shape, but I don't drop them like I did before,' Bahamontes said, 'but at least I'm not losing time on the flat, either.'

Anquetil tried his best to ambush Bahamontes before the mountains, attacking with Raymond Poulidor, Henry Anglade and Jean Stablinski on the long stage from Limoges to Bordeaux. However, Margnat combined with the Basque squad K.A.S. to pull back the move, prompting Bahamontes to tell journalists: 'Finally I am in a good team. Other times I raced the Tour as an individual. What do you think Van Looy or Anquetil could do without team-mates?' The difference between 1963 and previous years was that sometimes at least Bahamontes alternated his criticisms of his team-mates with dollops of praise. Margnat must have been doing something right.

However, while Bahamontes and his team rode far above expectations on the flat, things did not go to plan in the Pyrenees. All his attacks were neutralised, and though he took a solid hold on the King of the Mountains competition with some early breaks Margnat's only stage win came thanks to Darrigade, who secured the twentieth of his twenty-two career Tour victories. It was earlier in that stage that Bahamontes made a serious error. After attacking on one mountain section very early on, and despite having team-mate Claude Mattio with him for support in atrocious weather conditions, he then opted to sit up at a point where he could have inflicted serious damage on his rivals. 'He missed out because he listened to his director's instructions to wait for the peloton,' *MARCA* claimed later. 'If he had not done that it would have been Bahamontes on the highest step of the Tour de France podium that year.' Others agreed and also blamed the team. 'Fede lost the race in the Pyrenees,' Rik Van Looy said later. 'He couldn't handle the rain. If he had been in my team he and no other would have won the Tour for the simple reason I would have thought for him. That isn't what those who directed him did.'

The Alps were a different story. After Jacques Anquetil gained a thirty-second time bonus on Bahamontes at Aurillac, Bahamontes fired back the next day en route to Grenoble when he launched a devastatingly effective, short-range attack over the Col de Porte. Just nineteen kilometres from the finish Bahamontes blasted away alone on the first category climb. After reaching the summit with a two-minute advantage, for once he managed to maintain the gap all the way to Grenoble. It was the city where he had taken the yellow jersey four years before; now he was just twenty-four hours away from recapturing it in Isere. 'It was one of the most brilliant operations the Spaniard has ever carried out,' *MARCA* claimed, before warning: 'But it did not get us the result we wanted. Unless Bahamontes takes five minutes in any one of these stages any earlier moves will have been in vain.'

Taking the yellow jersey was almost a formality. On the Iseran pass the leader Gilbert Desmet of Belgium cracked completely, but with no real reaction from the main contenders. Desmet slid backwards, the rest trundled upwards. Bahamontes and the rest of the top names grouped together between the three-metre high snowdrift walls at the summit with only one brief attack from Poulidor to liven up proceedings. Bahamontes sardonically observed later that it was the only one Poulidor made in the entire race. However, Poulidor was not uppermost in Bahamontes' mind as they came down from the Iseran. With Desmet out of the running, Bahamontes was now ahead of Anquetil. One major Alpine stage and one long time-trial remained; the duel for the 1963 Tour, Bahamontes observed, was about to begin.

One of cycling's hidden attractions is that a lot of what remains memorable in an event is not what happens in the race but what happens around it. In the 1963 Tour it was the off-race controversy surrounding the crucial last Alpine stage that has come to dominate fans' memories, even though the key incident lasted all of twenty seconds. At the foot of the Forclaz, the last key climb of the race, Anquetil raised his hand to denote his bike needed repairing. Raphael Geminiani sped forward and cut the brake cable on Anquetil's bike with a pair of pliers when the officials, even the one in his car, were either not paying attention or could not see it. As a result of the 'broken cable' Geminiani was able to claim Anquetil should have a replacement bike, and quickly provided him with a lighter model. As a result of those twenty seconds, the three weeks and three thousand or more kilometres of the 1963 Tour were delivered into Anquetil's hands. Because as Geminiani puts it: 'If it hadn't been for the Forclaz, Bahamontes would have won the Tour.'

Sitting at his kitchen table now, Geminiani says: 'Bahamontes was the big rival we defeated that day and Poulidor lost seven minutes, but it was the organisers who made a mistake.' To say that Geminiani relishes discussing the Forclaz, and the tale of Anquetil's cable, is no exaggeration. He gives a lengthy, no-holds-barred explanation of what happened. He freely admits he cut the cable, but insists the fault was not his: it was the organisers' for failing to spot it.

'That year, before the race, it was said that on that stage we'd go over the Grand St. Bernard pass, go down to Martigny and then take the A road over the Forclaz. Not a hard climb. But there was a landslide [he laughs heartily at the memory] and that blocked the Forclaz. So . . . I was lucky enough that someone told me beforehand we would have to go over the pass on the old sheep track that we'd gone over in 1948 when everybody went up it on foot. I looked at the pieces of paper the organiser had given us, and there was no change on it . . . but I knew that we'd have to be careful and change bikes, which was prohibited. So I prepared another bike with a twenty-six-tooth sprocket [which was far more suitable for an untarmacked climb]. I told Anquetil what we'd do, but obviously we'd need some kind of mechanical problem.' He chuckles again. 'So I made the problem happen: I cut his cable. I told the official watching that Jacques' rear cable was broken and that we'd need a replacement bike. And that is how, when Bahamontes attacked on the Forclaz, he dropped everybody, but not Anquetil. Not on his light bike.'

That was not the only thing the officials failed to notice that day, Geminiani points out. He outlines a second, less well-known, game-changing piece of cheating. 'When we got to the other side, I gave Anquetil his old bike back, but with his time-trial gearing instead of his usual mountain gearing to do the last, flatter, thirty kilometres to Chamonix.' Bahamontes had tried his utmost to shake off the Frenchman, but he had been outwitted. When the pair reached Chamonix, Anquetil took advantage of the latest switch of bikes to outsprint Bahamontes and win the stage. The time bonus of a minute – Bahomontes received a thirty-second bonus for second place – meant Anquetil landed the yellow jersey by a comfortable margin of twenty-seven seconds.

With only Anquetil's strong suit of a time-trial to come, Bahamontes' dream of a second Tour had evaporated. For all MARCA claimed that he lost the Tour in the Pyrenees, and rebuked him for attacking earlier in the same day and wasting energy, the Forclaz had been his great opportunity to regain that time and turn the tables again. But thanks to Geminiani's sleight-of-hand that was rendered impossible. 'Bahamontes' defeat by Anquetil shows he had real talent,' Geminiani recognises. 'At Chamonix, it took a really strong Anquetil to beat him. And, like I said, if it hadn't been for the Forclaz, he'd have won the Tour.'

When Geminiani reached the finish he faced a storm of protests about cutting the cable. But he tackled them head-on.

'Remy protested for Bahamontes, [manager Antonin] Magne for Poulidor and I was surrounded by officials and journalists, and so on,' he remembers. 'Magne said, "You cut the cable!" And I said, "Did you see it? That's slander, be careful, eh?" So I said to the race official, "Can you tell this gentleman what happened?" And he said,

"I saw there was a mechanical problem." And I said, "Do I have the right to change a bike if there's a mechanical?" – "Yes" – "Well that's what I've done." And Remy said, "Well I could have done that, too!" and I said, "Well, did you?" – "No" – "In that case, your rights to do so are denied".' He howls with laughter at the memory.

'Me, though, I'd done my job, respecting the rules,' Geminiani insists to me, tongue clearly in cheek. Then he chortles at having beaten officialdom and the opposition in one fell swoop. Not to mention winning the Tour.

Apart from his specific accusation that Geminiani tried to buy the race from him, Bahamontes has very mixed feelings about the 1963 Tour. Keenly aware that he could have won the race, a torrent of resentment runs just beneath the surface when he discusses it. 'Geminiani was really scared of what I could do that year,' he says. 'When I attacked over the Grand St. Bernard, he got everybody he could to chase after me. I'd gone on the attack, waited to see if anybody came, nobody did, and [Margnat director] Raoul Remy came up and said, "Where are you off to?" and I said I just wanted to get to the top to settle the King of the Mountains competition. And then when I got to the summit of the Grand St. Bernard I had five minutes. And if you're at the top of a climb with five minutes' advantage, what do you do?' So on Bahamontes went, despite being weighed down by a large potato, kept in his back pocket to try to prevent an over-large *maillot jaune* from ballooning out. 'All the teams were chasing like crazy, the Belgians and the Dutch and Gem's team, because they knew I could win the Tour. Then there was only the Forclaz left and Geminiani was there with Anquetil. Geminiani gets a kick these days out of telling people how just at the point where it got toughest he changed Anquetil's bike and pushed him up the climb round the steepest corners. On the climb itself Poulidor got dropped when I attacked and there was just Anquetil left. He sat on my wheel and he was suffering badly because I went up on the left-hand side so he'd be riding into the wind as well. But Geminiani had changed his bike, cutting the cables with some pliers, and then he pushed Anquetil round each bend. On the descent Anquetil attacked, I didn't have good brakes and my foot came out of the pedal on a bend and he got fifty metres on me.'

After Forclaz, on a bike with gears suited for a sprint, wrapping up the race was easy for Anquetil. 'There must only have been three kilometres left when Geminiani told Anquetil to ride like it was a time-trial, but I was ready for that attack,' Bahamontes recalls. 'Then a motorbike belonging to the race organisation came up – it had no right to be there – and helped Anquetil attack again. And that wasn't the only time that happened by a long shot.'

At other moments, though, Bahamontes was capable of recognising that Anquetil rode the 1963 Tour 'like a great champion. He was well organised, he had no need of Poulidor'. Yet almost in the same breath, in an interview with *L'Equipe* at the finish in Paris, Bahamontes once again accused Raymond Poulidor of 'working for Anquetil on the Grand Saint-Bernard. Without that, I would have got six minutes. I'm not mad. I saw them talking together two days before that'.

MARCA said in their post-race analysis: 'He is the best Spanish rider in history and he deserved the triumph had it not been for those errors he made. At thirty-five, to go on being a great figure in his sport at the same level as the winner has its merit.' The Franco regime woke up to the fact that Bahamontes was back on top of his game, though it was noticeable that they took advantage of José Pérez Francés's third place behind Bahamontes, as well as Angelino Soler's sixth place overall, before singling out Bahamontes only briefly. It was a long way from the ecstatic reception and political exploitation that Bahamontes' Tour win had received four years earlier. 'I congratulated him and all the Spanish who have made the race Spanish again,' commented José Antonio Elola, who remained in control of sport. 'Even in different teams, you [the Spanish] cannot deny that your style of racing and sporting strategies have united you above brand names and tactics.'

The most intriguing analysis of Bahamontes' near-miss came from Damian Pla, Pérez Francés's director, who claimed that had it not been for Anquetil, 'Bahamontes would have lost twenty minutes on the flat', and with it all chance of a podium finish. 'Anquetil ended up blocking the race [by being so strong], he made everybody race more conservatively,' he said. That sounds like sour grapes because Bahamontes finished ahead of Pérez Francés. Besides, barring that crucial error of not opening up a gap in the Pyrenees, he hardly raced conservatively: as early as the first stage Bahamontes was taking time from Anquetil. As for Bahamontes' claims that Anquetil had been helped to win the Tour, the issue was skilfully fudged by *L'Equipe*. The newspaper shrewdly pointed out: 'Federico accuses, comments and regrets with the same degree of sincerity.' However, the writer then dodged the issue of Anquetil by focusing on another rider altogether: Poulidor, who finished eighth. 'His arguments lack any foundation . . .' *L'Equipe* blithely added. 'Poulidor was always behind him, he was never able to bring back this devil of a man who flew towards the summits.' Anquetil did, however, even if occasionally he needed a pair of pliers and a shrewd, piratical manager to be sure.

Chapter Thirteen
The Master and the Apprentice

In 2011, Luxembourg's Andy Schleck jumped away from the pack on the Alpine stage over the Izoard pass and up the mythical Galibier climb and rode the sixty-five kilometres to the finish alone. His closest pursuer was two minutes seven seconds adrift and it took him within fifteen seconds of the yellow jersey. Ultimately he finished second overall in that year's Tour de France.

The move was hailed as a throwback to the glorious days of long-distance mountain attacking. Indeed, it was almost a carbon-copy of another devastating break by Federico Martín Bahamontes back in 1964. Bahamontes attacked at the foot of the first of four Pyrenean cols with just one other rider, Julio Jiménez, for company. After riding over the Peyresourde, Aspin, and Tourmalet together he dropped Jiménez on the Aubisque and reached the summit alone. Forty-five kilometres later he crossed the line in Pau nearly two minutes before anyone else. As a result Bahamontes moved to within thirty-five seconds of the yellow jersey in second place. He finished third overall in Paris.

The similarities between the two moves, forty-seven years apart, are clear. Bahamontes' spectacularly long breakaway provided perhaps his greatest stage win of all in the Tour. However, outside Spain his two hundred-kilometre dash for glory is still considered merely a sideshow in the drama of the 1964 Tour. For proof of that lack of interest you could do worse than look at *L'Equipe*'s mammoth 1,500-page history of the Tour: Bahamontes' two wins in 1964 – in Briançon and Pau – do not even earn a mention. In fact, the only reference to the Eagle of Toledo is in one (wildly inaccurate) headline: 'Poulidor climbs better than Bahamontes'. His lack of recognition that year is down to the fact that he was considered the third man in what is still viewed as an epic two-way duel between Jacques Anquetil and Raymond Poulidor. Often cited as one of the five most exciting Tours in living memory, it was the year of Anquetil's near-collapse coming out of Andorra, of Poulidor's clown-like mechanical problems near Toulouse and of his stunning fightback to Luchon. Above all, it is the year of the Anquetil-Poulidor *tête-a-tête* duel, shoulders straining against one another, on the slopes of the Puy de Dôme. Bahamontes actually finished ahead of both of them on the Puy, but he was never considered to be a serious challenger. In the words of Raphael Geminiani, Anquetil's director: 'Bahamontes was all spectacle. He wasn't a threat.'

Yet when Bahamontes rode alone across the summit of the Aubisque he had an advantage of six minutes on the pack and the lead in the Tour de France was within his grasp. Bahamontes remains convinced that he could have won the Tour that year. Geminiani, as a biased observer, might not agree, but an astute neutral like André Darrigade says: 'He's not wrong; he could have.' Darrigade explains: 'When Bahamontes attacked that day in the Pyrenees Anquetil used the Pelforth team against him. There was a sort of conspiracy, or manipulation of events, against him.' And then, of course, there was Julio Jiménez.

Remembering how difficult Bahamontes' relationship was with his predecessor as Tour's King of the Mountains, Jesús Loroño, it is perhaps reasonable to suppose that Bahamontes' relationship with the man who succeeded him was never going to be a marriage made in heaven. As Darrigade points out, though, it is ironic that on that stage from Luchon to Pau in 1964 Jiménez was the man who held the key to a second Tour victory for Bahamontes. But Bahamontes failed to reach out and claim the crown. 'If he'd been a bit craftier,' Darrigade observes, 'he'd have said to Jiménez, "You take the stage win, and I'll go for the Tour". If the two had ridden together and worked together all the way to the finish Bahamontes could have done it. He could have won the Tour.'

True, with Jiménez riding for K.A.S. and Bahamontes for Margnat, the alliance of Spain's two great climbers on stage sixteen was never going to be more than a temporary fusion of mutual interests. Of course, both wanted to win the King of the Mountains title, and both wanted to finish as high in the overall classification as possible. But under normal circumstances an understanding between the pair was far from unprecedented in cycling. Putting as much daylight between themselves and their rivals as possible was to their mutual advantage and far more likely if they combined forces. After that the two could divide the spoils, Bahamontes going for the Tour and Jiménez for the stage and the King of the Mountains title. The problem was that while Bahamontes wanted the overall, he did not want to relinquish the King of the Mountains jersey. As a result, his best chance of winning the race that year disappeared on the long road to Pau.

Bahamontes made his move after three kilometres. 'I attacked early to see if I could get rid of the *domestiques*,' he claims, 'and force the leaders to come across. When I heard Julio Jiménez was trying to bridge across my director, Remy, told me to wait. I let him move ahead on the summits of the three climbs that followed. But when he had taken them all and moved ahead of me on the mountains classification he then refused to work any more. At the top of the Aubisque I had six minutes thirteen seconds on the bunch, more than double the advantage I'd had at the foot, but that was when the suffering started. I had all that way to go to Pau, but I was alone, nobody was there to work with me and that's what I needed, above all, when I had a group with Anquetil, Poulidor [and nine other riders] chasing behind. With a head-wind in the last ten kilometres the ride to the finish seemed to be interminable, and behind they rapidly reduced my advantage. But I still had nearly two minutes on them at the finish.'

With Spain able to watch the race live on television for the first time that year, what proved to be Bahamontes' last full Tour, and his last stage win, turned into a memorable dessert to serve for his supporters back home. 'It was,' Bahamontes once said, 'one of the most meritorious days of my career, but my hard work did not allow me to reap the full rewards. The distance from the summit of the Aubisque to the finish in Pau was so far that it allowed the chasing group, unable to beat me individually, to beat me as a unit.' Overall, though, Bahamontes had made serious inroads, moving to just thirty-five seconds behind leader Georges Groussard, while Anquetil was fifty-one seconds back and Poulidor at a minute.

Though Bahamontes took a trouncing in the time-trial that followed the next day, losing four minutes in forty-two kilometres, there was still an outside chance of regaining time a few days later on the Puy de Dôme, the race's final summit finish. Instead, Bahamontes was unable to follow Julio Jiménez's attack late on, admitting that he miscalculated, and his second place at the finish line simply allowed Bahamontes to consolidate his third place overall. A podium place was no mean achievement for a thirty-six year old and his two mountain stage wins were confirmation that he was still capable of mounting an aggressive campaign, and not just riding conservatively.

On occasions Bahamontes has attempted to explain away his defeat by saying that he wanted to finish third in the 1964 because he had already finished first, second and fourth overall. At other moments, though, more realistic feelings take over. '[In 1964] I took my sixth and final overall classification in the King of the Mountains,' he once wrote. 'But above all I felt that I had missed a great opportunity.' The real shame was that in all the hullabaloo surrounding Poulidor and Anquetil hardly anyone outside Spain noticed.

Bahamontes stood on the finish line in Briançon, a week into the race, and pronounced: 'I have prepared myself exclusively to try and win the Tour de France.' At that point, after the first major mountain stage of 1964, he was clearly the best placed of the favourites to do so. There was only one rider ahead of Bahamontes after Briançon – Georges Groussard – a reliable but not exceptionally talented *domestique*. The Frenchman had played his cards perfectly by getting into a break in the Vosges mountains and being allowed to go clear by the big names. Two days later he was into a lead he would hold for nine stages. For once, though, Bahamontes had managed to come through the first week of the Tour without losing too much time. Compared to Anquetil, the key reference point, he was around two minutes down, most of it lost in a twenty-kilometre team time-trial on stage three. However, it was one thing for a veteran like Bahamontes to stay in contention, another to move ahead. But Bahamontes, being Bahamontes, took the first opportunity he could. His declaration of war on the Tour's eighth stage was anything but subtle: he let his troops soften up the opposition in the first one hundred and seventy kilometres, before going clear on the second category Telegraphe. He widened the gap yet further on the most challenging Alpine climb of them all, the Galibier, then maintained his advantage on the long drop down the valley to Briançon. Second home was Poulidor, at ninety-two seconds, with Anquetil finishing a further seventeen seconds back. Overall Bahamontes was behind Groussard, but he was thirty-two seconds up on Poulidor, with Anquetil eighth nearly two minutes back. Asked if he dared attack the quadruple Tour winner, Bahamontes answered defiantly: 'The aim is to try. Both Anquetil and his *domestiques* want to stop me; they'll have to suffer.' However, Bahamontes' onslaught was not quite as beneficial as it could have been: in hindsight, a later, punchier attack on the Galibier, even if it did not rack him up as many King of the Mountains points, might have been more productive in terms of the overall.

The next day Bahamontes' attack over the La Bonette-Restefond climb enabled him to crown what was (and remains) the highest tarmacked mountain pass in France alone and ahead of the field for the second time in three years. It was a magnificent achievement, and Bahamontes wheeltracks – in the Tour at least – remained unfollowed for nearly thirty years until Scot Robert Millar became the next rider in the race to cross the summit of the pass, in 1993. Though not exceptionally steep La Bonette Restefond is daunting for its exceptional length – twenty-three kilometres – and its fifteen hundred metres of climbing. The altitude is another intimidating factor since anything above two thousand metres, like La Bonette-Restefond's summit, causes oxygen debt. The appalling road surfaces also pose problems. In 1964 it was only a gravel descent and in 1993 I can remember driving along poorly tarmacked roads, barely a car's width across and with no barriers separating us from a vast, impossibly deep ravine.

Millar told British magazine *Cycling Weekly* at the time that he had been 'honoured' to be the first rider to reach La Bonette-Restefond's summit since Bahamontes, and in a curious echo of Bahamontes' rider four decades earlier, Scot and Spaniard employed identical tactics on the descent. Just as Bahamontes had done in the foggy drop off La Bonette-Restefond in 1962, I can recall Millar saying he used the race motorbike's brakelights to guide him down as fast as possible, too. When the motorbike braked, so did Millar.

However, there were more parallels – none of the attacks worked out. Just as Millar's lone break in 1993 ended with him being caught on the flat roads that followed La Bonette-Restefond, so both of Bahamontes' breaks proved fruitless. This was no surprise the second time round in 1964 as the stage ended in Monaco, 130 kilometres further on. To add insult to injury, Anquetil outsprinted Tom Simpson at the finish for a minute's bonus: so for all his exploits, including taking the lead in the King of the Mountains competition, Bahamontes ended up losing time on his main rival.

For Bahamontes the big problem remained the same as it had been in every Tour since 1954: the summits were too far from the finishes for him to benefit. As a descender whose ability ranged from poor to mediocre, it was a real disadvantage. In 1964 that handicap became evident on the Bonette-Restefond stage; five days later, on the road from Andorra to Toulouse, when the whole field had Anquetil up against the ropes, the message was really rammed home.

For Bahamontes the planning for the Andorra stage started twenty-four hours earlier when he learnt that Anquetil was spending the rest day at a barbecue. 'They told me, "Anquetil's having a right party in the house up there, he's drinking champagne",' Bahamontes recalls. 'So I said to myself, "Tomorrow all that champagne's going to be coming out of his ears", and I got hold of [team-mate José] Segu and I said, "Tomorrow we'll have breakfast three hours earlier than usual, and then ride the twenty-five or thirty kilometres to the start"' The objective was to be fully 'warmed up' as soon as the race started the first ascent of the day, the twenty-kilometre Envalira pass out of Andorra which began almost before the stage had left the start town of La Vella. 'When we started, we were all fired up and – boom! – we went off – boom! – on the attack. After two kilometres they came up and told us that Anquetil had abandoned, and then the whole of his team had had to drop back to help him get over.'

Bahamontes was far from being the only one with the idea of putting Anquetil to the test on the Envalira, even though it emerged that his abandon was no more than a rumour. The photograph of Anquetil at the party stuffing himself with lamb from a barbecue, and Geminiani pouring him a drink, rather than embarking on the usual rest day's light training, had appeared in that morning's newspapers. Geminiani is adamant that it was just a mock-up for the press. Mock-up or not it was certainly unwise: Henry Anglade and the Pelforth team, defending Georges Groussard's yellow jersey, along with Raymond Poulidor, all went training before the start with the same intention. The mass attack they then staged was arguably the only way to sink so strong a rider as Anquetil, and the Frenchman was four minutes adrift by the summit of the Envalira, albeit partly as a result of his alleged indigestion.

Not for the last time, with three mountain stages ahead, and only two minutes down, Bahamontes seemed to be in the driving seat. But then Bahamontes and Poulidor, who led over the summit in dense fog, made two strategic mistakes. The first was not to wait for the first chase group, all of whom would have been more than happy to collaborate to eliminate Anquetil from the running. Secondly, they underestimated Anquetil's self-esteem: he pulled out all the stops on the descent, taking risks in the fog that neither Bahamontes nor Poulidor had been prepared to, and regained his position in the peloton. 'The fog saved him,' Poulidor would later say. 'The cars had their lights switched on because of the fog and that was a reference point [for Anquetil on the descent]. Without that fog, we would have waited for the group behind and he would never have seen us again.'

'Anquetil was kaput,' recalls Geminiani. 'They had all attacked and he'd been dropped one hundred metres after the start.' But his star rider's problems had nothing to do with the previous day's lamb or wine, he said. 'The problem was that some astrologer had predicted he'd die on stage thirteen and it had been published in *France Soir*, the biggest newspaper around at the time. All the *Poulidoristes* had sent him copies of the newspaper, and Anquetil was like, "What do I do? Go home?"' Anquetil was so worried that Geminiani even got his wife to visit to persuade him to calm down and not pull out. Anquetil spent most of the rest day in bed. Geminiani says: 'I got really pissed off with him lying there in bed and dragged him off to that barbecue. But the next morning he didn't want to get on his bike. I made him do it. One hundred metres after the start he was dropped. He was so far back he was the last rider over the Envalira. Then, at the summit, the fog was so thick it seemed like the end of the world. And I was so pissed off I went up to Jacques and yelled at him, "Hey! If you're going to die like that astrologer says, die at the head of the race and not in front of the broom wagon!"'

And that, by and large, was that. What had started as a mass mutiny against the winner of the three previous Tours fizzled out. Anquetil pulled off a stunning descent, first catching the Groussard group and then Bahamontes.

It is difficult to disagree with Bahamontes when he says the Tour was weighted in Anquetil's favour. It was not just the route or the lack of summit finishes, it also helped Anquetil that the organisers split the individual time-trials into three different stages. Each had a one-minute time bonus and they were all won by the Frenchman. Additionally, the Tour's decision to revert to trade teams made it impossible for Bahamontes to exploit any disunity between the major stars in the French team like he had in the 'bad old days' when the Tour was run with national squads. With television cameras now filming the race it was far harder to work against theoretical allies or pull a fast one on your team-mates without anybody noticing All Bahamontes could do was play Anquetil at his own game and try and form alliances with rivals to out-manoeuvre him. And who better, in theory, than Julio Jiménez?

Julio Jiménez settles back in the armchair in the first-floor flat he calls home in Ávila. Now well into his eighth decade, and nearly five decades after one of the defining moments of the 1964 Tour, when asked what his problem was that day with Bahamontes, Jiménez's answer is 'he [Bahamontes] wanted everything.' This is the Julio Jiménez so memorably described by the late Geoffrey Nicholson in *The Great Bike Race* as a 'small, bird-like figure . . . he was also balding, grey-faced and never looked particularly well, but on the first steep slope he would prance away as if he had springs in his calves'. Jiménez, who weighed fifty-seven kilos (eight stone thirteen pounds) when in form, has thickened with age. However, he still zooms about his living room at speed and with a bounce in his stride that would do credit to Zebedee in *The Magic Roundabout*. He constantly picks up and puts down pieces of paper and photographs, his head darting from side to side and talking nineteen to the dozen. Clearly none of the nervous energy that saw him secure three King of the Mountains titles in the Tour and Vuelta, and finish second in the Tour in 1967, has been lost. In his own slightly skittish way Jiménez is as keen as Bahamontes to ensure the visitor cannot miss the scale of his success. For one thing, he uses the pennants that he received for each of his five Tour mountain stage wins as rather painful head-rests (they are studded with brass knobs) for his sofa. And if the hat-trick of stags' heads he received as best climber in the Tour's Alpine stages between 1965–67 were lined up a little lower in his hallway, a tall guest might be tempted to hang his coat on them.

Delve into Jiménez's personal and sporting history and there are many other similarities with Bahamontes, right down to them both wearing grimy, non-regulation sports jerseys in their first races:

Bahamontes in his basketball shirt complete with shoulderpads, Jiménez in 'an Ávila football shirt that had been washed so many times you could barely read the letters'. And the parallels continue: both come from working-class backgrounds in central Spain. Though not as poor as the Bahamontes family, Jiménez's parents could not afford any luxuries like bicycles, either. In fact, Jiménez only acquired his first bike because his mother worked as a maid for an army general who had several. Jiménez spent so much time staring at them, he recalls, that the general felt sorry for him and ended up buying Jiménez a tricycle. Both Bahamontes and Jiménez started their professional careers late: Bahamontes at almost twenty-five, Jiménez at twenty-seven. Finally, they both spent large parts of their early twenties making their own way across Spain to races. Just a few years after Bahamontes, Jiménez would travel up to five hundred and fifty kilometres to Asturias and the Basque Country for his first big races. But in a sign of Spain's slowly improving economy he did so on a battered Vespa, not a racing bike like Bahamontes.

Jiménez was nicknamed the 'Watchmaker of Ávila' because that was his original trade. He also cut his cycling teeth in Barcelona, staying in Santiago Mostajo's house. He received his first professional contract in 1961 with a small Catalan squad. Three years later K.A.S. gave him the chance he so desperately wanted: to ride the Tour. Jiménez's first stage win came with an attack on the approach roads to the Envalira pass into Andorra in 1964. Like Bahamontes, he was a poor descender, but he still retained enough of an advantage on the pack at the Envalira summit to make it down to the finish to victory. It was on stage fourteen to Pau that Bahamontes and Jiménez, the old master and the young apprentice, found themselves together at the head of the field for the first and last time. There were four mountain passes ahead of them. As radios across Spain transmitted reports of the developing breakaway, crowds gathered in bars and the nation held its collective breath. With two such adept climbers at the head of the field who knew what would happen?

Back on the road in the Pyrenees, however, there was a problem.

And it was not an easy one to resolve. 'The thing was we were a bit pissed off with each other,' Jiménez says now, 'It wasn't like we were working together at first. We would each make long accelerations on either side of the road until his director came up and told him to work with me. At that point, the idea was, "I would be the first across each climb" – which Jiménez was – "and he would go for the [yellow] jersey.". We did a couple more climbs together. The break was going all right, [even if] Fede was sprinting for the points at the top of the climbs.' That, of course, went against their agreement. 'Then on the last climb I had a tough moment and I got dropped,' says Jiménez. Strategically, if Bahamontes really believed he could challenge for the overall it would have made more sense for him to wait. However, Jiménez claims that he did not have the courage to ask Bahamontes to do so, and Bahamontes never suggested it. 'To tell you the truth, I'd done absolutely everything I could to help him in that break and I was shattered. He even told me, earlier on, not to go so hard because there was a long way left to go. So that was it. We exchanged a couple of words and he went on. He was my idol; it was my first Tour. How was I going to say to him, "Go a bit easier because on the other side of the Aubisque there's sixty kilometres to go and you might need me there?"'

As Jiménez hints, that kind of distance without any further climbs, is an extremely long way for any lone rider to fend off a group of chasing rivals. But Bahamontes and Jiménez could not agree on a tactic that would benefit both of them. 'He wanted everything: to go over the top alone and win the stage and he forced the pace deliberately [to drop me] because you can tell when someone does that,' Jiménez says. 'So I went up at my own pace, and I said to myself, "If I manage to catch him, I'm going to attack him and he's going to pay for what he did".'

By the time he was halfway down the other side of the Aubisque Jiménez was under no illusions that he would catch Bahamontes again. He stopped and bought himself a Coca-Cola and sandwich in a bar. These days that would probably get him fired from his team; back then it was seen as perfectly normal. While he knocked back his Coke, his director told him to hurry up because a large chasing group was about to go through. Sure enough, about five minutes later the likes of Poulidor, Groussard and Anquetil came hammering down the road. Jiménez gulped down his quick snack and latched on to the back. He insists, perhaps a little too much, that he did not assist in the ongoing pursuit of Bahamontes, something that Bahamontes claims both Jiménez and K.A.S. team-mate Francisco Gabica had done. 'I got on their wheel and I barely moved from the back, I swear, though I didn't take one turn on the group. I swear it,' says Jiménez. 'But in any case they were flying and when we got to the square in the middle of Pau he just had a couple of minutes. However, if he'd waited for me we might have gone up [the climb] a minute slower, but I think on the flat we'd have held them off for longer, and he'd have been closer to getting the yellow jersey.' Instead, Bahamontes' determination to retain the King of the Mountains jersey had betrayed him and ultimately the greater prize eluded him.

The tale has been told and retold so often that the reality of what was actually said between Jiménez and Bahamontes is irretrievably buried under a blanket of half-truths. But Bahamontes' desire to take both the King of the Mountains title and fight for the overall, rather than sacrifice the first, was not the only problem. When asked if Bahamontes could be trusted in 'gentlemen's agreements', whilst Bahamontes insists he respected all deals with Jiménez, Jiménez answers straightaway, 'Not in my case.' That, it emerges, was the reason for the lack of collaboration at the start of the stage which lost them both time: Jiménez claims he had already been too badly burned in at least one previous breakaway with Bahamontes. 'I don't remember where, but there was some mountain stage in the Tour that year [almost certainly stage nine to Monaco where Bahamontes took the lead in the King of the Mountains], and where he'd told me the day before, "Look, if I go on the attack, don't follow me because it could ruin the break, and I'm going for the lead". And I thought I'd respect that because he was a god, an idol, in Spain and I was a piece of shit in comparison. However, when I talked to my director, Dalmacio Langarica [Bahamontes' director in 1959], he said, "Don't trust him". But I did. And, sure enough, Fede attacked and got away. But then his team-mates started fighting me for the points that remained on the third category climbs in the King of the Mountains. When I asked him later what was happening with his team-mates I realised that he wanted the King of the Mountains competition, too, and that he didn't care whether he finished second or third in the overall. The Mountains was the one he was after. That would be fair enough, but it was the way that he did it. That wears you out and pisses you off, and you end up feeling like you're stupid.'

Jiménez is not the only one to claim he had this sort of problem with Bahamontes. Poulidor, too, has recollections of Bahamontes – who says he cannot remember the event – 'pulling a fast one' on him the first time they raced against each other. 'After Bahamontes won the Tour in 1959, I was an "independent" [non-sponsored] rider and we both got in a break in the Bol d'Or de Monedieres-Chaumeil. I attacked alone on the climb and the only one who could get across was Bahamontes. He said he wouldn't go for the King of the Mountains prize at the top, which surprised me because I knew that was almost more important for him than winning. But I fell for it, we worked together, and then he outsprinted me at the summit. Then he told me as we rode towards the finish that he wasn't going to work any longer, but I didn't fall for it a second time. And even though we had two minutes' advantage at twenty kilometres we were both caught and finished fourth. To tell the truth, he gave me a very poor first impression of him.' Fast forward five years to the 1964 Tour and Jiménez felt the same as Poulidor. But this time Bahamontes arguably paid a heavier price.

Fast forward another thirty-five years and Jiménez is still resentful that Bahamontes will not give him the recognition he feels he deserves. He recalls when he and Bahamontes went to visit the Vuelta and Bahamontes was handing out postcards with his *palmares*. When somebody told Jiménez that Bahamontes had left him one and he went to pick it up, he saw it read, 'To my friend and *domestique*, [signed] Federico Martín Bahamontes'. As Jiménez points out, quite apart from being a put-down, he could never have been Bahamontes' *domestique*, given the two never rode in the same team!

Once started Jiménez cannot stop coming out with examples of Bahamontes' unwillingness to acknowledge his merits. There is little to be gained in listing them all, but several illustrate the point about how Bahamontes' pride did not permit him to admit that riders he claimed 'could never beat me', had in fact done so. At times it seems Bahamontes is trying to re-write history. 'There was the Subida [hill-climb] a Urkiola, where I beat him, and Bahamontes said he'd never ridden it,' says Jiménez. 'I had to get someone to download some classifications off the Internet and show them to him; that was the only way he would accept it. I said to him, "Look, you didn't even finish second behind me, you got third!"' Then there are the calculated putdowns. Jiménez scoffs at Bahamontes' insistence that he 'let' him win on the Puy de Dôme in 1964: 'And I joked to him maybe I'd have let him win, if he'd come up with a ruddy great cheque. I wasn't anybody then and needed the money' Another time Bahamontes was quoted as saying that his only rival in the mountains was Charly Gaul. 'And only when it rained.' Jiménez was not even mentioned.

At the root is the age-old rage of the apprentice who knows he is outstripping the master but who never feels he gets the recognition he deserves, and the master who feels his time is passing but is determined to go out anything but quietly. Dignified it is not, but there is no denying it is part of human nature. Jiménez says: 'The most reasonable thing for a star to say [on approaching retirement] is that "the young riders are breathing down my neck". And that "my successor was the Watchmaker of Ávila who won three Kings of the Mountains and should have won a fourth".' That is how numerous other stars have behaved, Jiménez says. Bahamontes, though, was always a case apart. Ultimately, these futile spats boil down to the fact that neither rider was willing to let the other gain predominance in the public eye if it meant they risked losing out. That, perhaps, was why Bahamontes was not prepared to let

Jiménez share in his ride to glory in Pau; he wanted to prove he remained the boss even if it meant losing the Tour.

Nor was this rivalry straightforward, either. While Jiménez admits that every Spanish climber was naturally keen to beat Bahamontes, because outdoing the star of the sport automatically brought added recognition, there were outbreaks of friendship and camaraderie. The two have travelled together to countless events around Spain. As recently as 2010 they went to the Vuelta presentation in Benidorm 'in a benzene-powered Audi with the race director all the way from the Paseo de la Castellana [in central Madrid]'. Yet amid the bonhomie, fast cars and backslapping, the resentment and mistrust lingered. In 1970, with Bahamontes long since retired and Jiménez desperate for a team as his career faded, he approached his old rival's professional team, La Casera, and asked for a ride. Jiménez did not have the nerve, or perhaps he had too much pride, to ask Bahamontes directly. In any case the answer came back immediately through an intermediary: No. 'I suppose that was because he thought they would forget about me quicker,' Jiménez says. And echoing Josu Loroño's words about Bahamontes, he says: 'It was all me, me, me . . . only he existed.'

In fairness to Bahamontes it is possible that Bahamontes rejected Jiménez purely because he did not think he was worth having on his team; he was at the tail-end of his career, after all. However, if it was the case that Jiménez paid the price for Bahamontes' unwillingness to share the glory in 1964, that reticence seems to have backfired completely. Others think it would have made no difference. When I interviewed Geminiani he claimed he did not believe that Bahamontes could have challenged in the 1964 Tour. 'He and Jiménez were welcome to put on all the shows they wanted to, but we knew how much time he had and we based our game around that. Apart from on the Forclaz [in 1963] he was never Anquetil's rival.' However, the way Anquetil forged alliances with Pelforth to reel in Bahamontes, both in the Alps and Pyrenees, suggest the opposite. Darrigade also feels that Bahamontes could have won the Tour. He might not have been a major threat like Poulidor, but threat he was, hence their frantic chase on the descent of the Aubisque. You can not imagine, either, that Anquetil would have forgotten Bahamontes' victory in 1959 or how close he came to winning in 1963.

That day in the Pyrenees the mistrust between the two top Spaniards was arguably what cost Bahamontes the chance of winning the Tour. The King of the Mountains had been 'his' for too long for him to give it up so easily. Most likely Bahamontes preferred to hedge his bets, thinking that even if he worked with Jiménez there was no guarantee that he would win overall. But if the two pair had worked together in 1964 the history of the Tour might read very differently indeed.

Chapter Fourteen
Into the Bushes

It took Federico Martín Bahamontes five months from the moment retiring from cycling first crossed his mind to his final, irrevocable decision. The process, during 1965, was in keeping with much of his career: occasionally farcical in appearance, often controversial in substance and nearly always driven, beneath the surface, by hard economics. The first and biggest sign that Bahamontes, now thirty-seven, was nearing the end of the road came in the 1965 Tour. After finishing second in 1963 and third in 1964, he had regained the status of favourite, particularly in the absence of Jacques Anquetil – allegedly because the Frenchman felt he had reached his sell-by date and did not want to risk being beaten. However, Bahamontes abandoned on stage ten, blaming knee injuries at the time, but later suggesting his main sponsors, Margnat, had not been paying him. 'The whole company was going to the dogs,' Bahamontes says, 'and they didn't pay anybody – neither me, nor Otaño, nor Darrigade.' André Darrigade has denied this was the case and that he was paid regularly by Margnat during his time there. When I passed this information on to Bahamontes he looked, to say the least, thunderstruck. Bahamontes says he had a major argument about the lack of money with his sports director, Raoul Remy, in the morning before the start of stage nine between Dax and Bagneres. When Remy dodged the issue and suggested he talk to the company director, Bahamontes rode off in a huff. He finished second last, forty minutes down.

Yet more fruitless discussions followed that evening in the team hotel. The next day on another Pyrenean stage from Bagneres de Bigore to Ax-les-Thermes, Bahamontes went on the attack just before the Portet-d'Aspet climb 'to show them what they would be missing'. However, if anyone expected him to reach the summit alone and at the head of the field as had been the script of so many Tours, they would to be sorely disappointed. Instead Bahamontes opened a gap, then when out of sight bizarrely rode off the road and into some bushes. 'I wanted to give them all a surprise; it was a joke,' he tells me thirty-six years later, still smiling to himself at his antics. 'They wouldn't be able to find me, the bushes were quite high. Of course, when they did find me all hell broke loose.'

For someone famed for his eccentricity and individualism it is somehow appropriate that the final image of Bahamontes on two wheels in the Tour de France is arguably the most surreal of his entire career: he is riding a road-bike, but he is not actually riding it on a road. Taken from behind, in the photograph Bahamontes can be seen heading over a broad grassy verge, well past a motorbike parked on the side of the road, and pedalling towards a dense bank of long grass with a line of trees beyond. A couple of seconds later and he would have disappeared completely. With the end of his career beckoning, the picture gives the impression that roads and civilisation no longer interest Bahamontes; complete with bike, team kit and bottle of water he is off to find himself in the jungle like the lead character in Joséph Conrad's novel *Heart of Darkness*. In fact, Bahamontes' Kurtz moment quickly passed. The next photographs taken that day show the cyclist putting on a tracksuit beside a team-car, talking with his director, and ready to abandon. It was his first step on the road to retirement and arguably the most important.

His Margnat team-mate André Darrigade recalls: 'When he left the Tour, it was a big disappointment. He was the team leader, after all; we'd all worked for him. Nobody could see it coming.' Bahamontes said at the time that he could not continue because of the knee injury, and 'you can't race the Tour on one leg'. Given he was in a breakaway when he abandoned that excuse is unconvincing. It was, though, consistent with previous controversial abandons. His antics were also highly reminiscent of the child-like behaviour he had shown back in the days when he staged go-slows in the Vuelta or pulled out of the Tour after two stages. Perhaps it was another indication that after years of self-control in the Margnat squad, Bahamontes was reverting to his 'true' self.

Coincidentally, the first rider across the Portet-D'Aspet that day was Julio Jiménez, who had won the previous day's stage after a breakaway. 'I heard Bahamontes had been dropped and turned on the heat,' Jiménez says. 'To be honest I wanted to pay him back for 1964.' That was not lost on the press either, and Jiménez was again hailed widely as Bahamontes' successor. Extensive interviews appeared with both riders with the Spanish magazine *Actualidad Española*, on 15 July, the day after the Tour finished. Tellingly, Jiménez, who won the King of the Mountains jersey that year as well as stages in the Alps and Pyrenees, has a full-page photograph on the cover and receives four pages inside; for Bahamontes, there are just two pages. There was no doubt who was the coming man. The interviews revealed that the rivalry between the two was now a full-scale power struggle for the top spot in Spanish cycling: Jiménez was determined to see Bahamontes gone, while Bahamontes was adamant that he would fight back. Underneath the headline, 'The Eaglet takes over from the Eagle', and resplendent in his Spanish national champion's jersey, Jiménez claims at first: 'I can't believe that he [Bahamontes] is finished, I'd prefer to think he's not gone ... he deserves a dignified exit'. But, perhaps rather too quickly, he reflects that Bahamontes' retirement is, in fact, 'due to happen soon', adding: 'Time waits for no man. Your natural abilities fade and if you don't abandon in due time you're bound to sink.'

Then Jiménez really sticks the knife in, suggesting that Bahamontes had failed to realise he was past his sell-by date. 'Curiously enough, he'd told me that morning that he was going better than ever in the flat, and that observation made me doubt that he was,' said Jiménez. 'He's a climber and I'm a climber.

Whenever I notice I'm going better on flat stages I know that my climbing form is going to be worse. Strange but true.' Sensing blood, the interviewer asks: 'Would you give Federico any advice?' Sure enough, Jiménez recommends that 'he should already have retired. Nothing better than an honourable retirement at the height of his powers. A minute later [on stage nine] and he'd have finished outside the time limit.' Leaving nothing to the reader's imagination, he added: 'This is the rider who forced so many others to finish outside the time limit when he won his stages and he was about to suffer the same fate. How humiliating for Federico!' Showing a keen knowledge of what drove Bahamontes on, Jiménez segued into the financial reasons for a retirement and argued that Fede's 'earning days' on the bike were long past. 'The best thing he could do now is stay at home. He's got a business going and he's not going to lack for anything. It's understandable that somebody is unwilling to renounce their best source of income when it seems like easy money. But sooner or later there aren't any rich [sponsors] left, and he shouldn't wait until they throw him out – not somebody as prestigious as Federico.'

As a declaration of how prepared Jiménez, already thirty and no spring chicken, was to step into Bahamontes shoes the *Actualidad* interview could hardly have been clearer. However, such a violent attack by one cycling star on another was also perhaps an indication of how unsure Jiménez was that Bahamontes was really going to retire. It was true that Bahamontes had ridden the Vuelta in 1965 for the first time in five years and finished tenth overall without any of his usual fireworks. 'It was,' as *Actualidad* put it, 'as if Bahamontes had abandoned the race, even though he was still there.' Bahamontes' disinterest in the Vuelta was such that Poulidor recalls he won a mountain time-trial, the Spaniard's speciality: 'I overtook six or seven riders, who had all started before me at minute intervals. The last one I caught was Bahamontes'.

But Jiménez was right to be worried. In other races that year Bahamontes had shown there was still life in the old dog yet. If you ignored the Vuelta and the Tour, Bahamontes had not had a disastrous season at all: not only had he taken second place in the

Arrate hill-climb he had captured an overall win in the Circuit du Provencal ahead of Jan Janssens, a future Tour de France winner, and Britain's Tom Simpson. Could Bahamontes really be finished? Not if his defiant first answer in the *Actualidad* interview was to be believed: 'I'm not dead, though. Me, dead? Leave off it, please. The deader people take me for the more alive I am.' However, the longer the interview went on, the more Bahamontes played it hot and cold, hinting at one point he could retire, but at another that his racing days were still not over. Presumably still holding out for payment from Margnat, Bahamontes blamed his Tour abandon on his old meniscus injury from 1955. However, when asked about the future, in different answers he was either unusually non-committal or adamant that his Tour days were finished. Something, the journalist concluded in the article, was brewing in Bahamontes' mind, but it was not clear what. 'I'm thirty-seven, not thirty-eight as some people say, and though I've lost some of my top-end speed, with time I've gained a lot of experience,' he said. 'I know I'm due to perform less well with age but I don't muck about as much as I used to.' That comment was barely credible given his recent premature exit from the Tour. 'I had and I have class,' Bahamontes nonetheless insisted. 'If I didn't I wouldn't be able to propose doing what I've got planned.' 'Such as?' asked the journalist. 'Well . . . things,' Bahamontes responded clumsily. 'Things that some people don't believe and which I don't care about if they do.' But he did reveal: 'This was my last Tour. You can be sure of that', adding by way of a rather trite explanation that: 'It's very hard.' As for racing the Vuelta, Bahamontes argued: 'That would depend on the sponsor.'

However, when asked directly if he would retire, Bahamontes seemed to leave his options open. 'It has to come some time. That's life. I don't race with the same idealism or willingness to sacrifice myself to the sport as when I started.' Such an offbeat, mixed response showed it was not going to be easy for Bahamontes to leave the sport behind. There again, he had not ruled it out. By September though, retirement had loomed a little closer when his sporting pride suffered a huge blow, thanks to the Federation.

Oddly enough, Bahamontes' beef with the Spanish Federation

this time was not down to disagreements over Grand Tours, his strongest suit, but an event in which he had never shone: the World Championships. Indeed, his best result in the World Championships was seventeenth place in 1961. Long after the World's road race, held that year in San Sebastian on 5 September, Bahamontes claimed that his dream had been to end his career in front of a home crowd and wearing the rainbow jersey of the world champion. Whether he would actually have retired had he fulfilled this highly unrealistic ambition is hard to say. But the humiliation Bahamontes suffered in the process of having to fork out money to watch a race he had desperately wanted to take part in was sufficient to tip him even closer to the edge. 'They didn't just not select me, they made me pay for my ticket to get into the circuit,' Bahamontes fumes. 'I'd ridden the Tour of Luxembourg to get into shape, and to get to San Sebastian in time I abandoned on the last stage thinking that I was in the Worlds. And then they didn't choose me. But on top of making me pay, when they [the organisers] realised I was in the stands they came up and asked me if I would cut the ribbon at the start. I said, "Don't come bothering me, I've paid for my ticket, I'm just a spectator – for one thing it's like you don't know me, and for another you come looking for me specially".' Bahamontes lays the blame on Gabriel Saura, the national coach, 'for being so envious of me. I had wanted to retire as world champion, but Saura was so jealous he made me pay for it, and I've never forgiven him for it, in all my life. I was ready to take part. Did he really not think I was one of the top eight riders in Spain?'

Bahamontes' assumption that he was one of the top eight riders in Spain, and therefore due automatic selection for the World Championships, was far from Saura's view. Bahamontes had already, without any reason offered, decided not to take part in the National Championships, which did not go down well. As Saura explained to *MARCA*: 'I can only say that Bahamontes has not raced anywhere he could have shown that he has recovered from his abandon in the French race, which he said was due to injury.' Abandoning the Tour of Luxembourg did not, contrary to Bahamontes' opinion, help his case.

On 8 September, following the row with the Federation, Bahamontes announced pointblank that he would not race any more. He then apparently called up the Volta a Catalunya organiser, the U.D. Sants cycling club, to tell them just two days before he was due to race there that he was retiring from the sport. 'I'm demoralised, and it's the right thing to do. I've thought about it, and when you have no morale, it's no good,' he told the Catalan newspaper *El Noticiero Universal*. He raced on, nonetheless, taking part in the Subida a Naranco hill-climb in Asturias where he finished eighth. Given the mixed signals, some like Margnat director Raul Remy did not believe he was going to retire. 'I consider Bahamontes to be a good rider, and with enough experience to continue for another year,' Remy said, 'though he should choose his races more carefully and pay particular attention to how he races the Tour.' The organisers of the Subida a Arrate hill-climb attempted to persuade Bahamontes to continue at least until their event the following spring. Even as late as 1 October Bahamontes was undecided, saying: 'It'll be me who decides whether I retire or not. I belong to a commercial firm [trade team] and the rest is rubbish. I'm still keen, I've still got fans, and I'm still keen to fight.'

Still wavering wildly over what to do, the final decision was not taken until he had ridden what was traditionally the race that brought down the curtain on the Spanish season, the Subida de Montjuic in Barcelona. Even more appropriately for Bahamontes' last race, Montjuic was his signature event, a hill-climb. It was held in two sections with a mass start and an uphill time-trial. Bahamontes did not win either. He was beaten into second place in both races by Raymond Poulidor. However, in warm sunshine, and watched by huge crowds, he received enormous rounds of applause in the city where his professional career had effectively begun. 'We saw Bahamontes, risen again from the ashes, and climbing formidably well,' claimed *El Mundo Deportivo*'s correspondent, before adding, a shade pretentiously, that Bahamontes 'received an effusive welcome from the fans who seemed inspired by enthusiasm [we would see] in the olden days . . . the public came here to savour the finest essence of cycling'. And for their main photograph to illustrate the event, what better than Bahamontes powering up a climb between a wall of fans one last time?

Bahamontes says he had barely finished in Barcelona when his longstanding Catalan business associate, Evaristo Murtra, told him in no uncertain terms that his career was over and that he should concentrate on his business in Toledo. 'He came up to me and said, "Right, now you are going to Toledo to sell bikes and motorbikes in your shop with your wife". I disagreed, saying, "Now that they pay me double, I'm going to stop?" Murtra replied, "It's not worth it. What's best for you are motorbikes and bikes and that's the future. That's where the easy money is."' With that alluring prospect in mind Bahamontes could have announced he had ended his career there and then. However, there were rumours that he would continue racing at least until the Six Days of Madrid track race, an exhibition event he had won the previous year. Here again versions vary of what actually happened. While Bahamontes insists to this day that he had decided to stop after Montjuic, the Madrid organisers told MARCA they were convinced he was going to be taking part in their event, because 'he wants to end his career in front of a home crowd, in Madrid'. However, it was claimed that a disagreement over the appearance money Bahamontes would be paid ruined what would have been a more spectacular send-off, especially as results are often pre-arranged in such exhibition events: he would have had a reasonable chance of going out with his arms aloft in victory one last time.

'He asked for two hundred thousand pesetas [£36,000],' the organisers told MARCA, 'which is what we paid him the previous year. But we offered him what [Spanish track start] Guillermo Timoner was going to get, and he didn't want to do the selection test for the event, anyway.' Afterwards, the organisers were adamant that 'his absence wasn't noticed'.

Whatever the truth of these claims, Bahamontes did not take part. He was moving on. An ex-cyclist now, he quickly adopted a new role as expert commentator on Spanish cycling. That winter he took part in a round-table conference in Bilbao with his old rival

Jesús Loroño, which predictably turned into a rose-tinted look back at their careers and how much better racing had been in the past. While Loroño said he believed Spanish cycling 'needed a rivalry like me and Federico had', Bahamontes claimed: 'If you take a look at my *palmares* there is no rider in Spain who's done better than me this year. [Top Spanish riders] Patxi Gabica, [Valentin] Uriona and José Pérez Frances could have got better results,' he claimed. In fact, Gabica and Uriona had both won two stages in the Volta a Catalunya, while Pérez Francés had won a stage of the Tour and finished sixth overall. 'But they just sit behind other riders' wheels [in the pack]. They're cold-blooded and never attack.' Since Bahamontes had just opted to retire because it made more sense economically this was at best a case of the pot calling the kettle black.

There is a certain irony that, rather than back out because he felt he had nothing more to give to the sport or that his time was up, Spain's top athlete of the 1950s retired using exactly the same kind of hardheaded financial logic with which he started riding a bike in the first place. In that sense, at least, Bahamontes had come full circle.

Chapter Fifteen
La Vuelta A Toledo

When you're going well, you don't suffer, you enjoy it. Nothing can go wrong because you can see that it's not you that's suffering, it's the rest of the field. Every turn of your pedal feels like a fresh round of applause a singer receives.

Federico Martín Bahamontes

August may be the hottest month of the year in Spain, but it still feels pretty chilly at 7 a.m. as dawn breaks over the broad, busy avenue in Toledo where Federico Martín Bahamontes' fan club, his *Peña*, is based. A shadowy group of men in their forties and upwards traipse back and forth between the building and a cluster of half a dozen vehicles parked nearby. As the sun rises the stickers on the hefty four-wheel drive cars become slowly legible. Across the top of the windscreens each one reads 'Vuelta a Toledo 2011'. The chain gang in shorts and T-shirts heaving boxes and folders out of the *Peña* are the race's back-up staff, and they are putting the finishing touches to that day's final stage of one of the biggest under-23 races in central Spain.

The reason for the painfully early start is simple: the race starts rolling at 9.30 a.m. and is finished by midday, well before the real heat kicks in. 'Fede? The boss doesn't come til later,' one says of those carrying boxes containing the trophies for the presentation.

Sure enough, just before 8 a.m., Bahamontes arrives in person, bustling around and barking orders. The convoy of six vehicles moves off soon afterwards towards the start, which is held in the most uninspiring of settings: slap bang in the middle of a semi-deserted industrial estate on the outskirts of town. On one side there is a line of wholesale dealers closed for August, on the other a huge metal fence and a severely under-used petrol station the size of a football stadium. It looks like the ideal location for a particularly gruesome gangland murder. However, the police motorbike planted in the centre of the road, blue light whirling, is only there to deter traffic. At one end a race steward in bright yellow safety vest guides team cars and race vehicles to their parking spots. In the middle Bahamontes blasts away on his whistle, stomping up and down the lines of cars to make sure they park absolutely where he wants them. The race's centre of activity is just in front of a shop selling knock-down furniture. Three girls stand behind a long trestle table and serve coffee and snacks to the handful of spectators, a trio of blue-shirted officials from the U.C.I. and the small army of organisers and hangers-on.

What the start lacks in scenery, though, it makes up for in good vibrations. The twelve-strong motorised corps of Civil Guards wander around munching croissants, chattering away cheerfully and, in the way Spanish policemen do, half-hiding the morning's first cigarettes in cupped hands behind their backs. Riders weave their way to the signing-on table just outside the shop, then dart back to their team cars, one hand on the handlebars, the other clutching a cup of coffee. Nobody seems stressed: for the organisers and police 9 August marks the last leg of their work, and though the classification is still undecided the participants know they will also be heading home soon. At one point Bahamontes waves over the race leader, a tall amiable Frenchman from the G.S.C. Blagnac club and demands to know: 'Tu aller gagner?' 'Je pense que oui,' replies the younger man with a broad smile before quickly pedalling away. Bahamontes, meanwhile, looks a shade smug about being able to speak the rider's language sufficiently well to hold the brief conversation. There is more of a communication problem, though, when the race doctor forms a brief huddle with the event's one injured rider, a Japanese amateur, whose knee and arm are a mass of injuries and seeping blood from a crash the previous day. The doctor bellows in Spanish at the rider's French director: 'Tell him he can take the bandages off in a couple of days.' The director looks blank, the Japanese rider even blanker. 'Two days,' the doctor shouts again before making strange handsigns.

Things, though, could not be friendlier. There are no restrictions, V.I.P. areas or team buses to deter the public from getting close to the riders. Though the location for the start is hardly ideal, the spectacular finish at the Plaza del Zocodover in the heart of Toledo's old town more than makes up for that. The riders and team staff look pleased with the warm weather and free food as they ogle the gaggle of publicity girls, barely out of their teens and teetering in white high-heels. To judge from the slogan plastered on one girl's T-shirt – ITV Ocaña – a government M.O.T. vehicle centre is a sponsor.

With no houses in sight there are few children present. One who is must be about two years old and he is clutching his grand-mother's arm. As they pass Bahamontes the boy receives a quick lesson in cycling history. 'That man is called Bahamontes and he won a big bike race called the Tour de France,' Grandma says. The two-year-old looks far more interested in the huge, empty filling station opposite than a grizzled man more than eighty years his senior, but it is a nice gesture all the same.

Like any sports event, part of this race's appeal is its predict-ability. Here, a PR vehicle consisting of a large man with a small microphone, a booming voice and a couple of loudspeakers strapped to the roof, draws up and begins informing everybody of what they already know. 'This is the Vuelta a Toledo, the fourth and final stage, and it's about to start.' Finally, after much to-ing and fro-ing and more pointless bellowing to corral the riders, Bahamontes dons the most incongruous headgear imaginable: a sailing cap. It clashes dreadfully with his sharply-ironed trousers, sensible brown shoes and immaculate white top and makes him look like a bank manager who has wandered into a landlocked marina. But as his way of indicating the race is about to start, it certainly stands out.

And the race starts with a bang, too. Running in a long south-westerly loop out and back to Toledo, the pack shatters almost immediately on two short but painfully steep climbs on the southern, rural side of the River Tagus. At the top of each one the bunch is in a line and gasping for breath, edging over the summit in groups of five or six. The race leader is just behind the first group of riders, looking far less happy than when he spoke to Bahamontes. On the roller-coaster roads which follow, past vast cattle ranches and foul-smelling pig farms, there is little chance of regrouping.

The twenty or so members of the race organisation act like sheepdogs around a worried, highly mobile flock. They warn the riders of upcoming dangers by waving flags or arms; they honk their horns at roadside fans to warn them the race is approaching; they power ahead to check that any obstacles have been cleared, then remove all the evidence of signs, barricades and bottles that showed Toledo's biggest bike race has just passed through. It is a non-stop operation but it proceeds smoothly. Since Bahamontes has been in charge for all the race's forty-six years, that is perhaps not so surprising. As for Bahamontes himself, he is a co-pilot in a two-seat, open-top sportscar, preceded by the two front-runners from the race's police escort. While a U.C.I. official runs the internal workings of the race, keeping an eye on the head of the pack, Bahamontes is responsible for ensuring any last-minute hitches are cleared. It is also impossible not to notice that as the spearhead of the race he soaks up the maximum attention possible. La Vuelta a Toledo is, in a sense, the Vuelta de Bahamontes, which is appropriate as Vuelta also means 'return' or 'comeback' in Spanish, as well as 'tour'. If on one level it is a race, on another it represents Bahamontes going back to his roots on a circuit of the villages and towns where he raced as an amateur. That said, despite being Toledo's greatest sports star Bahamontes is more than happy to knuckle down. He pulls down barriers, whizzes across from one side of the road to another at junctions with red tape to discourage oncoming vehicles, and yells and waves should any official vehicle be too close to the pack for his liking.

'Fede's never been one to work in a team and we're all used to that,' comments Basilio López, a close friend and head of sports at a local town hall, who drives a car for race guests and V.I.P.s in his holiday time. 'He's too hands-on to delegate responsibilities. I keep on telling him that he should just ease back and let others take over. But he's too keen to get involved. It's the philosophy of the workers who were born under Franco: you don't stop working till you drop.' Basilio has been part of the organisation for the last decade and reveals that the heart of the race is the Bahamontes' *peña* itself. While barely functioning now as a supporters' club, its main role is to run four or five bike races. In a town with no cycling clubs like Toledo that is hugely important. As the effects of the recession continue to affect Spain the number of teams has dropped though, by around a third. The chances of another rider following the wheeltracks of a former winner like modern-day Spanish Classics star Juan Antonio Flecha and making the big time are increasingly limited.

However, even if Bahamontes spends a large part of his year chasing up money from the towns and villages who host the tour – he has the list of debtors kept permanently in his inside jacket pocket – the commercial sponsors remain solid. Wurth and the M.O.T. centre at nearby Ocaña have been loyal for years, and if Coca-Cola's sponsorship of the signing-on table at the start is hardly the most generous of efforts by the biggest multi-national present, at least there are free cans of fizzy pop to drink as a result. There are national backers as well for a bulging portfolio of different prizes within the race: RENFE, the Spanish state railway, and the Spanish branch of Shimano, the bike components manufacturer, back two different sprint competitions. A local transport company has forked out for the King of the Mountains prize and a Toledo-based builder specialising in swimming pools funds the points jersey competition.

As usual in bike races the smaller the town and the further it is from the big cities the greater the interest. When the race passes through Galvez, a town where Bahamontes used to go to pick up bags of corn and wheat as a black marketeer more than sixty years ago, it seems that every front doorstep has a little child squatting on it, with grandma sitting on a canvas chair just outside and elder brothers and sisters lined along the pavement. On the outskirts of Toledo, though, barely anybody stops to look.

While returning to Toledo ahead of the race Basilio stops to give a co-worker a lift: it is the *peña's* treasurer, José Ignacio. The *peña* is still going, he reveals, but it is crumbling at the edges. Almost all its members are in their sixties or older and the days are long gone when its numbers ran into the thousands and they had separate sections for hunting and skeet shooting. Now the number of card-carrying *peñistas* is down to just one hundred. Ignacio remembers the day of glory in 1959 when Toledo was awash with yellow ribbons and the bars served 'yellow jerseys' and 'leaders' rather than glasses of beer. 'I'd joined the *peña* a few years before,' he recalls, 'but when Fede won I was on my honeymoon. Still, anywhere I'd go, the minute I told them I was part of his *peña*, it was drinks on the house for me,' he cackles. 'That's the spirit of Spain that we've now lost,' Basilio reflects. 'The old, real Spain.'

Bahamontes might have fallen out with the Spanish Cycling Federation after the events of 1965 but as a recently retired rider he had no intention of leaving the world of cycling. He bought his bike shop premises outright from its former owner after apparently helping to speed up the process by threatening to apply pressure in Toledo's town hall after the owner had been embroiled in a scandal involving a priest. Almost immediately he started directing the first in a series of amateur and professional teams. Initially encouraged by his success with junior teams, and using his fan-club headquarters as the logistics base for all these teams, the 'La Casera-Peña Bahamontes' ran as a ten-rider amateur team in 1968, and then with a squad of twenty-three in 1969. It became a professional team in 1970 and quickly moved into the middle ranks of the Spanish cycling hierachy. With the help of experienced co-director Miguel Moreno, La Casera took a stage victory in the Giro d'Italia in 1970 with Miguel Mari Lasa as well as the sprints competition in the Vuelta a España. Joaquim Galera even won Bahamontes' old favourite, the Arrate hill-climb in the Basque Country.

With Lasa gone, though, 1971 and 1972 were leaner years. But the team bounced back in 1973 when Pedro Torres took the team's first (and only) stage win in the Tour de France as well as the King of the Mountains competition. (José Luis Abilleira had pulled off the same 'double' in the Vuelta where La Casera also won the team prize.) Then in 1974 Abilleira landed the King of the Mountains jersey in the Vuelta a España for the second year running. However, with major arguments breaking out behind the scenes between Bahamontes and his riders that proved to be La Casera-Bahamontes' last season as a professional squad.

From Bahamontes' point of view, La Casera-Bahamontes was a victim of its own success. He became increasingly disappointed and frustrated with his riders, who, he claims, grew more and more demanding with each triumph. 'We built the team up category by category, from juvenile to junior to amateur to professional and we signed the best riders from all the other teams,' Bahamontes recalls. 'We had an advantage in that we had a big backer [La Casera] and the owner told me to do the maths and we turned pro. We had some good riders, and we were the first team out there to buy a bus for the riders to travel in to the starts. But after racing Milan-San Remo one year the riders wanted to go back by plane rather than in the bus, and I told them they couldn't, not after all the money we'd made the owner pay for it. If they didn't like the bus they could ride back home on their bikes.' That, says Bahamontes, was the beginning of the end. 'Then they started to make more and more demands [across the board]: they wanted to be Napoleon without having won the war. I had teams [amateur and profesional] for nineteen years. But [the professional team didn't fold] because of what it cost, the problem was what the cyclists demanded – and what they couldn't have.'

Bahamontes did not just run a shop and a bike team. Almost as soon as he retired his *peña* took over the role of Toledo's main cycling club, organising the prestigious four-day Vuelta a Toledo and other stage races. Another long-term project was a bike museum, located in the unlikely setting of an industrial tools factory, forty minutes' drive from Toledo. It contains around twenty frames from Bahamontes' career, as well as bikes donated by everybody who was anybody in Spanish cycling, from Miguel Indurain to Oscar Freire, the three-times world champion. It even includes the wooden-rimmed models Bahamontes used during his days as a black-marketeer. In addition, there are heavy woollen jerseys, posters, photographs and other paraphernalia from his past. Had Bahamontes' plans to transfer the museum to Toledo's city centre succeeded it would have been more appealing to normal tourists. But for bike fans the trip to the Wurth factory is well worthwhile.

Bahamontes had no qualms about milking the celebrity circuit during his retirement. For years he would travel the length and breadth of Spain, and occasionally France, in a gleaming Mercedes to attend everything from velodrome openings and cycling club prize-givings to annual get-togethers of former star riders. There is still no stopping him. In 2011 he twice presented the prizes at the finishes of different stages of the Vuelta, in Talavera and El Escorial, and was there again in Madrid, springing on to the podium to hand over the King of the Mountains' jersey to David Moncoutié, of France. He is always willing to turn up for cycling celebrations or ceremonies, sometimes uninvited, as Alberto Contador once discovered. He is a regular interviewee in various forms of media on the state of Spanish cycling, though he is none too polite about modern cycling in general. Indeed, he said in an interview a few years ago: 'It's no longer the same since it became pure business. It's got a lot softer, too compassionate. Breakaways in my time weren't like the ones [1988 Tour winner Pedro] Delgado used to do, in the last five hundred metres and with a big team. These days if somebody punctures the rest of the field is supposed to wait. Back when I was riding you'd use that to get an extra couple of minutes. Sport's no longer got that edge to it. It's like if you cut someone's eyebrow in boxing, should you stop trying to hit it? Of course not.'

*

To many observers, Bahamontes seems incapable of slowing down to a more settled lifestyle. It has got to the point where it is jocularly suggested that his multifarious activities would wear out someone twenty years his junior. 'Bahamontes or how to freeze time', ran the headline in Spanish sports daily *AS* during the 2011 Vuelta. Underneath was a photograph of Bahamontes at the race taking pictures with the Agfa Optima III camera he has had since 1960. 'Federico was a popular hero in a Spain that was just opening up to the world,' the article said, 'and a media phenomenon, perhaps the first of [Spanish] sport . . . [he was] over the top, provocative, extravagant, impulsive and vain. A genius of the bicycle.'

When asked the secret of his longevity Bahamontes always has two answers: the first, he claims, is that he did not take dope, with the tacit implication that others of his generation did and paid a high price. The second is work. 'If you come tomorrow, on Saturday and Sunday, you'll see me doing the same as I did today,' he told *El País* in June 2011 'I started work at eleven, flinging stones into a truck [when he and his father were road-menders]; now I work from the morning until two or three when I stop for lunch. And half an hour later I'm back in there again. I get up at seven [in the morning] and I don't stop.' In a sense it is a continuation of his life as a professional rider. He has always been 'the last to go to bed and the first to get up'. At weekends he occupies himself on his small area of farmland, checking and tending crops, but his week-day routine centres on office work at the *peña*. Much of his time is spent chasing up unpaid bills from recession-hit town halls who have hosted the starts or finishes of the Vuelta a Toledo. In one of our most recent interviews, he showed me the foot-high pile of paperwork detailing money due. Periodically he will drive off to hound the defaulters in person. It seems the final chapter of Spain's leading sportsman from the first half of the Franco regime could be that of an unofficial, ageing debt-collector.

His lifestyle will probably remain frenetic. It is in his genes. He told *El País*: 'My maternal grandfather had the same character. He was a small guy, but dynamic. My mother always used to say *"alto y flojo, como el hinojo"* ['tall and weak, just like fennel'] because when they [people] are taller, they can't reach down so easily and they can't work so hard.' And how did he feel about reaching eighty-three? 'You can't turn back the clock and be in the thick of the action all the time.' But if he did not work, he admits: 'I would be sunk.'

He is still married to Fermina and has frequent visitors to his *peña*, but there are still flashes of his old solitary self when he was the Eagle of Toledo flying through the mountains of France, Italy and Spain. When I asked him once if he had any good friends, either in sport or out of it, his answer was: 'Just one: Evaristo Murtra.' But that was all. And in interviews he gives the strong impression that his relationship with Murtra was founded on business rather than a personal friendship. However, that sense of isolation does not seem to bother him; it just sums up his life-philosophy. As he puts it: '*Solo me muevo mejor que nadie*' ('alone, I move better than anybody else'). And given what he achieved flying solo, can that really be doubted?

The *palmares* cannot fail to impress: six King of the Mountains titles and Spain's first victory in the Tour de France; two podium finishes in the same race when aged over thirty-five; seven Tour stage wins plus notable victories in every other major stage race of his time. The big unanswered question in Bahamontes' career, though, is whether he could have done even more? Or was he riding so far above his usual level in 1959 that further victories in the Tour were never really on the cards? And was he the world's best climber of all time? There will never be definitive answers. Yes, Richard Virenque may have one more King of the the Mountains title, and Lucien Van Impe more mountain-top stage wins and as many mountain titles as Bahamontes. But Virenque did not win the Tour and Van Impe never came close to Bahamontes' record of crossing Tour mountain passes in first place fifty-three times. And without Bahamontes, so the story goes, there might not have been a Van Impe at all: the Spaniard provided the inspiration for the Belgian to get on a bike in the first place. Indeed, it is said that Bahamontes used his influence to get Van Impe his first professional contract

after seeing him win the King of the Mountains title in the Tour de
L'Avenir, France's top race for promising amateurs. When I asked
cycling's all-time top rider Eddy Merckx what he thought of
Bahamontes' place in cycling history, he said: 'There are different
eras, different people and it's very hard to compare. But he was
certainly one of a very few, one of the very, very greatest.'

The question remains, though, whether a rider who could climb
so well that others, like Raymond Poulidor, say that to attempt to
follow him was to 'like committing suicide', might have acheived
more than near-blinding, but erratic, flashes of brilliance. So why
didn't he? Quite apart from Geminiani's skulduggery in 1963, his
failure to collaborate with Julio Jiménez in 1964, or even that elusive
telegram from the Franco Government during the 1957 Vuelta, the
single biggest factor in his failure to shine even more brightly must
be poor management. On a good day, he could be the best climber
there has been. However, lack of consistency was his biggest
downfall: to gain it a volatile, erratic personality like Bahamontes
needed a firm hand directing him; too rarely did he have one.

From Geminiani to a man I met near a graveyard in Val de Santo
Domingo, the common consensus is that Coppi was the best
manager he had, certainly in terms of his motivational skills.
Dalmacio Langarica was the one Bahamontes valued most for his
practical abilities, but Coppi was the one who inspired him to
greatness and the man with his finger on the pulse when it came to
technological advances in the sport too.

The tragedy, though, is that even if the Tricolfilina-Coppi team's
financial difficulties had not existed, Coppi's untimely death in early
1960 leaves unanswered the question of what Bahamontes' career
might have been with the Italian by his side for longer. And
Langarica, his other guiding light, was only with Bahamontes for
one Tour. For that reason 1959 became a watershed for
Bahamontes. When he had the natural strength of a young man
he did not have the team or director he needed; then when he did
have the team and the directors, particularly post-1959 with Raoul
Remy, he no longer had the natural power of a younger man.
Remy, in any case, made some strategic errors such as when he

ordered Bahamontes to sit up during his Pyrenean attack in 1963. It was only in 1959, when Bahamontes was thirty-one, with Coppi overseeing him and Langarica's faultless guidance of the team in the Tour that the twin elements of brute strength and sound strategy fully blended. When that happened, nothing could stop the Eagle of Toledo.

One indication of just how perfectly the planets lined up for Bahamontes that year is that he remains one of only six riders to win the Tour's overall classification and the King of the Mountains in the same race. It is surely no coincidence that Coppi, Bahamontes' mentor, took both titles in 1949 and 1952. But since 1959 only Eddy Merckx (in 1969 and 1970) and Carlos Sastre, by default in 2008 after Austrian Bernard Kohl was banned for doping, have managed the difficult double.

It was inevitable that such a huge triumph for Spain was exploited so ruthlessly by General Franco's regime. Starved of international recognition, and in constant need to justify its existence to the Spanish population as memories of the Civil War faded, sport provided both a pressure valve on social unrest for the Franco dictatorship and as a propaganda vehicle. As a Castillian taking what was arguably Spain's biggest individual athletic triumph since the Civil War, Bahamontes' Tour de France win was too good an opportunity to miss. As such, Bahamontes acts as a bridge between the two key periods of the Franco era: a reminder of the harsh, post-Civil War recession and international isolation of the earliest years, and the transition to the economic well-being of the 1960s and 1970s.

In terms of sport, at least, Bahamontes is one of the last, and certainly the most important, link between the two eras. But even today in Spain he is rarely cited as such. One of the rare high-profile analyses of Bahamontes' significance for Spanish society came in a keynote speech made by *MARCA's* former editor, Eduardo Inda, to celebrate the seventieth anniversary of the newspaper in 2011. In it he singled out Bahamontes as the one person who 'gained our affection because he confirmed that the "botched-up" Spain was giving way, little by little, to the Spain of excellence. His Tour and his six Kings of the Mountains prizes carried us to seventh heaven'. Inda went on to describe what the success of Bahamontes and other athletes meant to the people of Spain at the time. 'We feel grateful, emotionally, to the most veteran members [of our sport] because you made our long night of dictatorshp more bearable. With sport, the suffering was less painful, even knowing that the former regime used sport generally . . . as a sleeping pill which would make us forget the anxiety we had for freedom and the harsh economic and social post-war reality . . . they gave colour to a black-and-white Spain, to that Spain we have recorded in our minds as if it were an interminable *no-do*.' As Inda sees it, Bahamontes and his co-stars at the time played a beneficial role even while they were being exploited by the regime to help justify its existence.

Then there is his continuing role as the father figure for Spanish cycling, as Pedro Delgado calls him, and in particular for their most valued facet of the sport, stage racing. 'I'm from a much later generation,' says Miguel Indurain, Spain's five-times Tour de France winner and for many his country's top all-time athlete. 'I grew up watching Merckx and Hinault, but we all knew how Bahamontes was the one who staged the break-through for us in the Tour. In the mountains, he was unmatchable, even if consistency never was his strong point.'

Perhaps thinking of Jesús Loroño and Vicente Treuba, Indurain says: 'There were riders before him who were important, but Bahamontes was the Tour pioneer. He was an impulsive, very fiery rider – and that's still the case now. He just keeps going, he never stops. But he was hugely important, particularly when you consider that back then the Tour de France was as big as [football's] World Cup here in Spain. Not like now.'

The pioneering aspect of Bahamontes is one of his most appealing legacies. Perhaps one of the hardest aspects for fans to accept is how big a part money had to play in his career. Yet he was far from being the only big name to view cycling as a business as much as a sport. In William Fotheringham's biography of Tom Simpson, he writes of the British star: 'His contemporaries all noted his financial hunger.' And according to Paul Howard's biography, one potential reason why Jacques Anquetil failed to go for a sixth Tour de France was that it did not make financial sense. 'For him [Anquetil], the notion of a palmares was absurd if it didn't add value commercially,' top French cycling journalist Philippe Brunel tells Howard.

Apart from the precarious nature of his profession, as Carlos Sastre points out, this was an era in Spain when the struggle for survival was not just a question of being better or worse off. Like a large percentage of the population, including many of its greatest cyclists, Bahamontes lived through an era in which the spectre of starvation was never far away. It is hardly a surprise that whatever 'life-philosophy' he and other Spanish professionals learnt then was applied so aggressively to their racing. If this explains some of the sport's less savoury aspects, then arguably the same fear of financial ruin also helped drive Bahamontes and his fellow professionals along the path to greatness. 'You mustn't forget he was living in a time when nutrition as we know it didn't exist. It was a question of survival, pure and simple,' Sastre believes. 'That made them fight hard for sustenance and that kind of fighting experience was what made them such tough cyclists. Now we have all we want to eat and we just think about stupid things like buying cars. In the jungle, you're looking for food, not for the best car or the nicest house, just to survive.'

Raphael Geminiani concurs with Sastre's analysis, but goes further. 'He was more worried about making money than anything else,' he says. 'And that's why he didn't do his job so well, because he wasn't sufficiently dedicated to his profession.' However, if money was the reason which drove Bahamontes to racing, and which spurred him on in his amateur years, ultimately it may have been what let him down, too. Right from the start the richer Bahamontes became, the more King of the Mountains titles he amassed, the less willing he seems to have been to opt for the riskier goal of going for the overall titles. Matters reached a head in 1964: had he reached a deal with Julio Jiménez that had worked, such as conceding the King of the Mountains title, Bahamontes could have found the ally he needed on the long road to Pau. The margin between himself and Anquetil going into the time-trial that followed would have been smaller. But Bahamontes could not give up his 'surefire guarantee' of the King of the Mountains and beneath that lies a fascinating contradiction: the less likely his attacks were to succeed in winning the biggest prize, the greater his reputation as cycling's best 'pure' climber, and as the dreamer who never gave up. Or, to use a very Castillian metaphor, the eternal tilter at windmills.

All great sports stars have their critics and there are those who believe that rather than Bahamontes' career going largely unrewarded, in 1959 he simply got lucky and was in the right place at the right time when the French started to fall out among themselves. Geminiani, who was riding in the French 'A' team that year as one of the 'Big Four', does not agree. 'Bahamontes was not the climber he's been taken for,' Geminiani says. 'He was more spectacular than efficient. But then just when Bahamontes was getting on in years, just when Charly Gaul was at the height of his powers, just when he has all of the top French riders – Anglade, Rivière, Anquetil – lined up against him, Bahamontes goes off and wins the Tour. It's true they say that he was able to take advantage of the war between the agents, but that's not the case. Anquetil did not want Rivière to win – true. Rivière did not want Anquetil to win – true. But that Anquetil and Rivière ganged up against Anglade – not true. They stayed out of it. It wasn't their fight. All we saw that year was an Anglade-Bahamontes duel. And Bahamontes deserved to win it.'

Another damaging factor for Bahamontes' career was his erratic, sometimes eccentric, personality. But at least in 1959 Coppi and Langarica were there to resolve those problems. The knock-on effect was noticed by the newspapers. 'He is as hyper-nervous as Coppi, but now his brain controls those nerves,' argued *El Alcázar* after his Tour win. 'That extreme nervousness is what all great champions have . . . Coppi, aware he was close to losing a Tour [in 1952], once told a mechanic to get the right wheel as soon as possible or he'd shoot his head off. That kind of temperament is a two-edged weapon. If used rightly then it's a huge advantage.

Bahamontes' issues make him seem what he is not – vain, proud and anti-social – when in reality he is simply childlike.'

In his role as a latter-day commentator Bahamontes is wont to say: 'People don't enjoy cycling as much as they used to because there aren't any more breakaways like mine.' Note the use of the word 'breakaways' rather than 'wins'. Therein may lie the nub of why Bahamontes remains such an inspiring figure: because his concept of racing borders on the artistic, or as *L'Equipe* once said of him, on the 'Bohemian'. It is almost an anti-sporting way of racing a sport. Climbing up mountains at the head of the pack just because they are there, not because of what you can gain, underlines the fact that sport is ultimately an exercise in futility, albeit a fascinating one. That futility can even have a subversive edge as when Bahamontes stopped for his ice cream on top of the Romeyere. The effect was unintentional, but to the world it looked as if he was walking away deliberately from his chance of glory. And given his self-destructive racing style in the years that followed, the tantrums and the multiple abandons, that is why the image of Bahamontes opting for an ice cream, rather than continuing, retains so much power. Even if he did not mean it, it looked like 'typical Bahamontes'.

Bahamontes lingers in the memory precisely because of his wayward eccentricity and love of seemingly pointless, impetuous, attacking. Unfulfilled potential is far more romantic than a series of brilliant results, as Bahamontes, talking to reporters after his fruitless break across the Bonette-Restefond in the 1964 Tour, was keenly aware. As he put it: 'This will have made the bars in Toledo a lot of money this afternoon.' However, there was always an eminently practical bent to it all, too: after blasting across the mountain pass at the head of the Tour, Bahamontes was also the same man who stuffed his suitcase full of spare bike parts to sell back home in Spain. He was the one whose first thoughts when he talked to reporters after winning the Tour in 1959 was how much money he could make out of it. And that is perhaps his greatest achievement, that Bahamontes was driven by a desire for financial gain, but simultaneously maintained the rather far-fetched but appealing image of the eccentric climber forging his own solitary, almost dream-like path far from the vices of civilisation.

To race just for the money is straightforward enough, and so it is to race idiosyncratically. To do both, simultaneously, for twelve years as a professional is a tough call indeed. It is something only a handful of athletes have managed to pull off as convincingly as the Eagle of Toledo .

If the grimy, run-down setting for the start of the Vuelta a Toledo was a pretty faithful reflection of life in the suburbs of post-industrial Spain, the finish could hardly be more 'teepical Spanish', as the natives themselves say when the country's caricatures are so brazenly displayed. It is staged in the central Zocodover square at the top of a sharp, cobbled rise into old Toledo. The feel that this is the touristy part of town is reinforced by the woman in a tight flamenco dress, and even tighter hairbun, standing on top of the podium and belting out traditional folksongs. The crowd of around one hundred is mostly foreign, too. Eventually an MC from the race organisation takes over. Not even his inane patter – 'they're coming very fast, the bunch is all over the place, they're coming very fast, what's going to happen?' – causes the crowd to thin. All that matters is that they are enjoying themselves: it is a fine, sunny day and they are about to witness a free spectacle. For bike races in the summer that is the way it has always been.

Meanwhile, at the finish, which stretches down one cobbled side of triangular square in the shadow of the town hall, Bahamontes is once again in full flight. Striding up and down between the barriers and under the finishing gantry, it is Bahamontes who waves through what little race traffic there is before the peloton itself turns up. He is constantly peering at the descent to see if the riders are on their way. He bustles, he fusses, he is never still for more than ten seconds. The characteristic energy he exudes is irritating and fascinating in equal measure. When the riders finally appear the barriers are thick with the public. Bahamontes disappears from view as a blizzard of glittering bike frames and brightly coloured, tensed bodies, roar past. One, a shovel-jawed, burly teenaged

Spaniard in a gaudy red, yellow and blue jersey, bellows with delight as he scoots across the line for both the stage win and, it later emerges, overall victory.

No sooner has the stage finished than Bahamontes is back in action. Beneath the curtain behind the podium his brown leather shoes can be seen darting around at high speed. The announcer spends a long time requesting riders, most leaning on team car bonnets and comparing stories before the long trip home, to come up for their prizes. Finally, perhaps half an hour after the race is finished, the ceremony starts. 'A big hand for Teresa, the godmother of the Vuelta a Toledo,' the MC says as another publicity girl teeters across the stage, clutching a bag of cakes and sweets provided by local manufacturer Miguelañez instead of bouquets or a trophy. The Frenchman who was leading the race overnight, looks gloomy at getting beaten but still receives the prize for best under-23 rider, courtesy of the M.O.T. centre. He cheers up appreciably when he receives a couple of kisses from the PR girls. Then, when a couple of slightly inebriated friends in the crowd start bellowing his name and pointing at the sky, he positively beams.

Each time the winner of a different trophy comes out, Bahamontes again dashes out from the wings, fidgeting behind the publicity girls, pulling at their sleeves to ensure they stand correctly on the podium for the photographs. There is one cringeworthy moment when he all but manhandles a small child, clearly the son of a sponsor and allowed on to the podium as a treat, out of the way of the prizewinner. 'Can't he just enjoy it?' says one member of the public, a bike rider himself judging by his shaven legs. 'He's so nervous about everything.' There are a few moments when Bahamontes is recognised: 'Fede, you're the best', one man shouts, and another asks for a photograph with the 1959 Tour winner. But that is it: his time, it seems, has gone. Or perhaps not. When the riders have all had their pictures taken, raised their arms and brandished their trophies, Bahamontes leaps on to the stage again clutching handfuls of postcards bearing his picture and a list of his palmares which he flings gleefully into the crowd. Is it a pure ego trip? There is only one answer to that.

However, in a country where the sport is drying up in the worst recession since the 1950s, his bike race endures. In fact, the Vuelta a Toledo is the only Spanish race of its level that has never been cancelled, not once in its forty-six-year history. And it is a world away from the Ministry of Education race held nearby that offered Bahamontes his start back in 1947. But the connection between the two persists in the shape of a man still driven onwards by the same manic energy that enabled him to rule the Tour de France mountains for more than a decade.

And the legend, albeit increasingly distorted, lives on as well. 'Bahamontes?' the taxi driver says as I head away. 'Not many people know who he is now, but he was the greatest in his time.'

These are perhaps the final images we should retain of the Eagle of Toledo, the ones from the Vuelta a Toledo in August 2011: Bahamontes, arms waving in the air, whistle blowing, as he guides his race through the province where it all began; Bahamontes, determined to maintain his place in the public's consciousness and act as an inspiration for the younger generations of riders even if it all comes down to an eighty-three-year-old flinging pieces of paper into the crowd; Bahamontes, standing at the top of the climb to the Zocodover square, alone again naturally, but waiting to see who will be the fastest rider to power up the hill and join him.

Bahamontes being Bahamontes, he might even get an ice cream.

Palmares

Federico Martín Bahamontes
Place of birth: Val de Santo Domingo, Spain
Date of birth: 9 July, 1928
Turned professional: 1953
Retired: 1965

1953 TEAM: BALANZAS BERKEL/SPLENDID

Wins
Tour of Asturias: stage 1 and King of
the Mountains (K.O.M.)
Circuito del Sardinero: stage 1
Tour of Malaga: overall
Volta a Catalunya: K.O.M

Selected places
Volta a Catalunya: 8th
Tour of Asturias: 21st

1954 TEAM: CIRCULO BARCELONISTA-YASTA/SPLENDID-D'ALESSANDRO

Wins
Mt. Agel hill-climb
Tour of Mallorca: stage 3
(first sector)
Tour of Asturias: K.O.M.
Tour de France: K.O.M.
Bicicleta Eibarresa: K.O.M.

Selected places
Tour de France: 25th; stage 18, 5th
Barcelona–Palamos: 2nd
Bicicleta Eibarresa: 2nd
Tour of Mallorca: 3rd
GP Cannes: 4th
Trofeo Masferrer: 5th
Spanish Regional Championships: 7th

1955 TEAM: PEÑA LA SOLERA

Wins
Tour of Asturias: overall, K.O.M. and
stage 6
Bicicleta Eibarresa: stage 2
Volta a Catalunya: stages 7 (2nd sector)
and 11

Mont Faron hill-climb
Clásica de los Puertos
GP Monte Carlo

Selected places
Vuelta a España: 21st; stage 2, 2nd

1956 TEAM: FAEMA/GIRARDENGO-ICEP

Wins
None

Selected places
Mont Faron: 2nd
Tour de France: 4th; K.O.M. 2nd
Vuelta a España: 4th: K.O.M. 2nd)
Giro d'Italia: stage 7, 2nd; stage 16, 2nd

1957 TEAM: MOBYLETTE GAC/ST-RAPHAEL-GEMINIANI

Wins
Vuelta: stage 3 and K.O.M.
Tour of Levante: stage 3
Tour of Asturias: overall, stage 1 and
   K.O.M.
Mount Faron hill-climb
GP Jerez

GP San Lucar de Barrameda
GP Toledo

Selected places
Vuelta a España: 2nd
GP Europe: 3rd
Tour de France: stage 3, 4th

1958 TEAM: FAEMA

Wins
Tour de France: stage 14, stage 20 and
   K.O.M.
Vuelta: K.O.M.
Giro d'Italia: stage 4
Spanish National Championships
Arrate hill-climb

Selected places
Vuelta a España: 6th
Tour de France: 8th
Giro d'Italia: 17th

1959 TEAM: TRICOLFILINA-COPPI/CONDOR/KAS

Wins
Tour de France: overall, stage 15 and
   K.O.M.
Vuelta a España: stage 4
Spanish Mountains Championship
Spanish Regional Championship
Arrate hill-climb
Antequera–Cabra–Antequera: stage 1
Tour de Suisse: stages 3 (b) and 5 and
   K.O.M.
Tour of Levante: K.O.M.

Tour of Cerdeña: K.O.M.
14 criteriums

Selected places
Tour de France: stage 17, 2nd; stage 13,
   3rd; stage 19, 4th
Vuelta a España: stage 1 (1st sector),
   4th; stage 1 (2nd sector), 3rd
Mont Faron hill-climb: 2nd
Spanish National Championships: 2nd

1960 TEAM: FAEMA

Wins
Vuelta a España: stage 13
GP Priego: two stages 1 and 2, overall
   and K.O.M.

Tour of Asturias: K.O.M.
Arrate hill-climb
3 criteriums

1961 TEAM: V.O.V.

Wins
Arrate hill-climb
Monaco–Mont Agel hill-climb
Nice–Mont Agel hill-climb
Tour of Cerdeña: stage 4

Selected places
World Championships: 17th
Spanish Regional Championships: 2nd

1962 TEAM: MARGNAT-PALOMA

Wins
Tour de France: stage 13 and K.O.M.
Arrate hill-climb
Mont Faron hill-climb
Mont Faron time-trial
Tour of Romandie: stage 3
Dauphiné Libéré: K.O.M.
4 criteriums

Selected places
Tour de France: 14th; stage 19,
  3rd
Dauphiné Libéré: 4th
Tour of Romandie: 7th

1963 TEAM: MARGNAT-PALOMA

Wins
Mont Faron time-trial
Tour de France: stage 15 and K.O.M.
Midi Libre: K.O.M.
Dauphiné Libéré: K.O.M.

Selected places
Tour de France: 2nd
Tour of Romandie: 2nd
Dauphiné Libéré: 4th

1964 TEAM: MARGNAT-PALOMA

Wins
Tour de France: stages 8 and 16 and
  K.O.M.
Naranco hill-climb
Mont Faron hill-climb
Mont Faron time-trial
Midi Libre: stage 5

Six Days of Madrid (with Rik Van
  Steenbergen)

Selected places
Tour de France: 3rd
Dauphiné Libéré: 6th

1965 TEAM: MARGNAT-PALOMA

Wins
Circuit du Provençal: overall

Selected places
Vuelta a España: 10th; stage 4, 5th; stage
  16, 6th

Montjuic hill-climb: 2nd
Urkiola hill-climb: 8th .
Naranco hill-climb: 8th

Bibliography

A NOTE FROM THE AUTHOR ON SOURCES

Among the many people willing to give up their time to be interviewed, for which many thanks, first and foremost is, of course, Federico Martín Bahamontes himself.

Many thanks, too, to the following willing interviewees (in alphabetical order) for their time and invaluable insights:

Ian Brown (8 March, 2011)
André Darrigade (7 April, 2011)
Raphael Geminiani (11 July, 2011)
Miguel Indurain (22 March, 2012)
Antonio Jiménez Quiles (15 April, 2011)
Julio Jiménez (13 September, 2011)
Josu Loroño (9 April, 2011)
Luis Otaño (8 April, 2011)
Miguel Poblet (21 March, 2011)
Raymond Poulidor (1 July, 2011)
Brian Robinson (29 March, 2011)
Bernardo Ruiz (18 January, 2011)
Carlos Sastre (15 January, 2012)

BOOKS
(Published in English)
Beevor, Antony – *The Spanish Civil War*, Penguin, 1982.
Borkenau, Franz – *The Spanish Cockpit*, Faber & Faber, 1937.

Brenan, Gerald – *The Spanish Labyrinth*, Cambridge University Press, 1950.

Brenan, Gerald – *The Face of Spain,* The Turnstile Press, 1950.

Fallon, Lucy & Bell, Adrian – *Viva La Vuelta*, Mousehold, 2005.

Fotheringham, William – *Put Me Back On My Bike: In Search of Tom Simpson*, Yellow Jersey Press, 2002.

Fotheringham, William – *Roule Britannia: A History of Britons in the Tour de France*, Yellow Jersey Press, 2009.

Fotheringham, William – *Fallen Angel: the Passion of Fausto Coppi*, Yellow Jersey Press, 2009.

Hooper, John – *The Spaniards*, Viking Press, 1986.

Howard, Paul – *Sex, Lies and Handlebar Tape: The Remarkable Life of Jacques Anquetil*, Mainstream, 2009.

McGann, Bill & Carol – *The Story of the Tour de France, Volume 1*, Dog Ear Publishing, 2006.

Moore, Richard – *In Search of Robert Millar*, Harper Collins, 2007.

Thomas, Hugh – *The Spanish Civil War,* Simon & Schuster, 1994.

(Published in Spanish)

Bodegas, Javier & Dorronsoro, Juan – *Con Ficha de la Española 1960 – 2003*, Uriziar Edizioak, 2003.

Bodegas, Javier & Dorronsoro, Juan – *Historia de la Bicicleta Eibarresa/Euskal Bizikleta*, Dorleta, 2000.

Bodegas, Javier & Dorronsoro, Juan – *Historia del Campeonato de España*, Urizar, 2003.

Garai, Josu – *Ciclismo del Norte,* Recoletos, 1994.

Martín Bahamontes, Federico – *La Sombra del Aguila,* Wurth, 2009.

Pérez, Chico & Guerra, Adrian – *Vuelta Ciclista a España 1935–1985*, Caja Postal, 1986.

Preston, Paul – *Francisco Franco, Caudillo de España,* Grijalbo, 1998.

(Published in French)

Various – *Tour de France 100 Ans*, L'Equipe, 2002.

PAMPHLETS
(Published in Spanish)
Bodegas, Javier – *Bahamontes,* Dorleta, 2000.
Bodegas, Javier – *Jesús Loroño,* Dorleta, 2000.

NEWSPAPERS AND MAGAZINES
(Published in English)
Cycle Sport
Velo News
The Independent
The Guardian

(Published in Spanish)
MARCA
El País
El Mundo
ABC
El Mundo Deportivo
AS
Deia
La Vanguardia
Urtekaria
El Alcázar
Informaciones

(Published in French)
L'Equipe
Le Dauphiné Libéré

Index